19.95

Love in a global village

A CELEBRATION OF

love in

INTERCULTURAL FAMILIES IN THE MIDWEST

a global

BY JESSIE CARROLL GREARSON & LAUREN B. SMITH

village

UNIVERSITY OF IOWA PRESS Ψ IOWA CITY

University of Iowa Press, Iowa City 52242

Copyright © 2001 by the University of Iowa Press

Printed in the United States of America

Design by Richard Hendel

http://www.uiowa.edu/~uipress

Frontispiece photo by Christy Mock.

Top: Viren, Jessie, Ellie, Lauren, Hassimi;

bottom: Emma, Myriama.

The publication of this book was generously supported by
the University of Iowa Foundation.

Printed on acid-free paper

Library of Congress
Cataloging-in-Publication Data
Grearson, Jessie Carroll.
Love in a global village: a celebration of intercultural families
in the Midwest/by Jessie Carroll Grearson
and Lauren B. Smith
p.   cm.
ISBN 0-87745-740-9 (pbk.)
1. Intermarriage — Middle West — Case studies.
2. Interethnic marriage — Middle West — Case studies.
3. Family — Middle West — Case studies.   4. Ethnicity —
Middle West.   I. Smith, Lauren B., 1963– .   II. Title.
HQ1031.G74   2001
306.84′5′0977 — dc21   00-045634

01   02   03   04   05   P   5   4   3   2   1

For our

three wonderful,

lively daughters:

Emma, Eleanor,

and Myriama

CONTENTS

ACKNOWLEDGMENTS

From the beginning, this book has been a collaboration, and we would like to thank the people who worked with us to turn an idea into reality.

First, our heartfelt thanks to all of the couples we interviewed, those whose portraits appear here, and those we were unable to include, for giving so generously of their time and their life stories. Without their interest and enthusiasm, we could not have written this book.

Also, thanks to our community of volunteers who helped us in a variety of ways: Mary Swander, Kishore and Jyoti Sapat, Anne Zahlan and David Radavich, Gretchen Knapp, Linda Coleman, Marianne Ferber, Dale Rigby, Viren Sapat, Hassimi Traore, Julio Cesar Ortiz, Barbara Oettgen, and Murtis and Nana Grant-Acquah, who put us in touch with intercultural families; Christy Mock and Corbin Sexton for their photographs of the intercultural families; Kishore and Jyoti Sapat, Arlynne and Douglas Grearson, Stephanie Hall, Azim and Golrokh Nassiri, Julie Spanbauer, Diarra Sereme, Olga Abella, and Besty Kruger, who cared for our children; Allison York and John Schmidt, Barbara Oettgen and Rob Gajarski, and Dean, Anita, and Eddie Makaluni, who hosted us for overnight stays during interviews; Jeff Gore, Ellen Turner, Corinne

Morrissey, and Jonelle Depetro, who filled in for us during work-related absences; and Merey Grearson, Arlynne Grearson, and Kurt Buehner, who commented on essays in progress. A special thanks to Viren Sapat, who read and boldly edited all the drafts, and who also supplied patient technical support; and to Ellen Turner, who read every word of this book — except these — and who pinpointed trouble spots with a patient persistence we very much came to appreciate.

Thanks to The John Marshall Law School for help and support, and particularly to Dean Gilbert Johnston, for his continued interest in this project; thanks to Eastern Illinois University for a grant that helped support our work.

Finally, our gratitude to our own intercultural families, who introduced us to many of the couples, transported and accompanied us to many of the interview sites, and supported and encouraged us with their belief in the importance of this project. To our marvelously kind and tolerant husbands — Hassimi Traore and Viren Sapat — and our lively, joyful daughters — Myriama Smith Traore, and Emma and Eleanor Sapat — our deepest of thanks. We couldn't have completed this project with different, less loving, or less flexible families.

When we walk into Barb Immermann's house, we see a gallery of her grandchildren's photographs crowding the mantelpiece of her rural Iowa home. Three of Barb's children chose to marry people from other countries, and the diversity of their families is reflected in these pictures. Even at a glance, we can see the panoply of visual differences: hair blonde and straight to jet black and curly; eyes brown, blue, green. It is because of these faces that we have come here. We thought it remarkable that a woman living in the rural heartland of the country, by reputation among the most homogeneous of places, would have such a thoroughly intercultural family.

Of course, in some ways Barb's family *is* unusual, but like many of the people we have met while working on this book, Barb approaches the task of nurturing her intercultural family as part of the work and the pleasure of everyday life. For example, when Barb's extended family outgrew her dining-room table, she built an enormous new one so that they could all eat together. She had never done any woodworking before, but that didn't stop her. Barb chose several long and perfect oak boards from the hardware store in her town of Kalona, Iowa, along with five sturdy pieces to serve as legs — one at each corner, and a fifth one in the middle for extra support. A neighbor helped Barb make the legs, each one in a different design, each departing somewhat from standard table-leg form. Sanded and finished, the table is impressive — strong, steady, and unique.

We see Barb's table, and her approach to her family, as emblematic. For us, Barb has become a symbol of the intercultural families we have met who settle and thrive in what may seem the most unlikely of places and by doing so challenge our stereotypes of American families and communities. For example, we tend to think of the Iowa countryside where Barb and her family live as isolated, rural, white, and monocultural. Indeed, all the faces we encountered when we stopped for directions to Barb's house *were* white, and the county highway led us to a gravelly dirt road that cut through cultivated fields and rolling hills dotted with livestock. When we arrived at her house, we heard chickens in the backyard, where ducks and an old white donkey made their way to a small pond. Barb, both welcoming and matter-of-fact, could easily have been the farmer's wife we might have expected to emerge from an Iowa country house like this.

The photos on Barb's mantelpiece, however, belie our stereotype of this region in a powerful way. We are struck by one picture in particular in which Barb sits surrounded by her grandchildren, who represent almost the entire spectrum of racial diversity and a variety of cultures. The thread of family resemblance can be traced from one cousin's face to another, even though their parents come from such diverse places as Taiwan, Iran, and India.

Barb's table has also come to represent for us the practical innovation we witnessed in the families we portray. Intercultural couples make a variety of decisions to accommodate diverse family members, and though many of these decisions are mundane (what shall we have for dinner?), over time such choices form the strands of family tapestries that are deeply original. Into these family tapestries are woven many features that we recognize from the families we grew up in, yet we appreciate how they are also shot through with unique and colorful differences.

.

We wrote *Love in a Global Village* because, as two American women who have married men from other nations, we wanted to better understand the dynamics of intercultural families, those formed by partners from different countries. How do intercultural parents raise their children? What kinds of cultural identities do they encourage in their offspring? How important are adults' cultural identities in the contexts of their multinational families? How do intercultural couples organize their homes and their lives to reflect these different identities? What potential losses and misunderstandings are involved in these choices?

In response to the lack of literature on intercultural partnerships, we had previously edited *Swaying: Essays on Intercultural Love*, an anthology of autobiographical writing that explores the challenges of such relationships. While readers enjoyed the stories of the professional writers we included, they emphasized their delight in hearing the voices of "real people" — those whose voices are less likely to be found in print. Readers who are themselves part of intercultural families, especially, craved the real-life stories of others with similar life experiences. We felt that a collection of interview essays would provide a portrait of an even greater variety of people, particularly those who might not submit work to a literary anthology. We also hoped that these essays would deepen the conversation that *Swaying* began by returning to the issues identified there and examining them as they are experienced by a range of people.

All of the interviews in this book were conducted in the Midwest. When we embarked on this endeavor, we had planned to focus our attention on the Midwest because we were curious about the communities in which our own families had settled, and because we thought that intercultural couples might face different challenges in different regions of the country. In fact, an interesting consensus did emerge in couples' perceptions of this region. For example, many felt a tension between their appreciation of the Midwest as a tolerant place where people could "live and let live" and their irritation that this tolerance often masked a benevolent ignorance about other cultures. Nevertheless, most described the Midwest as a place where they enjoyed much kindness and freedom whether they lived in rural locations or city neighborhoods.

Over the course of the interviews, however, we began to see that most of the couples did not perceive the challenges and opportunities they found in their communities as specifically Midwestern. Many commented, for instance, on an apathy about other cultures that was best characterized by George Ricketson: "Fiji's not here? Okay, that's all we need to know about Fiji." Yet most believed that this arrogant insularity and woeful sense of geography, which could shrink Brazil to the size of Iowa and locate Bulgaria in South America, were simply American and not particular to the region.

While we recognize that a book of this size cannot be truly representative of intercultural families in America, we are surprised by the variety of geographical, historical, and personal differences these fifteen essays include. The voices in this book speak across more than half a century in time, telling stories shaped by events that profoundly changed our country (the Civil Rights movement, the Women's Rights movement), and the world (World War II, the lifting of the Iron Curtain). Reading Shirlee Taraki's account of meeting her Afghan husband in the 1940s alongside Diane Her's account of meeting her Hmong husband in the late 1990s affords a vivid glimpse of just how much the world has changed — and yet how much it remains the same. Although Shirlee and Diane met their husbands in very different ways (the former on a university campus, the latter on the Internet), the risks each took — for love, for adventure — strike us as remarkably similar.

This project, when we undertook it two years ago, seemed particularly pressing to us. We had begun to experience firsthand the impact of an antiimmigrant mood in America. We worried about being separated from our extended families, about the effect of xenophobic sentiments on our partners or on our children, that the unique reality of our blended lives would go unacknowledged.

Our project seems even more timely now. As we finish this book at the end of the millennium, there continue to be stories of cross burnings and numerous reports of police brutality. Right here in our own state of Illinois, a white supremacist embarked on a hate-fueled shooting spree that targeted minorities. The one consistent response of the communities in each of these cases has been to plead for tolerance, respect, and appreciation of differences. The voices in the essays that follow have powerful contributions to make to such discussions because they speak from the perspective of people who have successfully embraced diversity in their lives, and who have often encouraged lively conversations about cultural diversity in their extended families, among their friends, in their schools, and in their neighborhoods.

The sense of urgency we feel is also inspired by the growth of our own families. In the course of writing this book, two daughters have been born and one daughter has grown from a toddler to a small child. We want to learn how to honor each element of our children's heritage in the context of an American culture that tends to consume and homogenize other cultures; we want to help create for our children a world that is free from bigotry and violence. And so we have sought out the stories of other intercultural families who have created environments in which every family member can thrive.

We've learned that none of the answers to the questions we ask in this book are simple. If anything, both the questions and answers have grown more complicated — and more interesting — as our work has progressed. We noticed fairly early on, for example, that "intercultural" rarely means "bicultural." Many of those involved in intercultural relationships themselves come from families with more than one national background; for example, Julie Dalisay Elzanati is herself the product of an intercultural marriage, and Violette Ricketson's family tree has its roots in many cultures. Also, we saw how partners from different cultures create, together, a unique family culture, a dynamic that is even more pronounced when children come into the picture. Vilma Seeberg and Thomas Jacobs, for instance, have drawn together elements from seemingly diverse German, African American, and Chinese cultures to create a home for their newly adopted daughter, Su Guan-lan, and the resulting culture of their home is infinitely richer and more complex for their decision to do so.

The choice to marry across national and cultural boundaries seems to either create or enhance an openness to multiple cultures for these couples; many have given up rigid national affiliations in favor of international identities. As such world citizens, the members of intercultural families claim a wide range of possibilities for themselves with respect to the large and small choices they make. Intercultural couples feel free to choose the best elements from their cultures of origin, while leaving behind the problematic. As a group, they most often choose inclusively — "and" rather than "or" — which means that Santa and the Easter Bunny simply move over to share space with other holiday characters; that a Thanksgiving turkey will be placed next to a colorful stir-fry in November; that a devout Mormon may find herself on a given Sunday listening to "Amazing Grace" sung with Hmong lyrics.

The couples we met also encourage such internationalism in their children. For example, Don and Marilva Zeigler's lifelong interest in other cultures, their "open-door policy," has fostered in their children a sense of themselves as neither American nor Brazilian, but as citizens of the world. Intercultural parents pursue this approach to parenting even when it requires of them an admirable energy and dedication — teaching their children to speak Chinese, for example, in the face of intense English-only sentiment, or celebrating the holidays of other nations in cities where Santa and the Easter Bunny reign.

Although open to new ideas, this is also a discerning group, and their voices provide both direct and indirect critiques of American culture. For example, Katy Stavreva and Doug Boynton resist what they call America's "junk culture" of fast food and Wal-Mart purchases, while Jim and Jean Hussey reject what they see as a lack of child-centeredness in American family life. Violette Ricketson expresses alarm about the lack of attention to extended family, seeing nursing homes as a symptom of a neglectful culture. Intercultural couples perceive American culture from a critical distance that offers valuable insights into American society.

Our conversations also illuminated the persistence of racial tensions in the United States. Americans, we were told over and over again, are extremely conscious of race, a subject that was a central part of every conversation with couples in which either partner was a person of color. Racism was a serious concern for ten of the fifteen couples we spoke with and a point of discussion for several more, even though we rarely raised the subject ourselves, having intended at first to focus on other topics.

We were discouraged to learn that racism is still such an obstacle for so many, particularly for people of African descent. However, it is heartening that the interracial couples with whom we spoke had almost invariably found a useful way of talking about race with each other, their families, and the wider community — despite the pain and difficulty of such discussions. Because they were able to confront racism honestly, these families were also able to create comfortable, positive environments for every family member. The conversations that took place within individual families were as unique as the families themselves, and they reveal a repertoire of different strategies. For example, Janet Ingle's approach emphasizes the universal nature of human beings ("In my house, we don't call color. . . . I see a man. . . . A good man.") while her friend Murtis Grant-Acquah's solution emphasizes the power of alliances within the black community ("black is black").

Presented by the couples as an often unresolvable problem was the loss of place, culture and family that resulted from one partner's leaving his or her home of origin. The immigrant partner in the couple almost invariably expressed a longing for his or her own landscape and climate, and a deep sadness about the distance from extended family members. Other topics that frequently arose were loss of religion and language. While many couples were originally optimistic about importing religion and language from their native lands, they found that the United States exerted a pressure to assimilate that was very difficult to resist. As a result, these essential elements of culture were preserved only through great effort, if at all. For example, while Hueping Chin has managed to teach her son to speak Chinese fluently, as he grows older, their dialogue in Chinese sometimes falters in the face of new topics: "How does the space shuttle work? I find it hard to explain that to him in Chinese." The words of Jat Aluwalia capture the sense of regret that some felt: "I admit defeat; I guess the sense of being Indian ends with me."

The guiding principle of this book has been that of conversation. We were put in touch with the couples we portray in *Love in a Global Village* as a result of conversations with friends, colleagues, and acquaintances, and we have come to feel that the voices speaking within this loose network of people who know us, who know friends of ours, who know one another, comment on each other in interesting ways precisely because they are part of such a network.

These interviews were also conducted as conversations and so have their own emphases and ellipses, something of the spontaneous nature of dialogue — they are a kind of informal town meeting on subjects that matter to intercultural families. In the course of writing this book, it was almost as though we could hear the people in the different essays talking to each other, sometimes debating, sometimes in such close consensus that it was difficult to recall who had first voiced a sentiment. In fact, we arranged the essays in the book in conversational clusters, placing couples in similar life phases with similar interests close to one another so that they might shed light on one another's stories.

The first four essays portray couples that are laying the foundations of their lives, and their voices resonate with the energy of hopeful beginnings. The second group of four essays depicts families poised at a critical moment of choosing: these couples are making hard decisions about language and religion, and where to locate their families — choices that will shape their family lives in the long term. The third group we think of as "householders" — three families who are cultivating lives already established and enjoying long-held family traditions. The final grouping includes four families that have weathered storms and come to a kind of hard-earned optimism about themselves, their communities, and the world. Arranged in this way, the essays form a kind of progression that suggests, though in microcosm, something of the development of such relationships over time.

Spending time with these intercultural families has been a tremendous gift, and we have been astonished by their generosity. Not only did they fit us into their busy lives and tell us their most personal stories, but, after giving us so much, they always insisted on offering more — whether it was a badly needed cup of coffee, a popsicle for a child, or a meticulous set of directions to their home. We think of Clara Kamats, who at the end of a sometimes difficult pregnancy still reached out to help us with our bags. We think of Vilma Seeberg and Tom Jacobs, who made room in their lives for our entire families, including three children, and who made us dinner and took us to the airport. We think of the Ricketsons who drove hours to meet us for lunch in an unfamiliar city, and of Karen Holmberg and Aria Minu-Sepehr who drove from Columbia, Missouri, to Champaign, Illinois, in a car that they "thought could make it." We think of Don Zeigler, who, as we said our good-byes, began to muse about hosting a party for all the couples involved in the book, and how when we demurred, saying that would be too much trouble for him, still called back to us, "It could be potluck!" Surely meeting people like this has been the best kind of luck.

We have found a kind of community through working on this book, made up of people whose courage and energy have inspired us to work harder in our own lives: if it is possible to teach children Mandarin in the middle of Iowa, then it is also possible to teach our own daughters Kutchi and Diula in Illinois. If a Ghanan woman's integrity can survive the transplanting to white, wintry Milwaukee, then we can give our own children a sense of pride in their heritage that survives the onslaught of American culture. If it is possible for couples to create vital intercultural communities everywhere from Shaker Heights, Ohio, to Kalona, Iowa, to Springfield, Missouri, then it is possible for us to do the same, especially now with the benefit of their advice and ideas.

But perhaps the most important gift these people have given us is a sense of optimism in the face of the unknown, examples of how to work toward the kind of change we yearn for in this world. Such clear-eyed optimism, a willingness to remain open to others even during a struggle, is best voiced by Kim Kranich: "Give everyone the opportunity to know you as you are and to learn. I live life with my sleeves rolled up—and I often feel embattled. But I will give people the opportunity to treat me with respect, and I will be hurt each time they don't."

The stories we have gathered here offer a vision of the ordinary and extraordinary acts of love with which intercultural couples weave their family tapestries. It is a vision that we hope will encourage conversations about human commonalities and differences—conversations essential to creating inclusive and vibrant communities.

I spin around you

KAREN & ARIA

Karen and Aria. Photo by Lauren Smith.

ne of the first things we notice about Karen Holmberg and Aria Minu-Sepehr is how easily they tell us their stories. When they describe how they met, for example, we are interested not only in the exactness of the details they offer but in the collaborative way that they relate those facts to us: if it is Karen who supplies the year they met, then Aria knows the month, the day; if Karen knows the time of day, then it is Aria who pins down the exact hour and offers details of what each was wearing.

Karen Holmberg and Aria Minu-Sepehr met, as it happens, on January 18, 1994, in a student trailer park in Irvine, California. Late that Friday afternoon, Karen (LOT B 13) was looking for a neighbor who had promised to fix her bike tire; in his absence, Aria (LOT A 37) offered, in impeccable, slightly formal English, to help her.

"Fixing the bike took hours," Karen says, smiling. "Now I know it takes hours for Aria to do anything, so perhaps I shouldn't have been so flattered, but he kept making these small changes, having me ride in a circle around him so he could inspect the angle of my hips, make sure the bike seat was adjusted properly." Karen, who says she was wearing a short black skirt at the time, estimates that she must have ridden a hundred times around Aria on that first meeting.

"Really, the tire just needed some air," Aria remarks mildly.

At first glance Karen, who was a graduate student in the M.F.A. program at UC–Irvine, assumed that Aria was an exchange student — guessed that he was young, didn't speak English well, wouldn't be in the country much longer. This may be one reason that she, by her own account, flirted with him so boldly on that first encounter. He was a handsome and temporary part of the landscape, their flirtation an afternoon's diversion. However, it wasn't long before she discovered her mistake — that this attractive man was articulate, close to her own age, and a native of Iran but a long-term resident of the United States.

Karen also explains that her audacity was connected to a mysterious understanding that arose between them right away. "He seemed very familiar to me on one level, as if I was meeting him again after a long time, but at the same time he was totally alien. He belonged to this other culture, had an accent. He was dark; I was fair. He wasn't like anybody I'd ever met, yet I felt immediately that I recognized him." She pauses to think about those old feelings. "That was confusing, powerfully confusing. But it all got decided very quickly."

How quickly? we ask.

"That was Friday," Karen says. "He went away for the weekend, and on Monday we went for a walk. We were sitting on a rock behind our trailers and he put his hand on my hand. 'Well, I guess it's settled then,' he said. 'I guess it is,' I said."

What did you mean? we ask Aria.

"That we had the same sense of purpose," he replies.

"The purpose was to be together," Karen adds, meaning that they were both interested in each other, that they both wanted to have a relationship, give it a try; but in retrospect that simple statement takes on a deeper meaning. Even to us, who have known the couple only a short while, and mostly through e-mail correspondence, their meeting seems fated.

Karen is almost apologetic for describing her relationship in what she perceives as sentimental terms, but she doesn't need to be. We are astonished by how much these two people know about each other. They tell their stories about their childhoods together, as though they had lived those childhoods together, sometimes turning to address each other rather than us. Much of what they recount, they tell us with relish, in graceful, almost scripted, dialogue. It is great fun to listen to them talk — Aria with dark expressive eyes and smile lines that arc down the sides of his face, always cheerfully ironic, ready for an adventure or a laugh; Karen awake to all the particulars of every tale, as if she can hear the words before they are spoken and feel the hot sun of Aria's childhood home on her face.

Soon after their conversation behind the trailer park, the couple moved in together. Karen used her own trailer primarily as office space, and they shared Aria's. "His trailer was so beautiful," says Karen. "It was the same one that Lucy and Desi Arnaz took across country in the *I Love Lucy Show*. It was this fifties beautiful old piece of junk with curved paneling in it — enormous! When you're living in a trailer, an increase in ten square feet is significant."

"And it had a full-size bathtub, too," remembers Aria.

It was a happy time in their lives. The trailer park, owned by the university, was an inexpensive place for students to live and was much in demand. "The trailers were arranged in a circle, and people had gardens. They'd put elaborate additions onto their homes," Karen reminisces.

"In fact," says Aria, "I helped my next-door neighbor make his trailer into a skyscraper. We popped the top off and took it up one more level; we installed a huge window on one end that you could look out of." Such modifications were typical of the trailers, which generations of students had helped each other individualize. "It was very communal," Aria finishes nostalgically.

Despite this idyllic beginning to their romance, separation loomed quickly. Karen was finishing her degree, and Aria was still in the middle of earning his. Karen moved to Columbia, Missouri, in 1995 to begin her Ph.D. work at the University of Missouri, and the couple lived apart for a year, though their connection remained strong. In 1996, Aria transferred to the University of Missouri to be with Karen.

Aria was unsure of the move, he tells us. "The culture I come from looks down on villages. In fact, if you want to disparage someone in Persian culture, you might say, 'So, what village are you from?'"

"It's L.A. or nothing if you're Persian," Karen agrees, "especially if you come from the class Aria comes from, the upper echelon of Persian culture. Your mother refuses to visit because she doesn't want to see how much of a life you can have in a village," she continues, turning to address Aria.

"Yes," he concedes. "She has not come out here."

Although Columbia, the couple tells us, is more culturally diverse and more progressive than its surrounding communities, even it presents certain constraints and discomforts to someone who is not a part of the majority culture. "People like Aria are considered very exotic," Karen explains. "He placed in a bicycle race, and they had film footage of him on the news. I was very proud of him, but the newscaster slaughtered his name: 'A-REE-Ah Men-OO-see . . . Men-OO-see-fear. One of the reasons they featured him was because they wanted to show 'a diverse Columbia.' But people will constantly stop and ask him, 'Where are you from?'"

To this, Aria often replies simply, "L.A." "Because that's where I lived for seventeen years," he says.

"No," people insist. "*Before* that. Where were you from before that?"

.

In fact, since Aria's father was one of the military aristocracy of the Shah's Iran, Aria spent his young life on air force bases in that country. Aria's mother was a relatively traditional, upper-class Iranian woman, but Aria describes his father as very eccentric. He believed that "life is risky," and he brought this attitude to parenting. Aria remembers being allowed to fly his father's plane — "a four-passenger Beechcraft Bonanza, very fast and fully aerobatic" — at seven years old. His father would tell Aria to "just hold it steady, keep that heading and altitude." Then he would take a nap.

Once, when father and son were out flying together, they heard on the radio about an oil pipeline that had burst. When they flew to that location, they saw not much smoke but lots of flames. "Want to do something really fun?" Aria's father asked him. "Of course I said yes." His father headed the plane just above the tower of fire, so it caught an updraft and rocketed up thousands of feet in seconds, then plummeted the same distance as they moved past the flames. We are breathless when Aria tells this tale, and Aria appreciates our shock, as he relives the mixture of excitement and terror he experienced as a child. But still this is not the most remarkable story.

"Tell them about your Volkswagen," Karen prompts her partner.

"You tell it," Aria says generously, as though giving her a present, and she's the one who begins.

At the age of eight, Aria had a dune buggy that had been constructed out of an old VW bug. The car was orange with red flames and a black octopus his mother had painted on the hood. It had roll bars and a salvaged seat belt from a plane, "the serious kind that race car drivers have, that come up through the legs and around the shoulders." He also had "a white Evel Knievel jump-suit and a helmet," Karen continues, leaning toward us from her end of the couch. As young as he was, Aria was allowed to drive his car anywhere he wanted on the base, a freedom that astonishes us and fills Aria with nostalgia.

Eventually, the family moved to Tehran and took everything with them, including Aria's car. It was a terrifying place to be — Iran was in the middle of a revolution, and Tehran was the nucleus of the conflict. Many supporters of the Shah had already fled the country. Aria's father could easily have been executed. Never-theless, when ten-year-old Aria complained that his attention-grabbing car had remained garage-bound for so long, Aria's father took the car out. Here Aria can't resist taking over the narrative.

"'You drive it, it's your car,' my father said. So here we were, a ten-year-old and his father in the most visible car possible. We went to do errands, and sure enough, we were at a stop when revolutionaries pulled up beside us with their hand grenades and machine guns, signaling 'pull over.' I checked with my father who made a gesture to keep going, and said 'step on it.'" Here Aria imi-tates his father by making an exaggeratedly casual sign with his hands. "'Just step on it,'" he says again. So ten-year-old Aria did step on it, engaging in a car chase through the capital city of Iran with armed revolutionaries close behind. Aria's father directed him onto the highway, but the car stalled, and their pursuers pulled up behind father and son.

The men were furious, screaming, "We were going to kill both of you!" as they piled out of their car. When Aria took off his helmet, they were even more outraged. For perhaps a full five minutes they poured forth a torrent of words, screaming at Aria's father, who finally, calmly, undid the buckle under his chin and took off his helmet. "I couldn't hear a word you were saying," he told the men. Fortunately, Aria's father hadn't renewed his driver's license since he was in his twenties — and still a lieutenant. The revolutionaries, who were trying to recruit lower-ranking officers to their cause, thought they had a forty-year-old lieutenant on their hands and were instantly friendly. "We'll make you a captain," they told him. They concluded the incident with one last lecture on kids and cars, but Aria's father — always cool as ice — replied, "I recommend that you take him out for a spin — he's an excellent driver."

Aria's family fled Iran in 1979, living in London for a year before moving to Los Angeles, where his father still had military connections. Many of the military personnel had fled to what the Iranian immigrants call "Tehran-geles," the surprisingly large Iranian community in Los Angeles. "There's a big air force community in L.A.," says Karen. "They have meetings, get-togethers, monthly social events. When I met Aria, they still called his father *Timsar*, which means 'General.' Even your little cousin who is twelve years old would call him *Timsar*, and she was born here."

"Oh, I used to call my dad that, too, just for laughs," Aria responds. "Everyone else does, so there's nothing unusual about it. They've all maintained their ranks, right? And my dad is a general and somebody else was a colonel. In Iran, there may have been people in their midtwenties who may have been lieutenants, and now they're in their forties and they're *still* lieutenants. There was even a motion at one of the meetings to promote them to major or something — even though none of these former military men have been active for the last twenty years." The irony, Aria suggests, was not lost on the Iranian community — "Everybody thought it was extremely funny," he says.

"Something in me responds to all the freedom Aria had as a child," Karen tells us, after a lull in the conversation. "We also had a lot of freedom growing up, and we also knew life was risky. I learned to sail when I was eight — we were all taught to swim and sail and boat. We were taught to have fun, be careful, but have fun." Karen, the great-granddaughter of Swedish immigrants, was raised in the small town of Gales Ferry, Connecticut, surrounded by the members of her extended family, who jointly ran an orchard that grew apples, peaches, pears, plums, and raspberries, among other things.

From the age of thirteen, Karen also worked in the orchard. She picked apples and handed out baskets to pick-your-own customers. "I'd walk around making sure people weren't climbing the trees or breaking off the precious branches. My grandmother would go around scolding people for climbing the trees and plucking the fruit carelessly. 'You're taking off next year's fruit,' says Karen in nagging falsetto. "We lived on a cove, so there was water on the one side, the orchard on the other. It was very beautiful," Karen concludes. "It was our little village."

Karen attended college in Middlebury, Vermont, and went from there to Madison, Wisconsin, for a year, where she worked in the office of the Department of Slavic Languages. She tells us that she had learned Russian at Middlebury. "When I was fourteen I read my father's college copy of *Crime and Punishment* and I started reading all of Dostoevsky and Tolstoy. By the time I graduated, I'd read all the major nineteenth-century Russian novels." Her interest in these dark novels seems at odds with the picture

Karen paints of her childhood among the apple blossoms, but Karen insists that people of Swedish background have a very "morbid, depressive tendency."

Karen was surprised to discover that Russian culture is similar to Persian culture in some ways. "Americans can be very cool, nonchalant about things, and Russians and Persians are united in their dramatic expressions of emotion, like pleasure and gratitude, those things that we, as Americans, tend to downplay. In America, if someone gives you something you say, 'Oh thanks, that's very nice of you.' You wouldn't say, 'I will sacrifice myself to you now for giving that to me.' I spent time in Moscow when I was in college, and the Russians I met totally exhausted my poor narrow little American sensibility. Every moment, every encounter would be squeezed, plumbed for its emotional content. Men would profess their undying love to me the second time they met me. Mothers would say, 'You are like a daughter to me.' All this intensity. Persian culture's a lot like that."

Aria agrees that these kinds of expressions are part of Persian culture, though he wonders aloud whether self-sacrifice is as important a part of the Russian way of expressing gratitude. After some discussion, the two decide that tendency is more Persian, but both cultures do share a way of showing generosity that was particularly alarming to Karen the first few times she encountered it. "If a Persian woman is wearing a pair of earrings and you admire them, she'll immediately yank them out of her ears and say, 'I insist you have these.' The first time someone did that to me, I was really taken aback. I thought they meant it. I didn't realize I was supposed to argue, say no, give them back."

"She said, 'Oh, good, thank you,'" Aria jokes, making as if to pocket the goods.

"When I was in Moscow, it was Christmas. I admired an ornament on a friend's tree once, and she almost tried to force me to take it. She said, 'This ornament was my great-great-great-grandmother's, but I want you to have it. You are like a daughter to me.'"

"Persian culture," says Aria, "is exactly like this, if not even more extreme."

How do you know what to do? we ask.

"Well, you don't," says Aria. "You have to learn to read between the lines. The thing wasn't really her grandmother's, and she didn't really want you to have it."

Karen has learned something about how to communicate more effectively with her Persian relatives. When she was in a dilemma about when to begin calling Aria's parents by their first names, for example, she talked to one of Aria's cousins. In a low, dramatic voice she repeats her side of the conversation, while Aria sits back to enjoy the performance. "I'm in a quandary," Karen begins. "I have to confide in you. I feel like I can't go on in this state of painful confusion. I feel as though I am a daughter to Abdi and Lila, but I have been unable to call them by their first names. At what point may I? 'Oh,' the cousin told me, 'you can't wait for them to ask you. You have to worm your way in. You have to force them to be intimate with you.'"

"That is so un-American!" Karen exclaims. "I used to think America was a cultureless culture, but incidents like this make all your cultural assumptions just pop out in relief."

Karen freely admits that she has made mistakes, some, she insists, that Aria's parents have yet to forgive. "When Aria and I first started seeing each other, his grandmother had just died. I told his mother in person that I was sorry, but I never sent her a card.

There's a ceremony where a year after a person dies you send a card. So I thought I would make up for it by sending that card, but I didn't know when to stop. I've been sending a card every year since then — five years now."

Recently, Karen asked another of Aria's cousins about this tradition. The cousin responded with an incredulity Karen imitates. "What? You're still sending a card on the anniversary of our grandmother's death? She's gone. No, she doesn't matter anymore. She's dead and it's *over*. No, you don't have to send a card anymore."

Aria has had better luck with Karen's family. Her father likes Aria, appreciates his formal expressions of courtesy. "Oh, my father understands the game of it," Karen says. "He'll tease Aria at the doorway — 'No, after *you*, sir. No, I insist, after YOU.'"

"You know that cartoon, the polite crows?" Aria asks. "They used to show it in Iran, dubbed in Persian — these three crows, all stuck in a doorway because all of them kept insisting the others should go through first. That makes a lot of sense in our culture."

"It's true!" Karen exclaims. "The first time we went shopping with the family, I said, 'wait a minute, where did all the men go?' You look back and there are ten men congregating around the door trying to figure out who should go through first."

"Elevators are the worst," Aria remarks dryly.

Karen's mother also likes Aria now, though it took her longer to get used to him, partly because of such extreme displays of deference. His solicitude went against the grain of her New England spirit. Aria would trail after her, they tell us, offering one more piece of cake, one more cup of coffee, one more cookie until finally, Karen reports, her mother yelled, "Aria, stop following me around!"

"Is that a fault?" asks Aria, looking to us for sympathy, his dark eyebrows raised.

"My mother is extremely suspicious of flattery, too," Karen continues, "and Aria would pay her these extravagant compliments — 'Mrs. Holmberg, I must say, you are looking par-TIC-ularly beautiful,'" she imitates.

"Karen would say things to me like, 'Don't flirt with my mother.'" Again Aria looks at us as though we might help him plumb the mystery of such a comment. "I'm not flirting with her, I'm just trying to say nice things."

Karen has been unable to move to a comfortable footing with Aria's parents, and this is sometimes painful for her. For one thing, Aria's parents perceive Karen not just as an outsider but as a foreigner. Like many Iranian expatriots, they live in Los Angeles, but their intention has long been to return to Iran, though this is extremely unlikely. Because they never meant to stay in the United States, they have never tried to assimilate into American culture. "I feel a lot of tension, like I need to change myself to fit in better. I have to assimilate into *his* culture even though they moved here," she tells us.

"What's funny is that when they refer to Americans they say 'foreigner' — all Americans are *farangi*," says Aria.

"It's a self-preservation thing," suggests Karen. "Their culture is under an onslaught by American culture."

"What culture isn't?" asks Aria.

"But some people come to America because they want to assimilate, they move here for economic reasons. It's just so different," Karen tries to explain.

In particular, Karen doesn't conform to Mrs. Minu-Sepehr's ideas about what a woman should do and be. Karen, much to the chagrin of Aria's mother, is without doubt a villager. Not only that but a farmer, who grew up on an orchard and is proud of the gardening dirt wedged under her fingernails. Aria has not, he states emphatically, told his mother about the two tons of manure-enriched earth that Karen recently had delivered for several garden beds that she was working on. "My interests are things that she would find beneath a woman of her class," Karen explains. "Most of the things I do she would find puzzling, unfeminine. It's good for a woman to have higher education, that's a sign of class, but you're not expected to have a career. Your mother had a career, but it was to do good works, run the school, that sort of thing. Your mother has a difficult time figuring me out," Karen tells Aria, before turning back to us.

"I am like a man in Persian culture. I'm a professional, I have a higher education, my career's important to me. I'm not the desirable ideal of the Persian woman — someone who makes the home pleasant and lovely, someone who makes it easy for Aria to get through school, cooks and cleans, makes life orderly and harmonious, the fifties housewife stereotype."

·

Aria asked Karen to marry him on April 29, 1997, at a birthday party he had arranged in her honor. We hear the story of their engagement in response to a question about plans for their house in Columbia, which is under lengthy construction. The renovations, Karen says with sympathy in her voice, are very hard on Aria, who likes things to be beautiful and for whom surfaces (now covered in dust) are very important. "Right, well — why buy a dining-room table when you have yet to finish the dining room?" Aria asks, with a kind of resigned, if slightly pained, good humor. "But," he says, brightening perceptibly, "we do have nice silverware."

"Apparently Aria had been planning to ask me to marry him for years," Karen begins the story.

"But it had to be done in a dignified way," Aria adds.

Initially, Aria and the friends he'd consulted decided that presenting Karen with an engagement armoire filled with gifts would be just the thing, but this idea was regretfully abandoned in the face of "logistical problems" — he would have had to cart the whole thing two thousand miles east to Columbia. "Instead, what we came up with, again collectively, was the idea of nice cutlery." Something substantial, he says, something to represent permanence. The silver, purchased in L.A., had been hidden for a year in a file drawer in Missouri, and the couple had been together for three years when Aria finally began consulting another Columbia friend about the proper time to ask Karen for her hand.

Karen reports wondering why Aria was moving at such a glacial pace. Aria explains that the year was taken up with executing another part of his plan; he wanted a jeweler to make one of the silver spoons into a ring for her. "Here things just fell into place," he says with great enthusiasm. This mutual friend, in whom Karen had confided her frustration over how long Aria was taking with the proposal, found a jeweler who could make the ring — using the rest of it to fashion a baby spoon — in just one day.

"So it seemed like fate!" says Aria, who had made many fruitless inquiries about this task at jewelry shops in L.A.

At the birthday/secret-engagement party, Aria made an emotional speech to the gathering about the couple's new house, about permanence, and about making a commitment. "And I still didn't get it," Karen muses. "I thought, 'Why's he making such a long-winded speech?' Next he made me count out the silverware in front of everyone — 'OK, four forks. Four knives as well. Wait! Only three spoons!' Then he thrust this box with the ring and the baby spoon at me." Here Karen's voice quiets, and her tone shifts dramatically to one more in keeping with a Russian or Persian sensibility. "I burst into tears. People leaped up, squealed. There was chaos. Fainting."

Despite the levity that suffuses their engagement story, the question of when and how to marry is among the most difficult that Karen and Aria have faced in their relationship. "We've been together for five years, engaged for two. My family keeps asking me, when are you going to get married, what's the problem?" For a moment, Karen shares their point of view and is frustrated.

"Just because they don't understand the problem, doesn't mean there isn't one," Aria remarks quietly, and a little sadly.

"Yes," Karen responds quickly, looking at him. "It's taken me five years to be able to understand, and to have some compassion for it, instead of just being angry."

Couldn't you just elope? we ask innocently.

"I have begged to elope. Cried. Pleaded," says Karen ruefully, as Aria prepares to enumerate the difficulties that have kept them from choosing a date.

First, there is the problem of the ceremony's location, given that their parents reside on opposite coasts. Then there is the question of its funding. "As you can well imagine," Aria begins somewhat wearily, "the wedding has to be of a certain size and caliber. So without the means, it's difficult." And in the background, Aria notes, is the inevitable reminder to his parents that this marriage will not be an opportunity to unite two Persian families. "They're not giving their son to a family with whom they can form a kind of merger, and that's very sad for them." As they list these obstacles, a heavy feeling accumulates in the room and both seem discouraged in the face of what appears to be a genuine impasse.

But when, a moment later, they change the subject, tell us about their plans for the ceremony itself and how it will indeed be Persian, both brighten, adopting once more their animated collaborative storytelling.

"The Persian ceremony is very ritualized," Aria begins.

"Many claims of undying love," adds Karen, eyes sparkling. "I'm supposed to refuse two times and accept the third. I like that element."

"Actually, the first time, you listen to the whole thing and say, 'I don't know,'" Aria instructs Karen, turning toward her as though to rehearse. "So the priest goes through the whole thing again. Then you say, 'Maybe. I'll consider it.' Of course each time, the guy is getting more and more emphatic — "

"Urgent," cuts in Karen. "Desperate."

"Please Miss Holmberg, *please*, do you take this man — "

"For the love of God! *Take* this man!" Karen concludes in a dramatic escalation, at which point the two collapse in laughter together on the couch.

When we've all recovered from the ceremony, Aria circles back, somewhat cautiously, to a more sensitive discussion of the wedding dilemma. He has a plan and he would like to try it out on us, which he does, tentatively, his voice quiet and thoughtful. He is thinking that the wedding itself could be in L.A. but that the reception could be in New England, at the orchard.

"Ah," says Karen, with a touch of her previous bitterness.

"Then people won't think that you can't afford this wedding, it's just that the bride really wants to have it on the East Coast. I'm a pawn in this thing I don't want to have any part of!"

Aria continues, gently and as though he hasn't heard her. "I thought we could invite my closest relatives over there, and rent a house, take them around sightseeing in a bus. Doesn't that sound nice?" Now he is talking exclusively to Karen, who softens visibly.

"I know," she says after a moment, and links her fingers through his, though what she knows isn't exactly clear to us — whether she is acknowledging the insolubility of their dilemma or telling Aria that she appreciates his efforts, his attempts to make things right. She understands, she seems to be saying, that certain things need to be done a certain way, that she is a bit of a pawn and cannot help it, that she is lost to her fate settled on that sunny afternoon in January when she rode in circles around Aria, aware of the game, but helpless to stop herself from playing it.

Then she turns back to us. "And now I also know an expression in Farsi," Karen adds. "*Dorat begardam*. If you want to say you really love someone in Persian, you say, 'I spin around you.' Which is funny, because that's just what I was doing — even the first time we met."

Family photograph

SAAD & JULIE

Julie & Saad. Photo by Jessie Grearson.

I t was part of the liberal tradition," Saad tells us when we ask him about cultural influences on his 1995 wedding. From the beginning of our interview, we have been trying to understand how the two cultures of Saad Elzanati, a Lebanese math professor, and Julie Dalisay, an American graduate student in biology, have been woven into their marriage. Over and over again the couple insists on the international, the universal quality of their individual experiences and their lives together. They identify themselves by their politics, their choices, their intellectual interests rather than by ethnicity or nationality, and what we can see as we sit on their couch, with our tape players running, steno pads and cameras at our feet, reflects an intellectually committed universality. On the living-room walls are three paintings of human figures — abstract, primitive, brightly colored—that could have been inspired by African masks, European abstract expressionists, or children's drawings anywhere. There are books in the bathroom and the bedroom, and in the living room an extensive collection of international music. Both Saad and Julie wear blue jeans and T-shirts, the international uniform of the young and educated.

At first Julie's description of her family is subdued, almost apologetic — as though she is sorry her story is not more interesting — but as she talks, Julie's pride in her parents comes through clearly. Her internationalism is an inheritance from them. Julie's father is a doctor from the Philippines, and her mother is an American homemaker originally from Ohio. Julie's parents met in 1966 when both were working for the same Ohio surgeon, he as a medical intern, she as a secretary to the medical director in charge of the internship program. Despite the surprise and discomfort of both their families, they married. Their civil ceremony took place in Charleston, West Virginia, "only four hours away from Mom's hometown," Julie notes, though none of her mother's family members came. The couple had a bigger wedding in the Philippines, which was much better attended. "Dad wore the traditional white shirt," says Julie. "Mom wore the sleeveless Filipino dress, tight-fitting and very colorful." In any case, Julie tells us, the couple persevered. "Mom's family got over their disapproval when my brother was born." They lived in West Virginia for three years and in the Philippines for two more before moving to Hamilton, Illinois, a small town near the Missouri border, where they have lived ever since.

Evidently, Hamilton was not a bad place to have an intercultural childhood. We find Hamilton on our map — D7. It looks like little more than a village to us, close to the Mississippi River and a coffee stain, but far away from any urban center, with St. Louis and Chicago both at least a four-hour drive north or south. Despite its rural location, Julie describes a comfortable family life there. "I felt like a minority. I was darker, I stood out." But Julie emphasizes that the curiosity of the townspeople was friendly. They wanted to know who she was, how her family lived; they wanted to know about the mundane facts of her life, about the Filipino food her mother had learned to make. There were other Filipinos in a neighboring town, Keokuk, and Julie's family would get together with them to play mahjong and eat huge Filipino meals. Julie's memories of this time are very vivid. "And it was always fun to see our parents get tipsy," she adds.

Still, we sense that the biggest drawback of life in Hamilton was the relative lack of things Filipino for Julie to identify with. Because of this gap in Julie's life, a trip she took to the Philippines as a young teenager was especially important to her. It was a sad occasion because her grandmother was very ill and would soon die, but Julie rejoiced in everything around her: the landscape, the homes, the people, the food, the sounds of voices. Her Filipino family took Julie to historic sites and treated her like a special guest, stuffing the refrigerator in her room full of juice and treats. "I especially enjoyed the other kids, who threw me a party when I was leaving. They all wrote something for me in a little journal and gave it to me as a going-away gift." Julie's most vivid memories, though, are of the impoverishment and the beauty of the Philippines. "It was my first time to see in-your-face poverty, people living naked in cardboard boxes. I also remember how beautiful it was: waterfalls, rainforest, ocean — it was a sensory overload." She returned from the trip with a deep connection to her father's land, family, and culture, and she returned with a more developed sense of herself as not just different, but intercultural.

Ironically, it was Julie's father who expressed surprise when she announced her engagement to Saad. "You mean she's marrying a foreigner?" he is reported to have said, though both Julie and Saad insist that his reaction was more than a little tempered by irony. Julie's father sees himself as American now, and a conservative American to boot — though he is fiscally rather than socially conservative, the couple tells us. Mr. Dalisay knows we live in a complicated world, knows his own history, and is aware of how other Americans see *him*. When Julie told her mother about Saad, Mrs. Dalisay's reaction was more straightforward. Because she knew the complications of an intercultural marriage, she wanted Julie to know the challenges she might face and to learn about Saad's culture. But mostly, Julie says, her mother was happy for her. "I think she knew I was going to need a different kind of relationship because I was raised with the influence of different cultures."

"Plus I was such a wonderful guy," Saad interjects, grinning.

Saad's internationalism developed in opposition to the fierce ethnocentrism that shaped a civil-war-torn Lebanon. Saad grew up in the Christian Maronite village of Bfarwa, which has been rebuilt since the Lebanese Civil War and looks beautiful in the pictures he shows us. We see hillsides knotted with gnarled and unfamiliar trees and old stone walls. The earth is arid and red, strewn with small rocks and some cactuslike vegetation. The walls, which seem almost a natural part of the landscape, mark the lines left by an ancient system of inheritance that divides family farms into smaller and smaller plots so that a single family generally farms not one large plot, but many smaller ones. This strangely parsed farmland is beautiful, and Saad's family tends it skillfully, dividing their time between farming and running a real estate business.

Among the most impressive pictures we see in the photo album of Saad and Julie's 1996 trip to Lebanon are snapshots of dish after dish of food laid out on a long table, much of it grown by Saad's family. This bounty of colors and textures is the center of the social world Julie encountered when she visited Saad's family in Lebanon. "Every visit involved food. For days on end there were people coming into the house. They gave coffee to all the guests, Turkish coffee in little cups — a shot of pure caffeine — and little mints and chocolates," Julie remembers. "Then, whenever there was an event — the wedding, Christmas, New Year's — or when family came over, there were constant meals. They're very into presentation, too," Julie adds, pointing to photographs where the food is arranged in patterns on plates, and the platters are arranged carefully on the table. Saad lingers over these pictures with pleasure, explaining what is in each bowl. His family is quite self-sufficient, he tells us. In another picture, we see Saad's father leaning over a blackened barrel with a twisting pipe. It looks like a Prohibition-era still. "It *is* a still," Saad smiles; with it his father makes a drink similar to ouzo.

The tiny parcels of farmland and intricate pattern of stone walls in Saad's photographs might be seen as a symbol of Saad's ambivalence about his country of origin. The people who live here are productive and rich in resources, but their tradition of stewardship — the same tradition that has created this land's intricate borders and strange, patchwork beauty — also plays a role in the divisiveness and cultural isolationism that is a painful part of life in Lebanon. The conflict between Christian and Muslim Lebanese is so ancient and complicated that it is difficult to characterize. Christians, particularly Maronite Christians, have set themselves apart from, and have felt deeply threatened by, their Muslim neighbors, who have closely bordered them since before the Crusades. Because of their fear of Muslim *umma*, a concept of community that makes no distinction between religion and government, and because of their long history as a minority, the Maronites welcomed both the European Crusades and the much later colonization of Lebanon by France. French colonialism left behind an inequitable system of government (the presidency was reserved for Christians) and an inequitable division of wealth: among the Christians there was much less poverty. Finally, Lebanon's role in the Israeli-Palestinian conflict and the rise of Muslim fundamentalism in the Arab world has further hardened, if that is possible, the division between Lebanese Christians and Muslims.

In the village, Saad's father played an important role in healing the community after the war had finally come to an end. When the Israelis, whom the Christians had asked for help, began withdrawing from Lebanon, Saad tells us, they withdrew in stages. After each step in the withdrawal, Christian villages were attacked — so the Israelis wanted the Christians to relocate closer to the border. Half of the village left, but not Saad's family. "Dad said, 'No, we should stay!'" The empty houses were taken over by militants, but Saad's father, who has many Muslim friends, was the first person to build a house and invest money in the town again. "Everybody took it as a sign that things were going to be okay." Saad reflects for a moment. "I think it was very crazy, the war in Lebanon. We should have shared power instead of looking to the Israelis for help," he finishes.

Saad grew up in a world deeply divided by religion, region, and culture. He still expresses surprise that in the United States, the country is divided along racial rather than religious lines. "Unfortunately, we have religion on our identification cards, so I was shocked when I came to the United States and saw that whites don't really like blacks. Because my question would always be, 'Aren't they Christians, aren't you all Christians? What's the division?' The division in Lebanon was always a religious division, not ethnic, not caused by skin color."

The Lebanese Civil War started in 1975, though interreligious tension and hostility have a much longer history, and both cities and countryside have been deeply marred by the conflict. Beirut — sophisticated, wealthy, urbane — was all but ruined. Julie remarks on the disturbing wreckage of the once-elegant capital city, recalling the scars still visible on her 1996 trip: bombed buildings, unrepaired after six years of peace, a maimed cityscape that shocked Julie but seemed to go unremarked by the citizens of Beirut. "The buildings still had bomb pocks, like somebody who had bad acne." At the same time, she points out, a considerable effort has been made toward economic recovery. "One of my deepest impressions was that they're a growing society. They want to be involved in international commerce, but they're not there yet." As a result, there is a serious problem with pollution, among other things. One image that symbolized for Julie this struggle for economic growth was the tangle of telephone wires and electric cords that grew like strange vines between buildings. She shows us a photo, and we are amazed, like she was, at the unregulated snarl of cables and wires going in every direction.

Julie notes the bleak cityscape, but Saad speaks sadly, instead, of human losses and spiritual wounds. Usually generous with information about his family and homeland, Saad does not want to talk at length about these things. He remembers many of the people from his town who died or lost children, brothers, sisters, and he tells us how he feared for himself and for his family: "I got beat up at two o'clock in the morning," he says somberly. "They came in looking for my dad and would probably have killed him if he'd been around."

Saad grew up with war or the fear of it, with bombed buildings and fields, news of friends, cousins, and community members killed in battles and raids. When we ask if he will ever live in Lebanon, Saad expresses uncertainty. "Before our visit, I was really worried that Julie would hate it. But she loved it, and we'd like to visit more — I just can't see myself living there. Maybe we'd retire there eventually, but I don't know about that . . . I don't like the idea that you can't criticize the government. You can't fully sleep knowing that somebody might break down the door and harm you just because of your beliefs."

Saad feels that this violence and fear have bred an entrenched isolationism that has even followed some Lebanese Maronite immigrants to the United States. He does not like the ethnic paranoia that continues to be part of many Lebanese — even Lebanese-American — communities. Because of this isolationism, Saad stopped attending a nearby Lebanese Maronite church in which he had hoped to find a sense of community.

It seems to us that a certain intellectual universalism functions as a refuge for Saad from the divisiveness he grew up with. His network of politically committed, internationally minded friends and colleagues serves as an alternative community, a place from which he can care about his own culture safe from those aspects of it that he finds disturbing. This community is one of the things Saad and Julie share, and their membership in it brought them together.

Both have a deep political and intellectual interest in the natural world, which prompted them to take jobs as summer field-workers for Dr. Scott Robinson, an ornithologist who studies birds in the Shawnee National Forest of Illinois. They spent the summer of 1994 together in the forest looking for birds' nests and monitoring their inhabitants. Julie and Saad felt an instant kinship and attraction, and soon insisted on taking work that required two people so that they could be together during the day. Julie tells us they spent all their evenings together, "talking and visiting with friends. Mostly, I remember Saad listening to me as I told him what I thought were sad stories from my life, about the hardships I thought I was having. He probably thought I was crazy, but he didn't say so. He didn't give advice, just listened and cooked meals for me."

"I was off in the middle of the woods," Saad smiles. "I didn't know there'd be girls there, but I liked Julie immediately. Two weeks after we met, I took a couple of days off to meet my friends.

While we were camping, she was on my mind as a new person in my life. When I thought, 'Man, I miss this person,' then I knew she was important."

They exchange a smile, and Julie continues. "After the summer, I had planned to move out West for graduate school, but instead I fell in love with Saad, moved to Normal, and began graduate school at Illinois State. Then I knew it was all over — single life — after I moved up here. Neither of us were thinking about marriage at that time, but we didn't want to be far apart, either." Saad bought Julie a plane ticket to meet him in Paris on a return trip from Lebanon. "Everyone teased me that he was going to propose," she tells us, "but I thought he was just giving me a very romantic holiday gift. We'd known each other for about seven months when he brought up the subject of marriage as we walked down the Champs-Elysées."

The ecumenical selection of readings Saad and Julie chose for their American wedding reflects the life they have chosen together, built with pieces from whatever in the world moves them, whatever they hold dear. Their ceremony juxtaposed selections from *The Lorax* by Dr. Seuss with selections by Edward Abbey and Kahlil Gibran. Even when they speak, their voices often lace together. They finish each other's sentences, one beginning, the other helpfully adding a detail or finishing a phrase. Nowhere is this more true than when they describe the thick, silver wedding rings they created together. As we listen to the tape later, it is hard to untangle their voices, to attribute to either person thoughts that clearly belong to both. The symbols carved in their rings, they tell us, represent the elements: fire, water, air, and earth. There is a cross, "that's the sun for fire . . . it also looks like the Christian cross"; a butterfly represents air, "that's for freedom"; the wolf,

{ *Family Photograph* }

"for earth and for wilderness"; and two fish, the Pisces sign, "for life." The pictures are all connected by a cube design, a mathematical symbol Saad uses in his work. In it, we see infinity, with ends connected to beginnings.

The future Saad and Julie imagine for themselves continues to reflect the international life they have forged together. Julie is determined that her children will speak Arabic as well as English, and to that end she learned some Arabic herself during her last trip to Lebanon. She got a book and a tape, and every time she learned a new word, she would write it down. The problem was, says Julie, "I always had to double check with Saad before I said anything." Worse, Saad's family would make a great joke out of her attempts at the language, Julie reports ruefully. "They would laugh at whatever I said, like I was a dog doing tricks."

Saad and Julie also plan to return to Lebanon with their children every year and a half to give them a sense of belonging in their father's culture. Naming is a more complicated matter. Saad speaks with a wistful respect for the old tradition of naming the first son after his father. But, he says, "The war changed this tradition. Now a lot of Lebanese parents are choosing Western names for their children, just so that if they leave the country, they won't have the stigma of a weird name. It will be easier on the kid." Saad has himself developed the habit of introducing himself by spelling his name ("Hello, I'm Saad, S-A-A-D"), and he does not want his child to have to cope with this problem. At first, he wanted to name their son Akira, after their favorite movie director, Akira Kurosawa, but that name presented the same problem. Finally, they settled on the name Michael, which translates nicely into Arabic.

In a sweet twist, their good friend — the American man who

had performed their wedding in a Unitarian church — named his recently born son after Saad. Saad is pleased and touched by this, and he says so, but he can't resist adding, "Poor kid, now he'll be spelling his name for the rest of his life."

Despite their cultural differences, Saad and Julie insist that they have more in common than otherwise. Besides their shared political convictions, both grew up as minorities, Julie as a racial outsider in the rural Midwest and Saad as part of an embattled Christian minority in a majority Muslim culture. Saad and Julie also share a religious background. They explain that, in practice, the Lebanese Maronite faith is very similar to that of the Catholicism Julie grew up with. The Lebanese service, for example, is much like the Catholic service Julie is accustomed to, and Saad and Julie's small Lebanese wedding did not feel like a departure from traditions she was familiar with. Although the ceremony was in Arabic, Julie tells us that the priest "translated the vows for me so I knew what I was vowing." In fact, the most significant cultural difference Saad and Julie mention occurred when Julie sat with her legs crossed during the ceremony. In Lebanon, where women sit in church with their knees together, crossing your legs in church is rude, and in a wedding ceremony, where Julie was the center of attention, it was worse.

How did you figure it out? we ask.

"My father nudged me," Saad responds, and the message was passed domino-style down the pew. A small difference indeed.

Saad and Julie even look like one another. "She could pass for Lebanese," Saad tells us with pleasure, pointing out pictures of Julie among his family members in Lebanon. She does, in fact, look like she could be part of the family, with her dark hair and skin, black eyes. Saad, too, could be part of Julie's family — which we see assembled in another picture. Among the Lebanese photographs, we were surprised to find pictures of Santa. At first, we thought they were American photos that had gotten mixed in with the others, but on closer inspection we recognized the interior of Saad's family home, which we had seen in the other photographs.

These were taken in Lebanon? we ask, confused.

"Oh yes," says Julie.

Weren't you surprised to go all the way into the Lebanese countryside to meet Santa Claus?

"I WAS Santa Claus," she says with a mixture of pleasure and embarrassment.

We look more closely and can barely make out Julie's cheeks and eyes behind her white beard. The irony is lost on no one in the room. We all laugh without any need to articulate the reason — though eventually we do, and laugh again.

The Julie we see in the Santa Claus suit has gone to a place that she must, at some level, have thought exotic. She is as far away from home as any of us ever go, in a Lebanese village of 400 people, among olive trees and ancient rock terraces — and then she finds herself dressed like a department store Santa.

"Oh yes," says Saad when we have stopped laughing, "we got Santa in 1978. Beirut had him earlier than that, but it takes things awhile to get into the countryside.

"In fact, I was our first Santa," he adds with a smile. It is something else they have in common.

Part of the family

KIM & UMEETA

Kim & Umeeta. Photo by Christy Mock.

he first time we visit Kim Kranich and Umeeta Sadarangani, we have difficulty finding our way because we are driving after a record snowfall that slows us down considerably and obscures our view of the road. When we arrive, Kim is still out shoveling snow — trying to get the last bits of ice off the front walk. Umeeta has just made a fresh pot of coffee and is sending an Internet message to her family in Bombay. The interior of the house is sunny, the glare from the snow reflecting cheerfully on the white walls inside.

Theirs is a new house in a new neighborhood, and Kim, who works with public radio, and Umeeta, a literature teacher at a nearby community college, have moved in recently. But the place already feels comfortable, lived in, perhaps because of the smell of coffee and the colorful, eclectic personal effects scattered around the kitchen: mugs, flyers, books, mail. It may be Kim and Umeeta's unequivocal welcome of even such inquisitive strangers as we are, or their obvious happiness in this house together as they settle down at the table to talk to us.

The couple met on October 11, 1991, National Coming Out Day, at Penn State, where Kim was working and Umeeta was attending graduate school. Kim was standing in the crowd at a rally where Umeeta was handing out flyers for a small group meeting that would take place a week later. Kim signed up, and when Umeeta called to remind her, they ended up talking for forty-five minutes. Umeeta remembers that Kim had a cold. "I said, 'I wish I had a car. I'd come and make you a cup of tea.'" She smiles, recalling their early flirtation.

At that first meeting, Kim and Umeeta talked again and decided to attend a benefit together. Not until after the benefit did they realize they'd been on a date. That evening, another woman, assuming that Kim and Umeeta were a couple, asked them how they had met. Without skipping a beat, the two made up a long, romantic story together about finding each other through a classified ad and falling in love, a collaboration that unveiled their mutual attraction. Three days later, Kim and Umeeta were on their way to the blissful state they'd described in their story. They went to dinner and coffee, but, says Kim, "I couldn't eat a thing."

That Friday, Kim showed up at Umeeta's house with a tape full of love songs and then on Saturday with some chocolate kisses, her hands behind her back.

"Do you want chocolate or regular?" Kim asked.

"Chocolate," said Umeeta, who didn't get the joke.

"I was really disappointed," says Kim, "but then she figured out what I was trying to say when she saw the candy."

"And I said, 'Can I change my mind?'" Umeeta contributes.

Pretty soon, Kim was spending much of her time at Umeeta's place, which she remembers as very different from her own. "It was cluttered with pictures, and it smelled different, too — like incense — and there were scarves everywhere." In contrast, she says, her own apartment was well equipped, nice television and stereo system, but still somehow "depressing, spare. Not even intentionally spare but like-there-were-things-missing spare."

"It was as though she had not made her home her own in any way," Umeeta reflects.

"That was my background," Kim shrugs.

Are you a Garrison Keillor Midwestern Lutheran type? we joke, thinking of his stoic, restrained characters.

"Actually," Kim says mildly, "I *am* Lutheran."

Despite the spareness of her own life, or perhaps because of it,

Kim felt happy and comfortable spending time among Umeeta's scarves and photographs — her own clothing now suffused with the smell of incense and Indian cooking. In a matter of weeks, Kim was all but living in Umeeta's apartment. "She would go home on Sunday," Umeeta remembers, "just so we could say she still had her own apartment." By March, they'd given up the Sunday charade, and, the following June, they moved into a town-house together.

One year later, Kim and Umeeta had a commitment ceremony, one in keeping with the first moments of their courtship. They took part in the 1993 March on Washington for gay, lesbian, and bisexual rights, which was preceded by a mass wedding on the steps of the IRS. Kim and Umeeta were one of the twelve hundred couples married that day by the pastor of the famous San Francisco Metropolitan Community Church.

"I guess it's similar to what the Moonies do," Kim laughs.

In the pictures, both wear Indian clothes, Umeeta in a bright sari and Kim in the more tailored pants and long shirt called *salwaar kameez*. They are surrounded by couples sporting everything from full-length wedding dresses to cutoffs and tank tops. Gay rights posters are everywhere, and the asphalt beneath their feet is covered with chalk-drawn hearts enclosing the names of the couples and the number of years they have been together. The photos are colorful, festive, and happy. Kim and Umeeta — who are in their twenties in these pictures — look young.

Back home in Pennsylvania, Kim and Umeeta celebrated with a reception under a tent in their front yard. Sixty friends, including a number of Umeeta's professors came. Some friends helped with the food — one made a three-layer cake with two brides on top.

It was a bittersweet occasion, however. No family member came to the reception or called to congratulate them.

•

Umeeta was born in India between Bombay, where her parents live now, and another city, Thane, where she went to grade school. However, she graduated from high school in Kuwait, where her father practiced medicine for many years, and attended college in Pennsylvania. Because she has lived in so many places, she says that her identity is "not easy to pin down," an issue about which she feels both sensitivity and confusion. When people ask her where she is from, Umeeta's response is often a tart "Pennsylvania," though she knows she is really being quizzed on her ethnicity. She is sometimes irritated by the assumption that a woman with an Indian face can't be from here, that she doesn't belong in the United States, in the Midwest, in a given small town or suburban neighborhood. But on some level it is also an honest answer to a difficult question: many of Umeeta's most important memories have Pennsylvania as their backdrop.

Nevertheless, Umeeta really does identify herself as Indian. Her academic work focuses on Indian literature; she eats Indian food, finds herself drawn in friendship to other Indian women, wears the long flowing *dupatta* Indian women wear. How she envisions family, the way she perceives time, and her feelings about personal space, all these things, she has discovered, are affected by her cultural heritage. For example, "In India," she says, "people share small spaces more, they choose to sit and walk closer to one another. I remember in eighth grade how we used to walk arm in arm around the school building — that was our recess. Here, people don't touch each other like that."

But Umeeta has herself changed since she came to the United

{ *Part of the Family* }

States, absorbed some elements of American-style interaction. "When I was in India recently," she says, "people would walk close to me, and I found myself moving away." Time is less elastic for her, too, than it once was. "Being in the United States has affected how I experience time. I wish I could spend more of it talking, sitting together with friends without a goal, never thinking about the hour. But I myself am on a schedule; work takes up so much of my life."

Despite these changes, Umeeta deeply values her sense of connection with other Indians, particularly her closeness to family and a network of Indian friends she has made in the last few years. Such a sense of connection, however, is relatively new for her. At college in Cedar Crest, Pennsylvania, she was one of only three Indian students on a campus of a thousand. For four years, she had very little access to her own culture, and there were many things about it that she just didn't know, although she was still expected to represent India to American students.

Her choice to love women complicated Umeeta's relationships with other Indian people, too — especially her family. Unsure how her parents might react, Umeeta avoided discussing the subject or anything else important with them for years, and they grew apart. A similar sense of uncertainty kept her from befriending other Indians. "Until lately, most of my friends," Umeeta tells us, "have been white. I've been more cautious about making South Asian friends because of my sexuality."

Umeeta's sense of alienation from her culture changed about a year ago when she and Kim attended a presentation, "From Dot Heads to Dyke Divas," at a gay and lesbian studies conference in Chicago. "At first, I was afraid to attend — that I wouldn't be radical enough for them," Umeeta tells us. "I was afraid I wouldn't be

Indian enough, lesbian enough. Then I was afraid I would be *too* lesbian." Despite her doubts, Umeeta introduced herself to the panelists, all members of a Chicago group called Khuli Zaban ("Open Tongue"), and they invited Kim and Umeeta to lunch.

During this and future gatherings, the women ate together in Indian restaurants, told jokes in Hindi, talked about family, walked along Chicago's Devon Avenue, past storefronts full of saris and glimmering bolts of Indian cloth, laughing, arms linked. Umeeta still marvels at their ease together, at how warm and welcoming the women were. "It was my first time to be in the majority. I wouldn't have known I belonged on Devon if it had just been me and Kim."

Before, Umeeta had questioned her own ethnicity, but now she asks different kinds of questions: "Who really is Indian? And who decides what Indian values are?" Although once Umeeta had felt presumptuous thinking of herself as a woman of color — because she'd grown up with certain class privileges such as financial security, education — now she claims that identity. Talking with her friends has made Umeeta think of herself "in a racial way." She pauses. "If we call ourselves 'women of color,'" she says, "we can make people feel our presence. That's one way we can change things."

Kim feels that this friendship with the women from Chicago has helped to bridge a potential gap between the two of them, whose experiences have been so different. Blond-haired and blue-eyed, Kim's understated, straightforward style is softened by her warm demeanor. She was raised in Racine, Wisconsin, a place she remembers with deep ambivalence. A small town with an often insular perspective, Racine is not the source of Kim's interest in other cultures, nor was her childhood. She grew up in a family that rarely even vacationed outside the state and had no international experience at all. "I was the first person in my family to travel overseas," she tells us.

Part of her openness to other cultures Kim attributes to growing up lesbian in rural America, which made her feel alien from other people in her town. She did things that were unique for girls. The way she dressed and wore her hair short, for example, meant that she was often "mistaken for a guy," and she expected to be allowed to do the things boys did, too. She played on a boy's baseball team and was one of only a few girls to have a paper route. "The boys would spit bubble gum on my papers because they didn't want me to be a paper girl," she tells us ruefully. Most remarkably, at the age of fifteen Kim filed a lawsuit with the EEOC because she'd been denied work as a "stock boy" at a local pharmacy. Because she felt her differences from other townspeople so keenly, Kim has little sentimental attachment to the place of her childhood or to American culture as a whole. "My idea of being an American is conflicted," she tells us. "I often feel like an outsider."

In any case, Kim's interest in other cultures has helped her develop an increasingly intimate relationship with Umeeta's family, whose closeness she much admires. Kim tells us that the Sadaranganis were kind to her right from the beginning, that they treated her like family even when they thought she was just their daughter's friend. This warmth characterizes the relationships between the Sadaranganis and other friends of the family, too, Kim says. "I could not tell the difference between the people we visited who were relatives and those who were just friends — the warmth and inclusiveness were so different from what I'm used to."

Kim is also impressed by the depth and strength of the Sadaranganis' devotion to each other. She comments, for example, on the commitment of Umeeta's brother, Yogesh, to his sister — a relationship that is "based on duty" but is also very genuine. For example, the weekend before Umeeta defended her dissertation, Yogesh took a red-eye flight from Chicago. Despite a hectic schedule of his own, he devoted an entire weekend to helping his sister pack and move. Yogesh, Kim finishes, also sent his sister flowers at her favorite restaurant where she was celebrating after her defense; and Umeeta's face lights up at the memory of his thoughtfulness.

.

Umeeta told her parents about her relationship with Kim during a trip to India in January 1993, her first step in rebuilding a relationship that had been weakened by her secrecy. When she relates this part of the story, her eyes darken and her usually animated face grows solemn.

"I waited until it was late," she tells us. "In India, that's the only time when the phone doesn't ring — at 1 A.M. I wanted to tell them when we were alone." She pauses. "It was a very difficult thing — very hard to talk about my sexuality at all, and my mother didn't know what I meant. She was confused." When they did understand, both parents were worried about what would happen to their daughter, about her being hurt. What would Umeeta do if Kim left her for a man? What if this was just a phase? "They did tell me at the airport that they would always love me, but then I didn't have any word from them for a long time." Later Umeeta learned that her father had been seriously ill, which explained their silence.

Umeeta cannot say that her family understands her choice — Mrs. Sadarangani still cries every time she sees her daughter. "What the community thinks of you is very important in India,"

Umeeta explains, and "the family looks forward to a wedding." But both Umeeta and Kim communicate with the Sadaranganis frequently, and they have made progress.

Mrs. Sadarangani has told friends about her daughter's life and her relationship with Kim, although she cannot count on these friends' support, and during Umeeta's last trip home to India, her mother had moved to another level of acceptance. On the way to the airport, mother and daughter stopped to participate in a religious ceremony. As part of the ceremony, Umeeta's mother put a powder called *sindoor* on Umeeta's forehead. To her surprise and pleasure, Mrs. Sadarangani also put the powder in the part of Umeeta's hair, which, Umeeta tells us, "indicates that you're married" — her mother's way of acknowledging Umeeta's relationship with Kim.

Umeeta admits she is lucky, that many Indian parents might be less accepting of their daughter's lesbianism — though Umeeta is not "ready to say this is a special case." Still, her parents have traveled around the world, and in their homeland they are not minorities in any sense of the word. They can afford, Umeeta suggests, a certain leniency in their perspective. "My parents are in a position of privilege," Umeeta says, "so they don't have to exert control over me."

Kim's coming-out story is a more distant memory, but the pain of telling her mother about her love for a woman is still vivid to her. "I didn't do it right," she says with regret. She'd been hurt by one particular woman and went to her mother looking for comfort — an unreasonable expectation, Kim says, and she didn't get the sympathy she wanted. Her mother's negative reaction exacerbated the pain Kim already felt and deepened a rift between them that had developed when Kim became an adolescent. Kim's mother had to take her daughter's lesbianism more seriously once she had committed herself to Umeeta and has since sent them gifts as a couple, though, says Kim ruefully, "she doesn't particularly like Umeeta" and their mother-daughter relationship languishes.

Kim's father and stepmother, however, have been making an effort to reach out to the couple. The last time the Sadaranganis were in the United States, Kim's father and stepmother met them in Chicago, where they all went to an Indian restaurant in a north-side Indian neighborhood. Another time, Kim's father and step-mother came to visit in Champaign when the Sadaranganis were in the States, and a real warmth was generated between the two sets of parents. Umeeta's mother cooked a variety of Indian dishes and sent Kim's father home with several favorites. Kim's father and his wife have made, furthermore, a good-faith effort to understand and appreciate Kim and Umeeta's values and ways of seeing the world. "When we went vegetarian," Kim says, "they learned how to cook vegetarian."

Kim's relationships with her grandparents have turned out to be her strongest family connections. Her attachment to her mother's mother, "Grandma Keith," has always been unshakably strong. "I'm her special grandchild," Kim says. This grandmother has loved and accepted the couple from the beginning, and they have even "had discussions about what it means to be in a lesbian partnership."

Kim has been close to her father's parents all along, but their relationship has blossomed further in recent years. The Kranichs, whose love for Kim did not flinch when she came out to them, have now begun to treat Umeeta, too, like part of the family. "They saw our relationship as an opportunity for growth," Kim says, "and they embraced it." The Kranichs hug and kiss both Kim and Umeeta when they come to visit; at Christmas, they give a card and a check to both; and the younger couple shares a bed when they stay at the Kranichs' house. Recently, the Kranichs even sent Umeeta a birthday card, the importance of which Kim and Umeeta both stress.

"They used to send things just to Kim. Then they sent things to both of us, but they always put just Kim's name and address on the envelope. Now I get my own card — *and my own envelope*," Umeeta says. She pauses, her eyebrows lifted, to emphasize this point.

The two especially like the story of a recent family photograph, which Grandpa Kranich insisted should include Umeeta. "Don't you think you're part of this family?" he scolded her, when she had initially stood aside.

Kim and Umeeta have cultivated these family ties carefully, the way you might tend a delicate plant. They treat the Kranichs with loving attention, bringing them gifts from their trips to India, helping around the house, always cleaning the mirrors and windows — a chore that is hard for the older couple.

Kim's relationship with the Sadaranganis has been similarly nurtured. Besides visiting the family in India, Kim has made a point of spending time alone with members of Umeeta's extended family, even taking them on trips to Washington, D.C., and Chicago, for example. It is Kim, more often than Umeeta, who keeps up a steady e-mail correspondence with the Sadaranganis. "We share all the stories about the things that happen in our lives. I have found a special place in the family by making sure these tales get told," Kim says.

Sometimes, a niece or cousin of Umeeta's will even confide in

Kim, ask her advice about issues not easily discussed with some other members of the family. Kim wonders if the unconventional nature of her relationship with Umeeta might sometimes embolden these relatives to discuss such sensitive subjects. "My connection with Umeeta's family is unique for them and for me," she says. "They're important to me and I know I'm important to them."

．

Much of the work Kim and Umeeta have done to reestablish and strengthen their relationships with family members has been done in the context of the Midwest — Champaign, Chicago, Milwaukee — a site many would consider especially unpromising for such an endeavor. Some might assume that the region is too monocultural and too conservative for an intercultural family, or a lesbian couple, to thrive there, but Kim and Umeeta disagree. "In this town, in Illinois," Umeeta says, "it is possible to have the kind of social network we want. There's a really big lesbian community — and a big Indian community." They insist that Champaign is a better place to live, more diverse, than the East Coast town where they met, and that Madison and Chicago, both cities they visit frequently, are better still.

Though Kim moved back to the Midwest with some reluctance — the move to Champaign brought her closer to difficult memories of growing up in Racine — she is nevertheless particularly adamant on this point. The area, she says, gets a bad rap. In fact, as a young woman, Kim had always been proud to come from Wisconsin, despite the problems she faced growing up there. Wisconsin was the first state, she reminds us, to ratify the ERA, and it has a human rights bill that protects its gay and lesbian citizens.

Kim tells us that there is a strong sense of fairness that makes the region what it is, and Umeeta agrees. People tend to "talk to each other one-on-one. And," she adds with admiration, "they're really willing to listen."

.

And when they do not listen, Kim and Umeeta will do their best to change this. Each woman has a long history of social activism, and this history extends back, for Kim especially, to even before adolescence when Kim fought to be allowed access to the same privileges boys her age enjoyed. In fact, activism is such a pivotal part of Kim's life that she risked, and lost, a job in order to remain true to her ideals. In her first position at a CBS-affiliate television station in Altoona, Pennsylvania, Kim helped produce the evening news. Later, she was offered the chance to work on children's news stories, which she found even more exciting. Kim took this opportunity to educate children on serious social and political issues, producing a show on apartheid South Africa, for example, and one on the Tiananmen Square massacre, but was warned that the show was "too geopolitical." Kim was fired for doing news stories on human rights instead of teenage rock groups, and so she found herself at Penn State's public station — on Umeeta's turf. "Getting fired," she tells us with a brief smile, "was one of the best things that ever happened to me."

Though her job as a promotions coordinator at the public broadcasting station in Champaign does not give Kim the same opportunities to do human rights education, she nevertheless continues to put herself on the line as a volunteer. Now, for example, Kim is the area coordinator for a gay rights campaign called "Equality Begins at Home," which calls for city-by-city and state-by-state human rights legislation. As part of that work, Kim recently found herself talking to her district's very conservative Representative Ewing. Her argument — that gays and lesbians should be included in human rights legislation — met with such dismissiveness that Kim found herself at home later, sobbing in frustration. It is hard for us to imagine Kim shaken by the opinion of a man whose views on most subjects are anathema to her entire social circle. "It just hurts," she says simply.

Still, Kim is not about to step back either from this struggle or from the pain it causes her, and she describes her determination: "I live my life with my sleeves rolled up, and I often feel embattled," she tells us. "But I will give people the opportunity to treat me with respect, and I will be hurt each time they don't."

This combination of vulnerability and bravery, warmth and toughness characterizes Kim and Umeeta both as individuals and as a couple, and strikes us as a remarkably effective way to approach the world. If it won't change the mind of Representative Ewing — and certainly stranger things have happened — it has already been successful in many ways. In any case, talking to them makes us feel happy and hopeful — that we can also create a warm bicultural community for our families, that maybe with people like Kim and Umeeta in the picture, our children will have a better world to call home.

Signs

DOUG & KATY

Doug & Katy. Photo by Corbin Sexton.

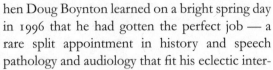hen Doug Boynton learned on a bright spring day in 1996 that he had gotten the perfect job — a rare split appointment in history and speech pathology and audiology that fit his eclectic interests exactly while allowing him to live in the same city with his academic spouse — it was not through official channels. He was walking down Iowa City's busy Burlington Street with his wife, Katy Stavreva, and with Katy's sister and brother-in-law, who were visiting from Bulgaria. The four had just stepped out of a restaurant called the Bread Garden, where Katy and Doug had, coincidentally, had their first date. "And one of the professors pulls over out of traffic and yells, 'You got the job!'" Doug's face brightens with the remembered joy of that moment.

"It was so neat, too, because we had with us this huge loaf of bread," Katy contributes with a matching flash of enthusiasm. "In Bulgaria, it is considered good luck if you see someone carrying a loaf of bread in their hands."

At first we are surprised to hear that Katy and Doug believe in signs of this sort, since such beliefs seem at odds with our initial impression of them. To us, they seem the consummate scholarly couple, witty and urbane, with a sophistication that sometimes borders on the sardonic. But when we listen to their love story, fate seems as good an explanation as any of how their paths converged. Their story, as they tell it, is such an accumulation of false starts and nearly missed opportunities that we are convinced, along with Katy and Doug, that whatever happened, they would have ended up — happily — together.

Doug grew up in the New Jersey cities of Middletown and Shrewsbury. "Bruce Springsteen country, blue collar, lotta ethnic communities, real diverse schools. There's Italian neighbah-hoods," he says, for a moment reverting unconsciously to his old New Jersey accent, "and Polish and African American neighbah-hoods." He lived his boyhood as part of a multiplicity of cultures that was just a fact of life for him as a child.

After he graduated from high school in the early seventies, Doug "hit the road," where he met an even wider range of people. "I wanted some adventure. I was looking for experience and truth and beauty," he tells us without irony. To some degree, he found what he was seeking, but, more important, he made friends who changed the way he looked at the world. "I met Native Americans, I met Mexicans, I met cowboys — that was all fascinating. I met *Californians*," he finishes dramatically.

Doug thinks that his predisposition toward an intercultural life may have begun with his attraction to deaf culture in the mid-seventies, when he had temporarily settled in Colorado. He was working at a preschool and became friends with a deaf coworker. "She took me to the deaf bar and deaf community events. I started hanging out with deaf people, and I realized they had a whole other universe. I was fascinated by this other culture in our midst and by the strangeness of their other, visual language."

Sign language also brought Doug "back to education," he tells us. His family still jokes about Doug, who, despite his earlier lack of interest in college, has turned out to be the professor in the family. "I took some sign-language classes at a community college, then wound up interpreting for friends, though at first I was really bad at it." Eventually, Doug moved to Seattle to attend an inter-preter training program, then to Oregon, where he worked at a small university, interpreting classes. Doug became so interested in one particular history class that he decided to take it himself, and ended up with "a bachelor's degree in history and an associate's degree in interpreting." The history of deaf culture has since become Doug's area of scholarly research. "But then there is the question of why I was attracted to that, too," he muses.

After further thought, Doug is inclined to trace his interest in other cultures even further back to his family's adoption of a Korean child when he was a teenager. "It was this great family project," he tells us. Doug was watching television with his brother and sister one night when they saw something about an adoption agency for Korean kids fathered by American soldiers. "One of us said, 'Oh, we should do that!' and my parents were like, 'Sure.' We kept mentioning it, really pushing it."

Finally, Doug's mother and father agreed, but because the adoption was expensive, the whole family worked on saving money for the project together. "We had this adoption jar on our table. We would contribute money from our allowance."

"When Lori came," Doug continues, "we all went up to Kennedy airport. It was a real high point of my childhood when she came walking off the plane — just this skinny, skinny girl who was terrified." Doug remembers the excitement of introducing Lori to her new world. "I was fascinated because she was from this faraway place. Showing her stuff was so much fun. She'd never seen television or used a telephone."

"And she squatted, right?" prompts Katy.

"Yes, we'd all lie on the floor to watch TV, but she would squat. We'd try, but we could never do that." Doug remembers that Lori "had a real hard time adjusting to American food. She kept asking for *kimchee*, but we didn't know what she meant. One time we served iceberg lettuce with French dressing, and she got all excited, she said, '*Kimchee*!' So this is what she had, every night for years, her own little bowl of *kimchee*."

.

Katy grew up in a different kind of intercultural world. Her Bulgarian hometown, Bourgas, is a port city of about 350,000, full of sailors, who bring with them a kind of worldliness not available in other medium-sized burgs, and tourists, who come to vacation by the Black Sea. There are also large ethnic populations of Turks, Greeks, and Armenians, who mingle together freely, as well as Gypsies — though, Katy tells us, "Nobody interacts with them at all; they live on the fringes of town."

Her family's neighborhood was urban and lower middle class, though she says it is difficult to distinguish classes "other than working class" in Bulgaria. Bulgarian children at the time were sometimes left home alone all day while their parents worked, so Katy developed a strong sense of connection with other kids, especially her cousins, with whom she often played. "We would go down to the port. Only authorized people were supposed to go there — you could fall in the polluted water and there was dangerous equipment — so of course it was our favorite place to play."

Katy remembers that there were Jewish playmates in her neighborhood and that she had many Armenian friends. "But I didn't think of them as different — except for their grandmothers, who mostly spoke Armenian and always yelled. Whenever we would pick plums off their trees without permission, there was this spurt of words in Armenian at the top of their voices, which we all found incredibly amusing." Katy laughs now both with the pleasure of recalling her old neighborhood and with the irony of having perceived these grandmothers as so strange, so foreign, when she would soon become a foreigner herself.

Bourgas offered a vibrant and entertaining street life with its coffee shops and public places. "It was a very street-oriented culture, you know, you didn't stay home," Katy says, and it was there that she developed a love of city pleasures, a taste for good coffee and sweets, and cafe conversations, which she shares with her husband now. She also developed a pleasure in multiple voices, and she took it for granted that she would be surrounded by different faces and languages. "The number of languages and people looking different — we were used to that," Katy adds brightly.

High school, she tells us, was "very international in focus." From high school, Katy went to the cosmopolitan University of Sophia which she describes as a midsized school, "the oldest in the country, very snobby," where she was first a student and then a teacher. At the university, things foreign were "just part of the landscape, part of my background." Before she graduated from college, Katy spent a semester in Great Britain. Like Doug, Katy did a lot of hitchhiking. "The first thing I bought was *The Hitch-Hiker's Guide to Great Britain*."

Given this history and that Katy had "traveled quite a bit" before she finally arrived in Iowa City to attend graduate school, it is not surprising that she found Iowa, even the university town in which she had settled, rural and isolated. "I was used to city grit and the pace of city life. I found it very strange that people here were smiling at you and not rushing. If these people aren't rushing anywhere, I thought, they must not have anything important to do." Worse, few people knew anything about her home country, including its location. "They would ask, 'Isn't that in South Amer-

ica somewhere?' Or, 'Is that part of Russia?' Or they would confuse it with Romania — and *that* was people in the comparative
literature department!"

Still, Katy had left Bulgaria because life was too difficult there
and because she needed the peace of mind to write. That tranquility she did find in the Midwest. "Wow!" she reports thinking,
"It's like a sanatorium here." What Iowa City lacked in "city stuff,"
it more than made up for in other ways. "Once I got used to
things, I found it an incredibly peaceful pace of life, and things
were organized, structured here; they worked."

·

Neither Katy nor Doug remembers when they first met. Both
were in graduate school at the University of Iowa, and they had a
few friends in common, so they know they mingled at occasional
graduate school parties in Iowa City. Doug only recalls thinking on
such occasions that Katy was bright and interesting, and Katy,
who was often "a little bit nervous around strangers," remembers
feeling surprisingly comfortable with Doug. But in the fall of
1995, the two began bumping into each other all the time. "And
being superstitious people," Doug continues, "we both took this
as a sign. Katy more than me, but I do recall thinking, 'Why do I
keep running into her?'"

And it wasn't just bumping into each other, Katy points out.
"Every time we met, we would end up talking, much longer than
you would with a mere acquaintance. We'd find an excuse to talk
a little longer." The wheels of fate had creaked into motion.

During this same span of time, Katy suffered a series of blows
in her personal life. Her father and mother died within months of
one another, and she was making her entrance into a very slow job
market. What she calls their "ah-ha" moment was set against this

dark personal time. "Maybe it was more *his* moment," she reflects, "because I was too dazed and confused from my parents' passing away." Katy and Doug were both in the post office mailing job applications on a depressing January day. Katy saw Doug and wondered whether she should greet him. "At that point, I didn't know if I could even bear to talk to anybody," she explains, with a trace of the sadness of those times. She did say hello, however, and the two chatted and walked out into the gray day together. As they approached the intersection, Doug invited her for coffee. Katy, who was in a rush, agreed to a future date, saying simply, "Okay, call me."

"What's your last name?" Doug remembers shouting after her. "I had no idea what it was! And the way she responded" — he flips his wrist expressing exaggerated disinterest — "'okay, call me.' It was extremely ambivalent."

So at first Doug didn't call. "At least not right away. But three weeks later, I decided to. Even though she didn't seem interested, we'd had these nice conversations, and I thought, 'What the hell, I'll give it a try.'"

"And he got the name right, which was pretty amazing because I didn't think he would."

"Another sign." Doug smiles wryly at Katy.

But when he did finally call, Katy responded to his greeting with a blank, "Doug who?" She was distracted, she admits. At the time, Katy's household had a weekly ritual of watching "Melrose Place," and the prime-time soap opera was on when the phone rang. She could see the television reflected in the kitchen window near where she was standing, she explains. "So I must have sounded a little —"

"Aloof," Doug finishes for her. "For the second time I asked her out for coffee, and for the second time I heard this lukewarm 'Okay, sure.' No enthusiasm at all. I hung up thinking this wasn't going anywhere." Still, the day of their coffee date came — with yet another sign. "We had agreed to meet at the Bread Garden, and there was this enormous blizzard; it was actually thundering and snowing at the same time." Doug, who was going out anyway, told Katy he would decide if it was still possible to meet in light of the weather. Not surprisingly, he decided it was.

"So he calls a few minutes later and says, 'Oh it's wonderful. It's snowing and so beautiful. And it's actually *warm*,'" Katy imitates Doug's breathless enthusiasm. "Well, it *wasn't* warm," she continues darkly, "and there was also fierce wind. I'm crossing the river and I'm all wrapped up. At one point, I decided that I had to cover one eye because if I lost just one eye, I'd still be able to see."

"But we made it there," Doug says, smiling at Katy as though encouraging her to cross through that blizzard to their happy outcome. "And then we had a really nice time."

When we ask Doug what motivated him to ask Katy out, it is Katy who responds first. "The buttons?" she queries mischievously.

"Oh, the buttons," Doug agrees, grinning. "When we met in the post office, she had this fascinating shirt on, a blouse with a thousand tiny buttons, a blue blouse with little red cloth loops over the buttons so there was this very intriguing half inch that went all the way down — maybe it was those buttons." But the more important attraction, he says, being serious now, was the ease of being with Katy. "We were comfortable with each other from the first conversation. I liked her. She was smart, she said interesting things." He pauses. "I think probably her accent and that she was from far away had something to do with it, too. I'm attracted to people from faraway, exotic lands."

"What attracted you to *me*?" Doug asks Katy. "That's what I want to hear."

"I think the main thing was the comfort, and he was also interesting. There are a lot of interesting people in Iowa City, but he wasn't pompous and that's a more rare combination. Also, he had a sweet tooth. I had a napoleon at the Bread Garden, and Doug finished half of it. That was a good sign."

Things went well right from the beginning, perhaps a little too well for Doug. After a month of dating, he began to panic. Doug had been married before, thought he didn't want to marry again, and, he says, the seriousness of his feelings for Katy frightened him. "It was much more complicated than this, but the way we think about it now is that I told Katy I wanted to break up, and she told me that I couldn't." We all laugh.

"The whole thing took about one hour," adds Katy, still joking.

Really, Doug says, she just reminded him that they could take things more slowly, that they didn't need to be as serious as Doug feared, that they could take one day at a time. "I hadn't asserted myself like that before," says Katy, "but I thought it was about time that I did."

"Good thing, too," adds Doug.

Four months later, Katy and Doug embarked on a trip to Bulgaria, a journey that tested and ultimately deepened their connection. In fact, it was not an easy trip at all. They flew into Istanbul and then, after their twelve-hour flight, had to take a twelve-hour bus ride from Istanbul to their destination in Bulgaria. "They have these wonderful buses that are made for superhighways," Doug recounts, "air-cushion buses. But on bad roads it's like being on a boat in a choppy sea." Both Doug and Katy make seasick noises here.

"Horrible," Katy continues. "Everybody smokes. Then we broke down. On the way out of Istanbul, the driver says something to the assistant, something about a red light. The battery was out. We had to travel without headlights — at night — on incredibly bad roads with terrible drivers."

Their stay in Bulgaria presented different kinds of difficulties. "Bulgaria was hard," Doug explains, "because Katy had to be my interpreter all the time. She was under the pressure of both speaking for herself and trying to make sure I got everything." To complicate matters, Bulgarians tend to repeat themselves several times, but without explaining this to Doug, Katy only translated once. "So he continually thought that he was missing something. And I'd tell him, 'But I *told* you what they said.'" Doug remembers asking Katy why she hadn't mentioned this cultural tic earlier.

"'Well, it never occurred to me,'" Doug mimics Katy's reply.

This was one of many elements of her culture that Katy just took for granted — like the Bulgarian penchant for teasing. "Bulgarians tease each other mercilessly," Doug says. "People kept making fun of me. Katy's nephew Chochi made fun of the way I walk, for example. Bulgarians have this very distinctive walk, very low down, bent knees, slouching, round shoulders." Doug gets up and hunches over to demonstrate. "But Americans tend to walk high and bouncy" — he takes another trip around the table in an upbeat manner — "and I am at the extreme. So Chochi kept making fun of me — walking on his toes and bouncing around. I was feeling very defensive." Finally, Katy explained that Bulgarians tease people they feel close to. "So it was a good sign. It was a way of making me welcome, like part of the family."

Differences in ideas about personal space and privacy also created discomfort for Doug. Katy takes obvious pleasure in narrating this part of the story. "The first time Doug goes to the bathroom and he comes back, the whole family's at the table." She pauses, thinking. "Did they applaud?" she asks Doug.

"No — but everyone turned and looked, eyebrows up, and I think it was her little niece Stella who said, 'How was it?' or 'How did everything go?' I had been a little constipated — a fact that Katy told everyone. This is the kind of information sharing that goes on!"

Doug expresses even more consternation, though, shaking his head even now as he remembers it, about the Bulgarian family's tendency to move together — in a group — from room to room. "As an American who needs his space," he tells us, "I'd get really tired. So I'd go into the bedroom to read a book in English, rest a little bit. Five or ten minutes later, somebody would wander in from the other room and then somebody else and somebody else until everybody was in the bedroom."

Sweet, we say.

"Yes," Doug agrees. "But it would drive me crazy! I just could not get away."

Despite all this, and partly because of it, the trip was a success, and on June 20, a month after their return to Iowa and six months after their first date, Doug asked Katy to marry him. He had planned a special meal for the occasion, an Ethiopian dinner from a cookbook they'd bought together. Ironically, this was the most disastrous dinner they had cooked during a courtship full of shared meals and culinary ventures. "Little did we know that this book was written for Ethiopians who already knew the basics, so there were shortcuts the recipes never explained. *We* didn't know you needed the bread to ferment for three days — the book never mentioned that," says Katy ruefully.

"So we basically made some bad crepes," contributes Doug.

"And part of the sauce had to cure for something like twenty days before that — so it —" begins Katy.

"— was inedible," finishes Doug.

Despite the ruin of the meal, Doug proposed that night and Katy accepted him. "It was a lovely evening," says Doug. "We had some wine. We were sitting out on the deck, and so it was nice — except that we were a little hungry."

"I'd been holding off for a couple of months, too," Doug reports when we express surprise at how quickly the two became engaged. He had felt sure much earlier and had been tempted several times to ask. "There was that sunset by the Black Sea," he says to Katy. "We kind of danced on the beach as the sun was setting — I almost proposed to you then." Doug resisted the temptation for a while, telling himself to "be sensible," but soon felt that waiting six months was sensible enough. "We just felt so natural together, really comfortable from the start. It was as though we'd known each other for much longer than we had."

Katy agrees. "I think in both our cases it was gradual," she says. "Well, quickly gradual," she amends, laughing, when we protest. "There was this sense of having known him for a long time from the very first intimate moments. I remember there was a storm once, and we had come into his house just to get umbrellas, and we started wobbling around with them in the kitchen, pretending that we were a seventy-year-old couple. It felt like a déjà vu, like we had already done this. So it wasn't a moment of revelation, just a series of incidents like this, that's what I mean by gradual."

Katy and Doug married, in essence, three times, which seems appropriate for a couple whose story is so rich with symbolism. The first ceremony was held in Iowa City in the summer of 1997 at the Unitarian Church, with vows composed from a variety of scripts provided by the church. The wedding was simple, a relatively traditional American ceremony with perhaps seventy-five people in attendance, and it went off without a hitch. "I was really nervous until my sister and my friend Svetlana and I went into the kitchen and had a shot of rakia — it's a very strong Bulgarian liquor — then I was fine." Such gatherings of friends and family members — in the kitchen, for lunches and dinners before the wedding, in clusters at the church and reception — were Katy and Doug's favorite part of this event. Even Doug's divorced parents, who hadn't spoken to each other in twenty-five years, made a kind of peace.

The reception was held at a friend's country home, surrounded by old oaks and hills of uncultivated prairie. The day was perfect, the sun turning the leaves to stained glass, everything yellow with light or dappled with shadows. It might have been the platonic ideal of an Iowa wedding — if it weren't for the Bulgarian guests dancing the *horo*, hands linked, and the *rakia* being liberally apportioned to the guests in the reception tent. That, Doug tells us, is a cultural difference. "Most of the American guests were drinking Diet Coke and the Bulgarians were drinking *rakia*. This was a wedding! You were supposed to be drunk, but most Americans don't do that anymore."

The next wedding came as a surprise. Katy and Doug had returned to Bulgaria in the summer of 1998 and had planned a second ceremony there, partly so that Katy's grandmother, a tiny intense woman in her nineties, could participate. "She is my only living grandparent, and I was named after her," Katy explains. "She and I have always had this very deep connection, so we really wanted her to attend our ceremony." Unfortunately, Katy's grandmother was too frail to leave her home, so Doug and Katy visited to show her their wedding clothes.

When Katy's grandmother saw the couple dressed in their wedding finery, she was so moved that she got out of bed, despite her weakness. Katy is herself deeply moved as she describes her grandmother's reaction, and she leans forward with the effort of conveying the moment's intensity. "I was amazed to see her lighten up and get this boost of energy. She was shaking a little, and clinging to us with both hands, but she started to do a condensed version of the Eastern orthodox ceremony for us. I was weeping through half of it." The occasion was remarkable partly because having a woman perform the ceremony is a serious infraction of church rules. "She not only broke the rules by taking the role of the priest, but she was also obviously ad-libbing the ceremony — the last time she had attended a wedding must have been fifty years ago."

We find the third ceremony, which we watch on videotape, very beautiful and mysterious. It takes place in a small, nineteenth-century church that feels somehow medieval, and some of the wedding rituals, Katy tells us, do hark back that far. "First of all, before you go in, they ring the bells, which I think is really charming because the whole village knows something is happening." In one of the more exotic portions of the ceremony, the couple has to wear crowns, called "wedding wreaths," made so long ago that they are too small for Katy and Doug, who balance them on top of their heads. The best man puts the crowns on Katy and Doug's heads three times, each time crossing and uncrossing his arms in the air as if playing a game of cups.

He then places the couple's wedding rings on their fingers in a similar manner — three times, each time crossing and uncrossing his arms in front of them. The wine drinking is less complicated, with the bride and groom each sipping from a cup three times, but is still solemn and meaningful. Finally, the couple walks around a table holding hands with each other, the priest, the best man, and the maid of honor. Such elaborate rituals bode well, we think, for Doug and Katy; we can't imagine a couple splitting up after such a ceremony. It is as though the priest, with all these ritual triads, is tying a knot too complicated to be undone in a human lifetime.

Admiring the formal beauty of this ceremony on video, we are struck by the depth of concentration that Doug, especially, focuses on the proceedings. When we ask whether he was particularly moved by the ceremony, he tells us that actually, he was in pain. He'd pulled a toenail off five days before and had been unable to wear shoes for a week. "I wore sandals everyday, everywhere we went, but I couldn't wear sandals to the wedding." The injury was serious and painful: "Even socks hurt. It got all puffy and infected. We went to the doctor. This is another Bulgarian thing — insensitivity to suffering."

"Yes, pain is no concern," Katy confirms. "Anesthetics are used rarely. In childbirth, only if you are having a C-section."

"So the doctor scrubbed my toe with alcohol." The stern-faced Doug we see in the video, it turns out, is concentrating on surviving the pain of shoes, and Katy's frequent, solicitous glances are expressions of concern for a suffering husband.

This wedding, too, was followed by a beautiful reception. This reception, held by the Black Sea, included an impressive spread, with bread for a final old-world ritual. "After the church wedding, the couple would traditionally go to the bridegroom's house, which is where they would live," Katy explains. "The mother-in-law would meet the newlyweds at the threshold of the house. She would give them bread dipped in salt and dipped in honey, feed these to each one." This ritual was meant to represent the difficulties and the pleasures of marriage, to prepare the couple for what lay ahead, but Katy's sister performed it in a more lighthearted spirit. In fact, the whole occasion, from what we see in the video, was celebrated with unrestrained gaiety. A small cousin of Katy's ran up to her at one point in the party to declare, "This is the best day in my whole life."

Aside from Doug's injury, those were good days for Doug and Katy, too, and they have been followed by others. The couple lives together in Iowa City now, in a small, pleasant house beside a neighborhood park. When we visit, everything we see reflects a harmony of tastes. Most of the furniture is antique; in the living room, we see paintings that Katy and Doug brought home from a Bulgarian monastery. There is European glassware in the cabinets, a handmade quilt on the bed. Katy moves around the kitchen and dining room, getting coffee and tea, with a happy energy. In a few months, the two will be moving to a new house, and soon after that, they will have a daughter.

Katy and Doug have decided to name her Anna Sophia because it is a name that they both like and one that works well in both Bulgarian and in English. "We especially wanted a name that wouldn't cause embarrassment in either language," says Katy.

"Like Doug — dook dook," says Doug, trying to imitate a Bulgarian accent.

"Anna is a family name on both sides," Katy continues. "It's Doug's mother's middle name, and my great-grandmother's first." In this bicultural spirit, Katy and Doug hope Anna Sophia will learn to speak both Bulgarian and English fluently, along with sign language and Spanish. And Katy and Doug will teach her about Bulgaria, incorporate Bulgarian traditions into their celebration of holidays, take their daughter to visit Katy's homeland and family.

Their ideas about parenting sound like a mélange of attitudes from American and Bulgarian culture. While they can't imagine being as strict with Anna Sophia as Bulgarian parents usually are, they like the idea, as Katy says, of "having some kind of structure," giving their daughter more guidance than American parents tend to. But Katy and Doug are most emphatic about struggling against what they see as the mediocrity of American culture. "It's really a junky culture," says Doug of the commercialism and media hype that take up so much space in our lives. Katy and Doug don't intend, for example, to get cable television or to allow Anna Sophia much time in front of the TV. They worry especially about public school — where, Doug says glumly, "Football is far more important than art," and where, Katy adds, "Smart kids don't get challenged enough."

Katy and Doug are not planning to incorporate any particular spiritual practice into their family life, although they would like their daughter to know something about religions, especially Christianity, because of its importance in the United States. But they also want to give Anna Sophia a connection to ritual, particularly old Bulgarian rituals, which they've already made a part of their lives together.

What kinds of rituals? we ask.

"Well," offers Doug, "we don't pass soap to each other."

"We don't shake hands with anyone across a threshold," says Katy.

"If you're going on a trip, someone should always throw some water on the porch in front of you."

"And you don't go back," emphasizes Katy.

"It doesn't matter if you forgot the most important thing," says Doug apparently remembering a moment from their past. "Even if you forgot your conference paper."

The couple honors Bulgarian traditions during the holidays, too: making Easter bread and Christmas *banitsa* made of feta cheese, philo dough, and eggs; burning incense on Christmas Eve; and picking the New Year twigs. "They're little pieces of the dogwood tree," Katy explains, "and you name each one with a fortune. Whichever twig you choose, that will be your fortune for the year." There are also days for the dead, and on these occasions Katy prepares bloated wheat with raisins and nuts, which she then gives away.

For both Katy and Doug, these traditions represent a connection with the past and a sense of continuity between generations. Their wedding in Bulgaria, they tell us, was attended both by young professionals, with cars and modern clothing, and elderly people in old-fashioned garb. "There's this real sense of generations," Doug continues, "the old people and the middle-aged people and all the kids interacting. I felt like I was not just joining a family but joining a historical progression. That's something you don't always get in the United States, where the old is often jettisoned."

For Katy, there's an additional spiritual element that she finds difficult to explain. "It's just what I do," she says, "how I interact with the world." She believes, she tells us when we push her on this point, in a kind of force, an equilibrium in the universe. "You don't mess with things," Katy tells us, "if you don't want to foul up the equilibrium." She laughs, but we can tell it is important to her. The traditional practices she incorporates into her life, and will include in her life with Anna Sophia, represent the ways that Katy's family and culture have tried to maintain such a balance.

So far, it is working. Not long after we spoke with Doug and Katy, Anna Sophia was born — naturally, and with only seven hours of labor. She was a few weeks early and a little small, but she is healthy, growing quickly, and all the signs point to continued harmony. "Doug knew just what to do the entire time," Katy tells us. "I was reduced to one-word commands but he became psychic. He even knew, during the worst part, when to comfort me by talking about my grandmother." It was as though Doug and Katy had done this all before.

{ *Signs* }

Amazing grace

DIANE & BLONG

Blong, Diane, & B. J. Photo by Jessie Grearson.

reparing to visit Diane and Blong Her's home, we feel a little anxious about finding our way. Their neighborhood is not, they have told us, in the best part of St. Paul, and on the phone Diane was more inclined to give visual landmarks (train tracks, a local grocery store) than specific street names. But it is a clear summer's day; there is a zoo nearby, perfect for entertaining our children; and a considerate friend, familiar with the area, has carefully translated Diane's landmarks into an orderly set of penciled directions with numbered lefts, rights, and the word "Directions" printed confidently at the top, so we set out bravely.

On the far edge of the city, we turn left onto University and right onto Western, following it past the railroad tracks, making another right onto Burgess Street. Suddenly, the upscale bakeries disappear, the McDonald's that looks as orderly as a post office is left behind, and residences are replaced by a battery of industrial complexes with empty lots and chain-link fences. When houses begin to reappear, they are noticeably shabbier and set closer together. The grass of their lawns is longer, and bits of plastic bags fly up around us as we drive. Two men working on a truck rise up from under the hood to watch us warily, vigorously shaking their heads NO to warn us off the first parking spot that we find near the family's apartment.

We enter the building now, armed only with a quick scribble from talking with Diane: *brick building, side gate to apt, go thru door on side, up stairs; turn into dark hallway.* Dark is right, especially as we have come in with our sun-dazzled eyes and a little girl who needs to use the bathroom bumping along the wall behind us. But then Blong opens the door to the loft apartment even before we can knock, and the light spills out with him, welcoming us up. For a moment, we stand in the long, sunny room that is their apartment. We let our eyes readjust and permit ourselves the simple enjoyment of seeing the people who, until now, have been disembodied voices on the phone, typed words sent out over the Internet.

Blong, from our first impression of him, radiates a kind of peace, a simple dignity that we both feel. An attractive man in jeans and a blue short-sleeved cotton shirt, he manages to look both attentive and at ease. He has a small, constant smile and a way of looking up candidly from beneath his dark straight bangs. Diane, who greets us at the top of the stairs, is her husband's height; she has long dark hair that reaches toward her waist. At first her manner is almost guarded, reserved, like a person posed in an eighteenth-century photograph. Later, however, when we are talking, her expression changes so completely — her light brown eyes animated, amused — that we feel we might have imagined this sternness.

We first learned of Diane and Blong Her's story because of their two-month-old infant son, Blong Junior, or "B. J." A friend who is a pediatrician told us of an especially beautiful child she had seen in her clinic whose father was from the Hmong community and whose mother was American. We were intrigued — what we knew of the Hmong suggested, if not a fanatically close community, at least one fiercely devoted to preserving its culture in the midst of the American heartland, one disinclined to marry outside itself.

Diane and Blong met, as it happens, on the Fourth of July 1997 at one in the morning, "just after the fireworks." Diane can be as exact about times and dates as her husband is hypothetical and vague — apparently the Hmong do not pay much attention to dates and do not keep birth records, which makes tracing events in Blong's eventful life difficult. "But she remembers everything," Blong comments indulgently about Diane's precision, as though making room for a somewhat odd American obsession.

We are ready to hear a traditional love story, complete with fireworks, but our image of a romantic summer evening shifts when Diane tells us that the two actually met in a chatroom on the Internet. Now we see a very different picture: two people, two remote rooms — one in rural Pennsylvania, the other in Minnesota. Diane (who signed on only with her initials, DRS, "plus some numbers") had expressed interest in talking to others in the 19–25-year-old range, and Blong (whose Internet address began "ilu4ever@ . . .") had written back that he was twenty-three. That's all it took. The two struck up a conversation that was immediate and, to them, uncanny.

It takes us a moment to picture this, to imagine how such an intense bond could have formed despite such tenuous connections. Was it his name that intrigued you? we ask. But what Diane actually liked and responded to was Blong's on-line profile, a brief description of himself that he'd posted. "What was it, exactly?" she asks him. Blong tips back his head, remembering, before reciting modestly to the ceiling, "I say, 'I love you more than the stars in the sky; and I will never let a mosquito to bite.'" Then he looks back at us serenely.

We are caught off balance by this unguarded sweetness and the poetry of Blong's words. Were you hoping to meet someone, we ask, feeling our way forward. Is that why you had a profile like that? "No, it was just conversation," Blong tells us. "But some people make up a profile about themselves. For me, my profile is true. I really make it from my heart."

Diane also denies that she was looking for romance on the Internet. "I'm Mormon," she tells us matter-of-factly, as though this explains almost everything about her. "For a while, I was planning to marry a Mormon, a returned missionary." The Church of Jesus Christ of Latter-day Saints — the Mormons — Diane tells us, encourages its members to marry other members, and Diane, who was baptized at eight, was seriously religious, taking instruction each morning for several hours throughout her high school years. A returned missionary — someone who went out to do the church's work and returned at the age of twenty-two or twenty-three — would be just the right age and probably looking to marry as well, she explains practically. Such a marriage partner failed to materialize, however. "And then I found *him* on the computer, and that was that," Diane concludes her explanation.

That Diane was even on the computer was a bit of a fluke; she admits that she never enjoyed school much and that she is not really a computer person; it was her little brother who introduced her to the Internet and to chatrooms. "We got a computer back in '95 or '96 and my little brother kept telling me how fun it was. I didn't want to get on it at first — I thought it was stupid. But then I tried it and started liking it and got hooked. I was on it all the way up to '97, when I met him."

Access to a computer was also a stroke of luck. Diane lived with her mother and brother in a trailer park, and the computer was a generous Christmas gift from an uncle. Similarly, Blong's computer seems out of place in the couple's austere apartment. In this one long room with its skylights and few possessions — the card table at which we sit is itself a recent purchase — the computer on its neat stand strikes us as a tribute to the couple's romance. It is their one luxury. We would wager that there are not many computers in this neighborhood, and we ask Blong what prompted him to make such a significant investment. He likes to be able to do "research" on the Internet, he says, to access information about current events, jobs.

"He likes talking to people," Diane says. "He can talk to people far away."

Like your family? we ask.

"My family — they don't have a computer, and it's far, far away," Blong replies, that second "far" implying something other than mere physical distance. The tonality of his native language imbues his words with a sadness that makes them sound like a fragment of song lyric. But then he brightens. "I like talking to American people, just say hello to everyone."

"That's him," Diane agrees. "He just says hello until he gets to know you. All it was for him was just 'hello' and 'hi' and then he'd go to the next room. But then he met me and it wasn't like that. They have IM — Instant Message — and that's what we talked on."

In fact, it was these Instant Message exchanges that quickly convinced both that they'd found true love. IM is a feature by which a message is displayed as soon as it is sent. When the two communicated, they'd often say "the same thing at the same time."

"Because of the IM, you can't see what the other person is saying, but as soon as I would send my message, his would pop up and it would say the exact same thing," Diane reports happily.

"Here we are, we think alike, and we're not even in the same state."

"She liked something, I liked the same thing," Blong agrees. "We just talked and talked and became to know each other very well. Having something in common, interests."

But when we ask for details about this immediate bond, what kinds of things they "talked" about, neither recalls. They do remember discovering that they shared the same straightforward life values — no drugs, no divorce, no cheating, that truthfulness was important to both of them. However, we can tell that they feel like their on-line courtship happened a long time ago, and in terms of large life events, they are right: within the year, they had married and had their first child. In any case, neither seems to think such details very important in the face of their early and unshakable certainty that they were meant for one another.

We get the impression that this connection was equally important to each of them. Their lives at the time seem similar — each yearned toward a future where things would somehow be *different*. Diane, who had finished high school, was working in a hotel "doing rooms," a job that she didn't particularly like. She would come home, sign on to the computer, and quickly become lost in the world of chatrooms and on-line conversations. Blong was working in a bank on an 11:00 P.M. to 7:30 A.M. shift, a job that he disliked because it confined him to a chair and cut him off from contact with most people. He would log on after waking and before going to work. For that time each day when their worlds intersected, the connection provided a kind of companionship and comfort that brightened their lives.

We are amazed to learn, although it would be six months before

Diane flew out to meet Blong, she bought a ticket to St. Paul within a month of their first exchange. "I would have bought a one-way ticket — I was always planning on staying — until I found out it was actually more expensive." When we ask about their other conversations, assuming that they must have begun talking by phone before taking such a step, again Diane surprises us. "Only once," she says, in her calm, understated way, as though this was natural to her. And this call was not even her idea — her sister-in-law decided to phone Blong as a kind of informal screening, to "see how he was." Diane, who was there but pretending not to be, wasn't even intending to speak to Blong at all, but he seemed so nice that her sister-in-law decided to put Diane on.

What did you think? we ask. Did he seem the same to you?

"Well, I was making a salad at the same time I was talking to him, and he said, 'make enough for me, too,' which is the kind of thing he would always write to me on e-mail when I would tell him I was going off to make myself some dinner," she says. Neither Blong nor Diane waver in their position that the tremendous risk they were about to take (at the time, Diane still didn't know Blong's real name) was at all remarkable. "I didn't feel anything strange," Diane tells us.

"Felt like it was right," offers Blong.

By then, Diane's mother had discovered her plans. Diane had begun moving her possessions out of her mother's trailer into her sister-in-law's house. It occurs to us that this covert-but-noticeable action captures the mixture of defiance and concern that Diane must have felt. At twenty-one, she was old enough to make her own decisions, but still young enough to care what her mother thought of them. Eventually, when Diane's mother noticed the disappearance of her daughter's objects, Diane revealed the ticket purchase. We wonder whether Diane's family was worried or if they shared the couple's confidence in fate.

"Oh, they were all scared," Diane acknowledges readily. "My mother was worried, but my older brother was the worst — he threatened to never speak to me again if I went out there. They told me, 'You don't know anything about him, or what he could be like.' But *I* knew," she finishes simply.

By December, Diane had saved up enough money to travel, and two days after Christmas in 1997, she boarded the flight for St. Paul. Later she writes to us, "When I moved here, it was my first time ever on a Plane," her Dickinson-like capitalization expressing the importance of the event in her life. Only days before the flight, Diane finally received a photograph from Blong with which to recognize him at the airport. "I'd sent him one right away, but it took him the longest time."

"Usually I don't have a photograph — I had to have someone take it at work," Blong explains, more to Diane than to us, as though still apologizing.

When she arrived in the terminal, Blong was nowhere in sight. "I was waiting for him and waiting for him — it was a late flight, too. I called up his apartment, thinking maybe he hasn't left yet, and I got his answering machine. Then I was a little worried — OK, maybe he's not going to show up, maybe he lied about that. So I had him paged as Jay Her, which was the name he gave me, then I waited in baggage claim." But because Jay is not his real name, Blong didn't hear the page. "He came down to the baggage claim anyway. And I stood up, because I noticed him right away. He was wearing the outfit in the picture, so as soon as I saw him, I recognized him." Even though Blong had arrived well before Diane's flight landed, he doesn't like to sit in the same place for a long time and, in walking around, had missed her as she exited the plane.

We are struck by the potential drama of this moment, although, according to both, there was nothing particularly dramatic about it. "He just grabbed my bag and we went out to the car," says Diane. The only detail that suggests Blong might have felt flustered was that he could not remember where he parked.

Not surprisingly, the beginning was awkward, though neither of them seemed to be thrown by this. "We were just quiet together," Diane offers. "We were even quiet on the way home. We didn't know what to say. We weren't used to *talking* talking."

"For me, when you talk computer talk, it's not face to face; it's a different conversation," Blong agrees.

"When I first got here to the apartment, it was pretty silent. It's easier to talk to someone when you can't see them. In person, you clam up."

"I don't know how she feel, but for me it's just a normal thing," Blong says, again with a serenity that makes commonplace even the extraordinary. When you have faith in your decisions, he seems to be telling us, whatever happens is normal, and whatever is normal is right.

When we who are intrigued by but lacking in this sort of faith ask Diane how in the context of such tenseness, such silence, she could possibly have felt confident about her decision, she relates two incidents, both small but emblematic. After she got to the apartment, Blong had offered her food and she had taken an apple. When she cut her hand on the knife, Blong went to get a bandage and put it on for her, a gesture that touched her and made her feel at home. "And then I knew that he was a caring person —

not everyone would have done that." Also, back then, the apartment had mice. "I put my stuff on the floor, and there were the mice. I jumped up and we both started laughing." This shared response reassured Diane that she had found someone with whom she could laugh at life's small and large difficulties.

Blong's certainty was also immediate. "As soon as I see her, I know she's the one," Blong tells us easily before we can even ask. "We talk to each other, we think alike — she's the right one. My cousin and uncle asked me many times to get married and I said no, it's not the right time yet. I told them I had to have a job, get a car, have a place to stay, prepare myself, stay strong, love yourself, then you can get on."

To this Diane adds, "It was more friends at first. Of course, we both said we loved each other — that was it. For a month, we were both quiet. But I knew after a while we would start talking."

We are quiet ourselves, trying to picture this comfort in such extreme circumstances, to imagine a faith so strong it could allow a grace period of silence while the two got to know each other. And after a while, as though waiting "a month or so" to talk is "just a normal thing" for two people who have been transplanted into a life together, Diane and Blong did begin talking, trading their life stories.

Blong's story is tied to that of the Hmong people, who are originally from China, where a long history of persecution prompted them to migrate further and further south to the more remote and mountainous regions of the country. At the beginning of the nineteenth century, about half a million Hmong migrated even further, to Indochina, first settling in Vietnam and Laos, later in Thailand. Blong's family, who took part in this migration, settled in a mountainous region of Laos, where they lived the typical farming life of their people, a labor-intensive but self-sufficient one, tied to the land and the rhythms of the seasons.

Even before the war that was to disrupt Laos, the Her family's life was not easy. Blong was the first child in his family — he had "three sisters and two brothers, but one sister and one brother had passed away" — and as the eldest, shouldered many responsibilities. "In my memory as a child, I have had a lot of struggle, some time happy, sad, want to live, want to die, which sounds funny. When I was young I don't have much time to go around with friends or go somewhere to play." Each morning, Blong had to care for his family's animals as well as himself: "I had to let the ducks and chickens out of the cage and feed them, sometime help my parents feed the pig too. After that I cook myself breakfast then get ready to go to school for the day." After school, Blong would feed the animals, put them back into their boxes and cages for the night, before preparing dinner for the family. "After I had done all the things I have to do, then I do my homework for the next day."

Those were hard times, though not without their pleasures. Blong recalls with particular wistfulness the self-sufficiency of his life in Laos. "We grow rice, corn, bean, tomato, potato, banana. Everybody works the farmland, a very happy life, you don't have to buy anything, just clothes. We build our own home." Life in the United States is very different, and Blong misses the immediate connection to nature, the lack of fishing and farming in his now urban life. When we ask him what he misses the most, he says it is the freedom to "go to the jungle, listen to the birds singing. Many things you can do there, you can go out there."

While Blong is saying this, we are looking at a recent picture of his mother's home: the walls are made of rough wood, the roof is thatched. It would be easy to romanticize this rural life, and Blong makes a point of acknowledging the advantages of his home in America, as though failing to do so would be impolite or ungrateful. He emphasizes the freedom he has here, then adds, "Some things are easier. In my country, if you want water, you have to go to the stream and get water. Here you have a tap." But for this precious freedom, he has paid a significant price, and for a moment we all pause, thinking of what has been lost.

The family's life was dramatically altered in 1975, the year Laos fell to Communist forces. Life became difficult and dangerous because the Communists were searching for soldiers who had cooperated with the CIA's "secret war." They were searching "for those who were involved with the CIA during the Vietnam War, to take them to jail, send them somewhere far from family. We know that a lot of those old soldiers caught by the Communists never returned home to see their family, and nobody knew what happened to them." Blong, too, was in peril. The Communists were seeking to recruit young boys to fight against those "still living in the jungle resisting the Communist regime. At that time, things were very hard for those who live in the country like us, so we have to escape."

Blong's father, understandably, refused to go. "Because we have many things such as cows, water buffalo, fish, chickens, ducks, pigs, goats, a farm, it is hard to just put these things behind and leave." Sadly, Blong notes that his father's decision to stay failed to preserve the family's way of life. "They suffered a lot because of the Communist regime. My family had to move from place to place, and they lost many things that we had. Now all they have is just a little house and couple of animals. They don't have money, good clothes, medicine, and good food."

We are struck by how difficult Blong's decision to flee Laos must have been. As the eldest son, Blong had great responsibility in the family, and only severe circumstances would have prompted him to leave his parents and most of his family behind for an uncertain future in Thailand. But by 1982 Blong felt that life had become unbearable, and he decided to flee Laos with his beloved paternal grandmother and a few other relatives to a relocation camp in Thailand. He explains, "Actually, my grandmother loves me more than the others, everyone says that I am her favorite, and she is like my mother to me. She decided to live with her two sons in St. Paul, and she would take her favorite with her, even though that made her family sad."

The dangerous journey from Laos to Thailand, accomplished on foot, took one and a half years. They had to go slowly, Blong tells us, "move one place to another and stay on for a while, then move on." All Blong took with him were two pairs of pants, one pair of sandals, a small flashlight, and a little rice.

The Thai relocation camp, Ban Vinai, where Blong stayed for five long years, was "a little bit better than living with the Communist rules, and it helped a lot for those living in a dangerous situation." Of course, the camp, with its thousands of refugees packed into tight quarters, had its own hardships, namely, a complete lack of freedom and privacy. "You cannot go out in Thailand, you can't do anything there, they control you," Blong offers briefly, not wishing to comment further on the loss of liberty he suffered in order to eventually secure passage to freedom in the United States. Blong worked at a variety of jobs at Ban Vinai; he taught Chinese to a neighbor (he speaks five languages — Thai, Chinese, Laos, Hmong, and English), and he also worked for the United Nations High Commission for Refugees, where no doubt this fluency helped in his work registering other refugees.

His grandmother left the camp before him, after three years, in 1985. Blong's uncles were among the handful of the earliest Hmong refugees who left Laos before the Communists took over. One uncle, Blong tells us, lost part of his leg to a land mine. "My two uncles sponsor my grandmother, because she's older, she have to come early. She don't have to stay and study or learn language or anything for school. After that I was alone, because I did not have a sponsor yet." At this point, Blong was still in his early teens. For a long moment, he sits with his head slightly bowed, looking at his folded hands, a gesture that translates roughly as time passing, difficult arrangements made. In July 1989, Blong arranged passage for himself to the United States, claiming to be eighteen when he was actually several years younger. "You had to do that because they say, 'You're too young, you can't travel on your own, you have to have someone take care of you.' So I had to make my age older, because I didn't have those things."

Blong arrived in St. Paul on July 7 and stayed with his uncle. He didn't know how to navigate this new world, having never seen a television, an electric light switch, a refrigerator before. "Soon time went by fast and it was December. It was cold," he remembers, "and everything was still new to me. But when I got used to it, it was just a normal thing," he says, again emphasizing the positive. "And I was happy to be with my grandmother again. She was like a parent to me," he reiterates. "Everything she has — some food, some fruit — everything she has, she saves something for me. Lots of people say to her, 'you love that one the best.'" We ask

Blong what he was able to bring to the United States with him, and at first he turns up his empty hands and smiles. Later he amends this, writes to us, "What I brought with me was HAPPY."

We ask Blong, who received his certificate of United States citizenship in June 1999, whether he feels any regret over making the break with his previous homeland, Laos, so final. His answer is definite. "No. My home is here. I live here. For me, everywhere I live is just my home." For one thing, in the United States Blong is at liberty to practice his religion. "I have always been a religious person," he says, and for a moment his voice is uncharacteristically hard-edged with disdain and something close to anger. "In Laos, you cannot go to church. Here you can, because you are more free. There, you cannot call freedom yet, over there in Laos."

Another reason Blong wanted to leave Laos was to seek education. Ironically, though he was high school age upon his arrival, on paper he was "too old," so he went directly to St. Paul Technical College, where, by working and taking advantage of scholarships, he was able to complete his major, data entry. It took him four years.

·

Diane's story, though less overtly dramatic, had its own upheavals, uncertainties, and early responsibilities. Her family moved several times during her childhood. Although she was born in Connecticut, her family moved to southern Tennessee when she was five, and her parents were divorced shortly after her youngest brother was born. "She left him because he refused to work," Diane says of her mother's decision. Diane's father then moved to Florida "for the surfing." He was, according to Diane, "a surfer, trapper, hunter, fisher," and when we ask Diane what he did to support himself, she tells us, "That was the problem — nothing!"

Yet when Diane speaks of her father, it is without judgment. During one lull in our conversation, we admire a carving that turns out to be his, a wooden boat, skillfully rendered, that she is eager to show us. She seems to regard her father affectionately, as a free and creative spirit, and when she tells us that he died — "from cigarettes" — an unmistakable shadow of regret and disappointment passes over her face, that he couldn't attend her wedding, couldn't meet her husband or son.

Diane began working early, at a restaurant through a school work-release program. "I didn't like school in the first place," she admits, and so after graduation she took a number of jobs working in different restaurants. Diane liked none of them in particular, and we get the sense that she was waiting for her life to begin when she met Blong in the chatroom. She had left high school knowing that she was searching for something but was only certain that she wanted to be married, to have children. She had always loved children.

When Diane tells us this, her face softens, and she looks toward her son, who has joined us in the arms of her husband. B. J. is two months old, with a round, perfect head and soft downy hair, eyes that shine black and are such a clearly defined, lovely shape that they might have been drawn with one perfect sweep of a calligrapher's pen. Diane would like to have lots of children, "as many as we can," she says, but Blong is not so sure.

"The exact number we cannot say," he says, looking down into his son's face.

We wonder whether B. J. helped break the ice with the families, but Diane and Blong agree that there was no need: after recovering from their surprise, both families were supportive of their decision. Blong didn't mention a word about Diane until she arrived. "They had to get used to it because some marriages they saw did not last long. So they were a little bit concerned that the marriage won't last with two different nationalities. My grandmother and two uncles were the first to meet her. They just said, 'Are you sure, both sure, that you really want to marry each other?' And we said yes, and then they supported us."

Weren't you scared, meeting them that first time? we ask Diane.

"No not really. Whoever I would have married, I would have been meeting their family," she replies.

We would have been intimidated, we confess. A little research on Hmong customs suggested that our cultural conventions are at odds on many points, that it would be difficult not to make an insulting mistake despite the best intentions. We mention, for example, the importance of extreme deference, especially to male elders, how it's not respectful to make eye contact, how one should wait to shake hands.

Blong looks amused at our homework. "A lot of Hmong people do that, but I think you are the same as me, you are equal, everyone is equal," he says kindly.

Diane, meanwhile, looks preoccupied, is apparently still thinking about all this, especially the eye-contact taboo. "I don't make eye contact with anybody anyway," she decides after a while, as though looking on the bright side of things.

From the beginning, Diane felt that Blong's family embraced her. "They love me," she said confidently when we first spoke. Blong's grandmother especially is "real sweet" and told Diane, through Blong, to call her "Grandma" when the two met for the first time. On a recent visit after B. J. was born, Diane was touched when Blong's grandmother tucked money into Diane's hand, folding it up tightly again.

Diane's own mother was soon equally positive about Diane's decision. "My mom was like, 'As long as you know in your heart that that's the way he is.' And I knew. And now she agrees — 'You were right about him.'" When Diane had B. J., Blong took off a week from work and never left his wife's side, a fact that her mother appreciated. "She told me, 'you're lucky to have a man like that,'" Diane recalls with satisfaction. "And," she adds, pointing to the baby's crib, decorated brightly with a little mobile that dangles above, playing a familiar, jaunty tune, "we wouldn't have that crib in there or any of the baby things if it wasn't for Blong, who worked a *lot* of overtime to pay for them."

We comment that Diane's family seems accepting. "Well, I do have a cousin from Taiwan," Diane reflects. "And I have a cousin who's black — my aunt's daughter married a black guy. I am myself a mixture of French, Irish, German, Polish, and Lithuanian — there may be a little Hungarian in there. Plus a little Native American. My mom's dad is completely French."

We express our interest, point out that there is still a lot of resistance to such families, that there are still many prejudiced people in the world.

"Oh yeah," Diane agrees quickly. "My grandfather's one of them! Which surprises me because we do have such a mix in our family. He's prejudiced against everything — he doesn't like people who are rich, he doesn't like different cultures." At first, when Diane told her grandfather about Blong, he was unenthusiastic. "But now," Diane tell us with pleasure, "my grandpa really likes him."

How do you know, we ask, expecting to hear about some subtle behavioral shift.

"It's because he said, 'I really like that man,'" she responds. By now Diane has an album of her wedding photographs out on the card table, and she points to a picture of her grandfather hugging Blong, who is smiling his sweet half-smile. Next, she points out a picture of her elder brother, the one who was never going to speak to her again, giving her away.

"And nine months later, we had B. J. We call him B. J., but his real name is "Blong B. J. Her Junior," Diane says proudly, showing me a framed certificate bearing that very name on the wall, decorated with two tiny, inky footprints.

"In my culture, we don't use that 'Junior,'" Blong adds, with a mix of amusement and pride. "I think he is the first one to use that."

When Blong is in the small bedroom taking care of the baby, we take the opportunity to admire his parenting skills, noting what a gentle and capable father he is. Watching Blong with the baby is touching. He murmurs to B. J. in Hmong (which he is determined to teach him) bending his head near, making soft, solicitous noises whenever his son moves or talks, as though always listening, ready to translate: "Now he is hungry. He needs a diaper. Now is time for him to sleep."

"When he comes home at the end of the day, I just hand B. J. to him," Diane says appreciatively. "B. J. is real spoiled, likes to be held all the time."

Like new parents anywhere, the Hers' life has been redefined by the birth of their son, and their goals and plans revolve around him. They live from moment to moment, with little time to think about daily rituals and blending cultures, although they are right in the middle of creating a life of interwoven traditions for their son. Blong works hard; he is now at a company called "Register Re-sales," where he helps put a computer chip in cash registers, a job he likes because he can be "his own boss" and can move around instead of being restricted to one spot. Diane is happy to stay at home with B. J.

One constant in their changed lives, we learn, is church on Sundays. We have spotted a calendar of the "Hmong Alliance Church," a Protestant church at which the couple worships weekly.

Is the service conducted in Hmong? we wonder.

"Oh yeah," Diane tells us. "So I don't understand. But I love it when they're singing, it's very pretty. They take the English hymns and use Hmong lyrics. They sing 'Amazing Grace' in Hmong."

What does that translate into? we ask Blong.

"Jesus love," Blong replies, and then promptly sings the first verse to us in a strong voice that lingers in the sunny air. At times during our conversation, because of the tonality of Blong's language, it has seemed to us that he was singing when he spoke. When he really does sing, however, in a sweet, true voice, the familiar melody of "Amazing Grace" pierces us, and we feel momentarily rooted to the spot. Perhaps it is the unself-consciousness of his song, or the familiarity of the tune despite its unfamiliar words, but for a moment it is as though we are in church, and grace seems very nearly visible, floating among the dust motes.

"That's my favorite one," Diane says with satisfaction, breaking the silence. "They stand up and sing their songs. I just stand there since I don't know the words, but I can feel it."

When we ask whether they plan to blend religions, Diane tells us that she wishes Blong would convert to hers. "I am hoping one day to get married in the Mormon temple, that's why I got a gown with long sleeves. I am hoping that someday he will switch to my church. I don't know how he feels about that. It's almost the same. But in his church you sit there in one spot for a few hours, where in mine you go to different classes."

"In their church, they don't have a pastor, but in our church we have a pastor — that preaches," Blong sums up what he sees as the main differences, clearly not worth the bother of conversion.

"For three hours," Diane says again.

"Two hours," Blong corrects her.

"9:30 to 12:00!" Diane counters with the conviction of one who has felt the hard pew. Later, she tells us that some Mormon missionaries visited recently to talk with Blong, which explains why he has two versions of the Bible according to the Church of Jesus Christ of Latter-day Saints on his shelf — one in Hmong and one in Thai. Blong apparently listened and concluded that they were saying pretty much the same thing that he already believed. Why convert?

We ask whether the Hers worry at all about their son's future, or whether they have received any ill-treatment here in the Midwest. We have heard that in some cities where Hmong families are concentrated, such as St. Paul, which has excellent refugee services, there has been some violently expressed resentment from the surrounding community. Diane acknowledges that they have received "some stares" when they are together and says that she worries a little about whether her son will be teased or face trouble in school. But Blong dismisses such concerns. He will teach his son to ignore those people, "turn his back, be strong and disciplined within himself." One value that Blong wishes to impart to his son is that of control, which he feels that the Hmong culture emphasizes more in parenting than American culture. "[Hmong] children are more under the control of the parents. In Hmong culture, the children will have to stand for the parent. So they are a little bit strict. I will try to be strict. Because it will help, when they grow up, to control themselves."

Diane and Blong plan to travel to Laos, a trip they hope to take by "the year 2005," Diane tells us, "if not before." The trip is a goal that requires careful planning, that they are looking forward to, working toward together. In the meantime, Diane is trying to learn some Hmong, an attempt complicated by the way that the sounds and spellings of Hmong words often don't seem to match. For example, "Hello" sounds to our ears like "Ya-jong" but is spelled *Nyob zoo*. The word for "drink" sounds like "how" but is spelled *haus*. "I also learned how to say 'what is your name' — *Koj npe hu licas* — it sounds like 'Com-bay hu-li-jah,'" Diane says proudly.

"Kombay hu lee CHA," Blong corrects her, spacing the sounds differently and spiking the last syllable. We listen to our own voices on tape, attempting to imitate Blong's. The tonal nuances of his language are much easier to hear than to replicate, and our efforts, compared to his, are clumsy, as though we have picked up a violin for the very first time and screeched the bow across the strings. "My language is not difficult," Blong says happily, just as we are coming to the opposite conclusion.

When we ask whether Blong still reads things in Hmong, he assures us that he does. "Mostly I read the Bible," Blong tells us.

"He's typing his Bible into the computer. So he can look things up easier." Diane laughs out loud in delight at this fact — here, finally, is something that strikes her as unusual, that she doesn't shrug off as unremarkable. Yet to us it is no longer astonishing —

certainly no stranger than stepping onto a plane toward a completely different, unknown life, a step both Diane and Blong were willing to take. In fact, the Bible project seems very much in keeping with the couple's approach to life, since it demonstrates the same kind of patient view toward the long term, the same accomplishing of big tasks with small steps, a willingness to postpone short-term pleasures for more important goals.

The Hers may have limited means with which to reach their ambitious goals, but they also have clear priorities and a practical approach. It may take them a while, but we believe Blong will finish the Bible project, that the trip to Laos will become a reality. We also cannot help but believe that B. J. will learn to speak Hmong, that he will inherit his father's peaceful, disciplined dignity. It is a fate that is especially easy to imagine listening to them here, in this sunny, empty room, so close to the beginning of things.

Hao yin (good luck)

JIM & JEAN

Jean & Jim with their children, Molly and Patrick. Photo by Corbin Sexton.

Driving up to Jean and Jim Hussey's house on its quiet Kalona cross street, we find the Husseys sitting together, rocking gently on the porch swing of their home, their children kicking a soccer ball back and forth before them. We park our car in the long driveway in front of an old wooden barn next to the Husseys' two cars and have enough time to note their license plates: — TAIWAN and NI HAO (Chinese for "hello") — before all four Husseys drift over to meet us, leading us into their pleasantly cool home for a brief tour of the downstairs.

Despite its classic Midwestern exterior (a picture of their blue-brick, Mission-style home can be found in *The History of Washington County*), we see immediately upon entering it that the Husseys have made this house their own. A wooden feng shui screen placed just inside the entrance and near the foot of the stairs, Jean tells us, provides a break in the path from the family sleeping quarters to the front door and prevents energy from sliding down the staircase and out of the house. "It's insulation," says Jean. An elaborate red knotted silk cord hangs nearby for good luck, and huge painted fans, tilted like birds wheeling in the sky, adorn the walls. The fans are hung at an angle like this, Jean explains, since placing them straight would be unlucky. In other rooms we see Chinese paintings, ink washes, calligraphy. On the living room mantel sits a smiling jade Buddha with a big belly and big ears; pennies are tucked under his arms, chin, and in his fat lap. "He has money, we will all have money," Jean explains cheerfully. "Plus, he has big ears, big ears mean long life." Even the family's answering machine begins with an expected English greeting but then segues into Mandarin: Hello. This is the Hussey family. *Wei. Zhe shi Hussey de jia.* Please leave a message after the tone. Thank you! *Ting huan bisheng shi hou. Xie Xie.*

This grafting of the Chinese and American in the Hussey's physical surroundings feels perfectly natural, graceful. We admire the cultural hybridity that is apparent in every element of their lives. Even the way they sit together as a family expresses a comfortable integration. Arranged on a couch opposite us during our conversation, they seem almost of one piece — Molly is draped across the lap of both parents, her head cradled in her father's arm, feet in her mother's lap. Patrick, perched on the arm of the sofa just behind his mother, watches us thoughtfully; he wears a shirt boasting the name of his T-ball league, the "Kalona Optimists." The children are striking with their dark shining eyes, tanned skin, thick chestnut hair.

The Husseys' composure is in pronounced contrast to our own feelings of dishevelment. While we search for pens and try to soothe a baby who is tired but will not sleep, they sit together serenely. No one jumps up; the children, despite their ages — seven and eight — do not interrupt or wander off. Patrick disappears only once at his mother's request to help Jean's parents, who have just arrived for an extended visit from Taiwan. They need help decoding the mysteries of the microwave, and Patrick heads purposefully toward the kitchen. We hear him far away at the back of the house, instructing them in Mandarin.

The Husseys consider our questions carefully and always answer thoughtfully, sometimes with laughter. Later, they take the same approach to our photo session, listening to the photographer's suggestions, making their own. ("Can you take our picture in this tree?" ask the children.) Even when our photographer has them posed sitting together on their barn roof, the Husseys do not lose their air of happy tranquillity.

.

Jim and Jean met, it turns out, neither in Iowa nor Taiwan but in Fairbanks, Alaska, where Jean had gone to study accounting and Jim was working as a television reporter. Jean remembers the shock of stepping off the plane in Fairbanks for the first time, in February 1986. It was twenty-eight degrees below zero. "When we arrived to Alaska, we were really disappointed. It was so cold. We couldn't believe people lived there."

"For a person who had seen a dusting of snow only once on a remote Taiwanese mountainside, it was a quite a change," comments Jim, master of understatement. "It was like living inside a freezer." But Fairbanks had much to offer, in particular an interesting degree of diversity: a sizable Taiwanese population, an even more pronounced Russian presence, and a Native American community that has survived better in Alaska than in most other places in the United States. "What's different about Fairbanks is that almost everybody is from somewhere else. Here you walk down the street and you only have the Yoders and the Hochstetlers. In Fairbanks, you have some people who've been there for 10,000 years, and everybody else is a newcomer."

Jim and Jean met in October 1986, at a gathering for international students and American mentors. Jim wasn't Jean's mentor but sat beside her, made her acquaintance, and invited her to a Halloween party. Later they went on what both consider their first date, to a restaurant called the Blue Marlin, after which they began seeing each other more often. The Husseys' manner is pleasant, but they are not forthcoming about this first date. They sit smiling at us, side by side, clearly treasuring the memory but not sharing it with us, our pens frozen above tablets, tape recorders turning silently.

When the couple describes those early days, we get the impression that Jim was sure of what he wanted in the relationship almost from the beginning while Jean was more cautious. "Why is he interested?" she reports wondering. "Some men not in love, just interested in meeting someone from a different culture." She had to know that Jim genuinely cared for her before she took him at all seriously, and indeed she eventually reached just such a conclusion — one that, twelve years later, she confirms with conviction. "I never thought I would marry someone from the U.S.," Jean tells us, "but Jim is a very good, very kind man. I think I made a good decision. Even today I am very happy." Jim does not say anything in response but shines with a pleasure that touches us.

Their parents created no obstacles for them. Jean's parents, who would have preferred she marry a Taiwanese man, already had one son-in-law from Ohio, so their slight misgivings over Jean's choice were qualified by experience. When they visited Fairbanks during the summer of 1987, they met Jim and, as he tells us, "despite my complete inability to speak Chinese, at that point, and their inability to understand English, everyone seemed to get along fine." And Jim's own family expressed no objections, although they'd little chance to know Jean since the relationship had developed so far from their Iowa home.

The Husseys' Fairbanks wedding was about as multicultural as possible. Jean wore the white dress traditional in Western cultures and common in Taiwan now, too. The organist, who was African American, played a mixture of hymns and gospel music, the reception featured an Irish band, and the food was international — representing the diversity of the Fairbanks community and of Jim and Jean's own friends and family members. Jim is matter-of-fact when he describes the wedding, but we get the impression that he is proud. "It was a lot of fun," he says, and we imagine a room full of warmth and light, people dancing or balancing plates full of wontons and potato salad.

Jean's account of the wedding serves as a kind of allegory about the happy life she has found now. "Outside it was raining. We went into the church, but I was crying. I didn't know if I was ready," she explains. "All the people were in there waiting for me. Then I thought, and I knew I was ready. After the wedding, people came and hugged us. And when we went outside, the sun was shining." The sun is a symbol for Jean of her own good fortune, a symbol that might sit beside the smiling Buddha or hang above one of the red silk knots if she could find a way to capture it.

Though Jim had anticipated that his time in Alaska would be short ("I figured I'd be there a year"), the couple stayed in Alaska until 1996. The Husseys show us a photograph taken there; in it a large group of friends and family stand posed against a backdrop of green mountains and gleaming water. The photo seems surreal in its beauty, and we wonder aloud why the Husseys chose to leave such a spectacular landscape. The couple discussed the move at great length, Jim tells us, but finally decided to relocate for several reasons. They wanted to be closer to at least one side of the family, to begin with. "In Alaska," Jim tells us, "a lot of kids grow up with limited knowledge of aunts, uncles, cousins, and grandparents who live 'Outside' in the Lower 48. We didn't want that to happen to our kids if we could help it." Jim also notes that other opportunities for their children would have been limited in Alaska, particularly in Valdez. "The schools are good, but the extracurricular activities are limited, and the chances of being around other excellent young musicians or mathematicians, for example, would have been as remote as the location."

Ironically, the beautiful environment we so admired in the photograph was another reason to leave. Fairbanks summers are both beautiful and "painfully short," and the average low for the month of January falls to less than twenty below zero. "In Valdez, we averaged thirty feet of snow each year, and literally had bears walking through our front yard," Jim tells us. The Hussey children could not enjoy an outdoor world where they faced snowdrifts twice or three times their height or where a bear might pay an unexpected visit. Jim and Jean both grew up playing outdoors and wanted that same pleasure for their children, so they looked to Iowa, where the family could enjoy all four seasons.

Jim's mother, Barb, admired Jean's courage in making this move. "It was just about the bravest thing I've seen, a real leap of faith," her mother-in-law told us. The Husseys moved to Iowa without a definite job for Jim. "I didn't have a career path," Jim tells us, "more like a career meander. I came down with the idea that I could either get a job or hang up my own shingle. Then this job with ACT came up, and that was beans on the plate." The Husseys took a similarly unconventional attitude about finding a house. Jim's mother found it for them: she took a video camera through the house, and Jim and Jean made their decision on the basis of that tape. We agree with Barb that Jean was brave to make the move to Iowa, especially with two small children to consider. But talking to us now, Jean downplays the drama, shrugs off the long-distance move as simply necessary — good for her family, good for her.

We are impressed during our conversation with the Husseys by how carefully thought-out their life together seems. Their choices, from large to small, have been arrived at through discussion and consensus; no decision seems too small or uninteresting to have thought about, talked about together. Perhaps this is partly because they approach things from two different cultural vantage points, which could make even the commonplace an interesting source of difference; in any case, they consistently make decisions in ways that honor both partner's personal and cultural values.

Most remarkably, the children speak their mother's language — a significant accomplishment in rural Iowa, where they are unlikely to hear their language spoken outside the home or to have ready access to Chinese books or videos. In fact, the Hussey children seem at ease moving between the two languages and the two worlds they represent, and proud of their bicultural heritage. When Patrick got the gist of our questions about his family's intercultural life, he went up to his room to get a book he made in school, a book about himself. "What is special about me? What is different about me?" Patrick shows us where he has written in response, "I can speak Chinese." Jean has taught the children Mandarin with the support of her husband, who has learned some himself, and when the children are with her or her parents, Mandarin is the language they use.

The Husseys feel that the advantages of this bilingualism far outweigh any potential costs. Because math is a universal language, and because their mother began playing number games with them when they were infants, Patrick and Molly's math skills are formidable. Both children can do long division sums in their heads, and their scores on the math components of achievement tests are off the charts. In contrast, their reading scores are more average for their age, probably because of their relative inexperience with English. Neither the children nor their parents seem particularly concerned with these scores, however. "You're raising American kids no matter what," Jim says, and language is one important element of Jean's culture that they can hold on to.

All this cultural grafting is quite deliberate on the Husseys' part. Jean has no intention of giving up the riches of her own culture, and she wants to make these riches available to her children as well. When she tells us about growing up in Taiwan, Jean's voice is full of happy memories of a small house crowded with people. Jean grew up in a family of ten children, "three, six, nine — bad," she laughs, explaining her mother's thinking. "Have ten. OK, that's enough!" The sixth daughter and the seventh child overall, Jean and her nine siblings grew up in a small village in the mountains approximately fifty miles from Hua Lien, a larger community on the east coast of Taiwan. She played outside all the time in the shadows of the mountains and frequently played teacher, collecting a number of her friends to serve as students.

Jean's parents both worked for the government, her father until he started his own business in heavy equipment, and her mother until she suffered a stroke when she was forty-nine years old. When she started high school, Jean moved to the city of Hua Lien, one of the most beautiful areas of urban Taiwan, and later she moved to Taipei to study accounting at a business college. Her mother's stroke brought her home in the early 1980s, and Jean spent much of the next few years caring for her and helping her recover before emigrating to the United States in 1986.

The bicultural life Jean has created with her family results, in part, from her very practical nature. Her attachment to her culture is not a sentimental one, and throughout our interview her observations of both American and Chinese cultures seem marked by objectivity; she chooses what she takes from the two cultures with a discerning eye. "We bring two cultures together," she says. "Each one has some good, some bad. We choose the good, leave out the bad. We're very lucky to have two cultures." Jean disapproves, for example, of the freedoms Americans often give their children. "American families let children be much more independent. Just give kids suggestions, 'Oh, do whatever.'"

"Jean is more directive," says Jim.

"Yes," Jean agrees. She prefers the Chinese way. "In Chinese culture, most parents tell kids what to do, give them clear guidelines."

She approves, however, of the way American siblings are encouraged to relate to one another. "In Chinese culture, the younger child has to listen to the older child. That's hard on the younger one. It's not equal. American way is all equal. If you have an idea, you can talk to the parents. It's more close, more open. I like that."

Jim's capacity to live a bicultural life seems to spring more expressly out of a lifelong passion to experience and understand multiple cultures. He cites the advantage of his parents' attitude about people from other places: "In our family, never once did I hear any kind of racial slur or joke; it was just never said and it wouldn't have been tolerated. We grew up benefiting from the kind of environment that encouraged intercultural ideas." Also, Jim's family lived in the university town of Iowa City when he was growing up, and Jim had friends from all over the world. He thrived in this international environment, and, when he went away to college, he tried to recreate it for himself. "I always asked for international roommates, and over the years I lived with students from Iran, Iraq, Japan, Sudan, and Puerto Rico. I was always glad to have an opportunity to meet someone from a different culture."

"It just seems natural to recognize and celebrate both halves of our lives," says Jim of their efforts to create an international household. "From my perspective, I honestly don't think there are profound differences among any of the cultures that I've encountered," he says, explaining the ease with which they have woven their lives together. "The differences seem to be primarily the ways in which those beliefs are expressed."

Like Jean, Jim feels lucky to be able to pick the elements of Chinese and American culture he thinks are valuable — and to leave others behind. "If I had to name something negative that I've chosen to abandon, I'd say that in America, people tend to spend more money than they have. I hope that marrying Jean has reinforced my desire to be appropriately frugal in most matters, and to invest our time, energy, and money in our children's lives, and — particularly important from the Chinese cultural point of view — their educations."

Jim also feels that some American parents tend to regard children as "accouterments" in their lives, and not the focus of them. Jim agrees with Jean that American parents can be too permissive with their children, give them too little guidance. "I do want my children to make the most of whatever gifts and talents they have. I have tried to give them the opportunities to do so and have not hesitated to 'encourage' them to develop their talents even when they might prefer to be doing something else at a particular moment. I believe that is a responsibility too often ignored in this country." But Jim doesn't focus on his children's achievements, test scores, and other measures of success — an element of Chinese culture he does not like.

.

The Husseys' confidence in their choice to honor both of their cultures has no doubt helped create acceptance in the surrounding community. Ironically, Jim also thinks that the relative homogeneity of rural Iowa makes it an especially safe place for cultural others, a safe place for his family. "I have never once been aware of anyone giving us trouble here. My theory on it is that if you are in a place where the majority is such a majority, where they never feel threatened, then there's no real reason to give anyone a hard time. In places where there is a closer mix of demographics, people might — incorrectly, but they might — try to blame others for whatever goes wrong in their lives. There's more potential for tension there. But here where you have ninety-eight percent white — there's not much threat."

Jean points out, though, that despite the apparent racial homogeneity, there is a kind of less visible diversity in their community. Kalona itself, she reminds us, is full of immigrant history and has a deep German heritage that is still evident everywhere. There is a Thai family just around the corner, Iowa City is less than twenty minutes away, and international students come every weekend to see the little German town, look for Amish farms, and eat at the family-style restaurants.

People from Kalona have access to Iowa City's East-West stores, Indian restaurants, import shops, and visiting performers from around the world, and they are quite open-minded, participating happily in those elements of her culture that Jean introduces to them. The Husseys celebrate the Chinese New Year, for example, with family and community members who are more than willing to eat Jean's food and learn about moon cakes and other elements of the New Year celebration. Jim and Jean usually bring a Chinese dish to local events. It is difficult for us to imagine Jean's gourmet Chinese cooking sitting on a potluck table beside a Jell-O and marshmallow salad, and it is hard to imagine the person who could enjoy those items on the same plate, at the same dinner. But Jim and Jean assure us that their neighbors' palates are sufficiently broad.

When we get up to leave, hours later, we feel somehow refreshed, more rested than when we arrived. Again, all four Husseys accompany us to the car, Jim carrying the car seat with the baby sleeping in it, Molly and Patrick thoughtfully pointing out the drainpipe to avoid at the corner of the house. Their shirts glow white in the country dark, and they seem to flow around us and one another as gracefully as fish. As we drive down a dirt road toward Iowa City, an owl flies up suddenly before our car, its great wingspan a swoop of gold suspended for a long moment in the beam of our headlights. Caught in the spell of the evening, we read it as some as yet indecipherable but definite sign, a piece of good luck connected, though we don't know how, to the tilted fans and feng shui screen.

The quilt

KATHLEEN & JAT

Kathleen & Jat with their children, Paul and Kiran. Photo by Corbin Sexton.

Kathleen Aluwalia saw her husband, Jat, for the first time as he was briskly rounding a corner in a corridor of the hospital where she worked as a nurse. "He was wearing this purple shirt and an orange tie — he had thrown it over his shoulder, like he was in a big hurry. And I said to myself, 'Now, there's the guy for me!'" Kathleen, who throughout her life has had eerie intuitions about the future, felt sure she would marry Jat, "almost immediately" upon meeting him. "I saw him, and I saw how he was," she tells us steadily, with a smile of retrospective amusement. She liked him for his quirkiness, his slightly unusual sense of fun, his outgoing and adventurous nature — all characteristics that coworkers associated with *her*. In fact, Kathleen says, everyone on the floor kept telling her, "'You know, he's single.' They said from the beginning, 'You seem like the same kind of people.' What that meant was we were both *different*, just a little weird," she tells us, clearly not offended.

It is perhaps these similarities that drew them together, though Kathleen and Jat tell slightly different stories about their courtship. According to Jat, they became friends naturally because they worked together. "She was interesting to talk to," he recalls. "To avoid stress at work, I try to make it into a joyful exercise by talking to people. And I enjoyed talking to Kathleen." Jat tells us that their early dinners and coffees were casual, his invitations motivated only by friendship, and that out of this friendship, romance gradually grew. He speculates that their passage from friendship to romance might have been "helped along" by the long impromptu voyages they took together, he to visit his Indian family in Toronto, and she to visit her sister in nearby Whitby, Canada.

But Kathleen's story is a bit different, a bit more detailed. In her version, this pleasant confusion over whether they were "just friends" was very brief. Kathleen, who knew Jat's schedule, signed up for extra work during his shifts; she knew Jat was interested in her, she tells us, because he hung around her station at the hospital, made himself available, paid attention to her. He would make wagers with Kathleen that always entailed one of them taking the other out to dinner, wagers he would usually lose, and she played the game because she liked him, because she found him urbane and funny. Kathleen assumed the dinner bets were dates, and eventually she invited Jat to her family's house for dinner, after which things got more serious. According to her story, their trips to Canada further established a relationship already long in the making. "He was always so excited about things, so interested, and I found that attractive," Kathleen tells us. "I felt comfortable with Jat, and he made me laugh. You know how you can be yourself with someone, and there's no pretending? Both Jat and I are very much ourselves in our marriage."

When we ask the couple when they decided to marry, Jat demurs, turns up his hands. "I remember," offers Kathleen. "Jat was taken by my curtain-making skills. I'd made some curtains for him. The woman down at Wal-Mart in the fabric section got to know Jat because he was always looking for fabric," Kathleen laughs. "You'd found some really wild material that you loved and you wondered if I could make a futon cover with it. And then in front of the washer-dryer section you said, 'You know, I think we should get married.'"

Jat doesn't remember this.

"I knew you wouldn't," Kathleen responds tolerantly.

Despite any differences in these accounts of their early romance, Kathleen and Jat agree about one thing: they don't feel their love story has much to do with culture, and they seem slightly puzzled by the idea of themselves as an intercultural couple.

Before we visited the two, we had stopped in at the home of Kathleen's mother and stepfather, located two miles away on straight country roads. Kathleen's mother, Barb, showed us a quilt she'd made of her neighborhood, complete with porches, trees, and windowboxes. On it we could see Barb's own home with its little duck pond, and the square blue house of her son Jim and daughter-in-law, Jean. Kathleen and Jat's, a sunny white farmhouse, nestled cheerfully nearby against a background of green grass and blue sky. Each house was detailed and unique, but together they projected a cheerful harmony of clipped lawns and big sunny windows. Nothing, Barb's quilt seemed to suggest, could be more happy, more ordinary, less in need of interrogation than these homes, these lives.

The house we visit when we interview Kathleen and Jat resembles the one sewn into Barb's quilt, both in its architectural details and its spirit. It is the best kind of Iowa farmhouse, we see from our approach on a dusty gravel road. With rolling Amish farmland as a backdrop, the house sits next to a defunct windmill atop a hill that is green with summer and dotted with oaks. The house has a screened-in front porch and a tall, stark front without the embellishments of columns, bay windows, or fancy trellises — none of the flourishes a town house of its era might have. Its windows are decorated only with shutters, like the tall, plain windows of country houses we admire all around the Midwest, windows that give these houses a cheerful, unblinking dignity that outlasts fierce winds and bad winters.

Out front, Jat and a man who turns out to be Kathleen's father are tinkering with a lawn mower. The screen door swings suddenly open and the Aluwalias' three-year-old son, Paul, bursts forth — a striking child with jet black curls, black eyes, and an Irish creaminess to his skin. Behind him comes a woman, a neighbor, who waves good-bye to Kathleen over her shoulder. It is early evening, and the sun is setting on what was a clear summer day. Everywhere around us is space, safety, and family activity. We are longtime fans of southeastern Iowa, and standing in the maple-shaded cool of this summer evening, draped in bags full of travel supplies, we feel a touch of envy. We have left our own families behind us in significantly less pastoral parts of Illinois, but it is easy to imagine them here, in the sun-drenched beauty of rural Iowa.

While we settle in at the kitchen table, Jat finishes with the lawn mower and Kathleen puts Paul to bed. As serene as their lives appear from the outside, the Aluwalias are very busy people, and we can tell how difficult it has been for them to find space in their lives for our conversation. Jat, a doctor of internal medicine, works in a hospital emergency room; his beeper is clipped to the waist of his running shorts. Kathleen, who is still working part-time as a nurse and is six months pregnant with their second child, has just arrived back from a trip to New Orleans with her mother — "just for fun" — and just in time to host a baby shower for a friend. There is a harried air of finishing up the day's tasks. By the time we begin, it is dark, and a certain exhausted peacefulness has come over the house.

Jat and Kathleen finally sit down together at the table. Certainly, we cannot tell by looking at them that they are an intercultural family. They fit into this environment as well as their farmhouse fits in among the others on Barb's quilt. Kathleen is red-haired and freckled with blue-green eyes, very pregnant, down-to-earth. With her cheerfully forthright, practical demeanor, one might easily peg her as the Midwesterner she is. Jat conveys a contained energy; even while he is relaxed at the end of the day, with his arms folded on his chest and his legs stretched out in front of him, he seems poised for the next activity. He is lean and tan, and unlike the other international people we have talked to, has almost no discernible accent. In his shorts and community "fun run" T-shirt, he too looks perfectly American, perfectly Midwestern.

Jat's ease in fitting into this rural Iowa setting is due in part to an adaptability he developed during the several moves of his childhood. Jat was born in India, where he lived until he was fourteen. Though he spent his entire childhood and early adolescence in that country, Jat's sense of self was not primarily established there. At first, Jat is hard-pressed to recall very many specific details about his young life, talking instead about his teenage and young adult years in multinational Toronto, where he attended high school and university.

In fact, if forced to identify a place of origin, Jat might pick Toronto, though the sense of "home" as a geographical place is not clear to him, and listening, we begin to understand that home for him is family. "Sometimes when I'm talking with my family we'll say, 'Well, in India — ' and I'll realize in the back of my mind that we mean Toronto, because that's where my parents are. I suppose subconsciously I end up thinking of home as Toronto, just because my parents live there. Yet, when I visit, it still feels relatively foreign because I didn't live there very long either."

It is easy to sense in Jat both his cosmopolitan nature and his distance from any clear concept of home. There is a certain worldliness and irony about him, an independence of thinking that is clear-eyed without being sardonic. Having been so influenced by a city made up of differences, Jat feels undisturbed by potential differences between himself and the members of the Iowa community around him, expressing sometimes a kinship, sometimes a distance from the people of Kalona. "Actually, I don't know where home is anymore," he tells us, more with a sense of clinical interest than regret. "I've become so adept at making wherever I am home." Indeed, we get the impression that Jat could live anywhere, that his sense of himself as a voyager, a person independent of place is an integral part of his identity. In some ways, the rural Midwest, with its peace and isolation, is as comfortable a home for him as anyplace else. "I think I welcome change," he reflects, "although I am a little averse to large cities, having grown up in so many of them. So here I am in the middle of Iowa. Here, where you can stay for days and never see anybody. You see their cows more often than you see them."

Kathleen has a similar independence about her, a similar enjoyment of the voyage. "I like to go places," she explains simply. Should she need to prove her point, she could remind us that she has just returned from a pleasure trip to New Orleans, which she took despite her pregnancy, despite the responsibilities of a small child, work demands, a still-recent move — despite the fact that she had agreed to host a shower and to meet with us almost immediately upon her return. Besides demonstrating a near-Herculean capacity for activity, the trip confirms a desire for adventure that triumphs even over the exhaustion of pregnancy, job, and motherhood.

Kathleen also shares with Jat a detachment from the idea of "home" as a specific geographic location. She grew up in Iowa City, a university town, where she works as a nurse now, but it is not the beauty of the landscape or any of the details of a childhood in Iowa that Kathleen remembers with fondness or clarity. What she recalls and appreciates, in much the same way Jat remembers and appreciates Toronto, is the cultural diversity of Iowa City. Her schools, she tells us, were filled with children from all over the world — the sons and daughters of international students and scholars.

Her mother attended college while Kathleen was in high school, and her mother's career as a university student offered Kathleen glimpses of an international, intellectual world. She remembers in particular the different international students that her mother invited to dinner sometimes, especially for Thanksgiving and Christmas. These acquaintances became an important part of her family's life and helped her develop a more international perspective. "At the holidays, Mother would invite home international students from her classes, and so it was natural for us to find people interesting, or to find interesting people of different nationalities who were out there. We never did put up a lot of the boundaries that people construct. My parents never made an issue of difference." She smiles, adding, "I don't think we went out there *collecting* people from other cultures, thinking, 'Who do we need now and from where?'" Her family, she suggests, was naturally captivated by people with a variety of national origins and experiences.

Kathleen liked this international atmosphere, felt at home in it, and developed her sense of self there. She grew up without fear of people whose clothes and food and ways of life were different from hers — grew up, in fact, with a healthy curiosity about and appreciation for people from other cultures. She also developed a sense of adventure and a sense of humor that comes partly from meeting people from other places and hearing their stories — qualities that were evidently useful in August 1995, when she and Jat decided to marry, a year after their first date, in a traditional Indian Sikh ceremony.

By now, the two have so downplayed the role of culture in their romance that we have almost forgotten it ourselves. When they show us photographs of their wedding, we are momentarily startled. We hardly recognize Jat in his traditional clothing; the beard and the turban, especially, transform his face. Suddenly, he does not look so familiar to us, so North American. Now he belongs to a different world than this one of shorts and fun runs and lawn mowers. Kathleen, too, looks like another person in her wedding photos. Indian brides may be the most glamorous on earth; and Kathleen, in these photographs, is transformed from an attractive Midwesterner in a print cotton dress into a dazzling woman decked in gold and silk. She is perfectly made up, with eyes outlined carefully in black, and a red *bindi* on her forehead. Wearing a shining fuchsia silk sari, she is decorated from head to toe in gold: a load of bangles worthy of Nefertiti, large and intricate earrings, a jeweled headpiece that dangles down onto her forehead.

"I was nervous about the ceremony," Kathleen admits, even though she had tried to prepare by watching her brother-in-law's videotaped ceremony. "At first it didn't seem like a big deal, but then when I was getting ready for it, I actually once fainted when talking to Jat on the phone." The elaborate celebration began the evening before, when she had her hands hennaed "while Jat was off being freed from impurities." She remembers how the female members of her Indian family helped dress her for the wedding, working from all sides as though decorating a Christmas tree.

"They brought out so much jewelry," Kathleen says looking down at a photograph, "including a clip-on nose ring about which they kept saying, 'No pressure, no pressure, you don't have to wear it.' But I did for this one picture."

The wedding was attended by a mix of the couple's families, including Kathleen's "real Catholic" aunt, who had called a week before the wedding and was shocked to find out that there would be no Catholic ceremony or priest.

"At first," reports Kathleen, "she declared that she couldn't come, and we said 'That's fine. If you can't be happy and come, don't come.' Then she decided that she could come, but once she was there she felt she could not sit down in the *gudwara*, the temple. So then she sees Jat in this wedding costume, and she was meeting him for the first time." Kathleen stops with a wry smile, imagining her aunt's discomfort. "She must have been thinking, 'Not only am I in this strange place where I don't understand anything and it's not Catholic, and now this guy with a turban turns out to be the groom.'" Later a friend of Jat's told the couple that Kathleen's aunt had interviewed the crowd at the wedding, asking various members of the party questions like "Who is this guy? Is he any good?" Evidently, Kathleen reports, her aunt must have been satisfied with the answers she received, "because she came for the family pictures. And later she called me and said what a wonderful time she'd had, and what a wonderful man Jat was."

The wedding was followed by a reception, and when we ask for details about that party, Kathleen is at a loss. "It was . . ." she searches for a description, then gives up, "just a traditional reception."

"Just?" Jat objects.

"It was fabulous," Kathleen amends quickly. "It was at an Indian restaurant."

Jat is mollified. "Not totally traditional," he adds, "not totally modernized, but a taste of both."

Just as she was finally beginning to relax, Kathleen explains, she encountered a final hurdle. "After we got married, I was informed that, according to tradition, I was supposed to make a meal for all my close relatives." Kathleen, who has told us earlier that she's never had much interest in cooking, has a slightly stricken look on her face, as though she is recalling the trauma of that moment. "My reaction was 'that's it! I'm leaving.' Because the women in his family are all such good cooks! Then I thought maybe Jat was joking. Nope, he wasn't joking."

Jat interjects, "It was meant to be symbolic more than anything. They didn't necessarily want her to cook the whole thing herself, but they did want her to help a bit."

"Fortunately for me this wonderful woman, one of Jat's aunts, came and said, 'Don't worry, I'll help you.' And I helped her as much as I could, and did the serving. I was saved."

The contrast between the very American couple sitting before us and the photos of an Indian bride and groom we have in our hands silences us for a moment. Both Kathleen and Jat are aware of this contrast, and both of them experience the disparity between their wedding and their everyday lives as a potential loss, though the intensity with which they feel this loss of Indian culture is different. Kathleen would like her children to know something about Sikh culture and spiritual practices so that, when they are adults, this religion will be one of their options and so that they will understand their father's family more completely.

She knows, however, that her children will have very little contact with Indian life — Paul is not fluent in Punjabi, his father's native language, and Kathleen has just now begun learning how to cook some of the simple, traditional foods of her husband's past. A cookbook we see lying on the counter — *Microwave Moghul* — serves as a testament both to the sincerity of Kathleen's effort and as evidence of just how American their lives are. Furthermore, Kathleen tells us, the family doesn't celebrate Indian holidays. "I've said to Jat, 'Let's celebrate Diwali, tell me the protocol, I'll do it,' but his mother took care of those details, so he doesn't really know how to prepare for the celebrations," Kathleen tells us regretfully.

Kathleen is grateful, however, for other benefits of Indian culture that are accessible to them, and she is touched by the degree of devotion Indian families show to each other. American families' professional commitments, she says, often force them to be more isolated and inward-looking, to rely more exclusively on their own resources. In contrast, Indian professional and social worlds seem to prioritize family, providing a flexibility in the face of extended family needs that is almost never available in an American context.

Last year, Kathleen and Jat tell us, they were the beneficiaries of this kindness. Since Paul had been born, Kathleen had had terrible nightmares that her son might fall and be seriously hurt or killed, and she was haunted with the fear that these dreams were really premonitions. Her fears were realized when she suffered a bad fall while holding her son, just after the couple had moved into their new home. Kathleen protected Paul by breaking her fall with a stiffened right arm, which was badly fractured as a result. She had saved her son, she felt, but it was Jat's parents who saved her from a very difficult situation. Kathleen had to cope with the recent move and a two-year-old child — all with only one arm. Although they had just returned to Montreal after helping Kathleen and Jat move into their new house, Jat's parents went back to Iowa to help Kathleen unpack and care for her son until her cast came off. "They never hesitated," she says with feeling.

Kathleen is impressed by the generosity of her in-laws, and Jat seems proud. His connection with his extended family is one thing Jat can claim of an Indian identity that, otherwise, he has a more tenuous grasp of. This connection is visible in the wedding photographs of Jat with his parents and siblings as they stand closely together — Jat looks, in fact, like a younger version of his father, and his responsibilities as eldest son keep him close to his parents. He makes time in his busy life for extended family visits and talks with his parents by phone several times a week. "If his folks haven't heard from Jat in about three days," Kathleen smiles, "they call and ask, 'What's wrong?'"

Although Jat embraced international Toronto during his early years, lately he has begun to feel some regret that he did not participate more fully in the Indian, specifically Sikh, culture that was available to him. Jat has begun to long for a memory of his homeland that is a fuller, more substantial part of his psyche, and in the absence of such memories, he has begun cultivating other ties to his Indian origins. The traditional Sikh wedding ceremony he and Kathleen chose was one expression of Jat's desire to partake in Indian culture. He has also begun to listen to Indian music, something he did not do when he was younger. Not only is this music beautiful, comforting, he tells us, but it also calls forth memories — some of them specific and some of them less so, smoky tendrils reaching up from a past that he cannot quite bring into focus.

The Aluwalias plan an extended visit to India as soon as their second child is old enough to travel, and Jat also tries to speak Punjabi with his son each day, knowing how quickly English will become Paul's only language if he does not. But even while Jat is increasing his efforts to reach out to a cultural history that he had almost left behind, he is very realistic about what he has lost. "I'm thinking of it more and more as I look at my child," Jat tells us. "When I look at Paul, I think about how his skin is lighter than mine, and at times I almost wonder if he looks like me, if he looks like my child at all."

He realizes how unlikely it is that his children will participate as much in his culture as he would like them to. It is sometimes a source of sorrow to him that his children will be first and foremost American, but he faces this reality squarely. "I am looking at it, and already I'm conceding defeat. I think the sense of being Indian ends with me. That's the saddest part. I think about that sometimes, not so dramatically, but I am realizing the significance of the loss now, because I have children."

Without dismissing Jat's sadness about the difficulty of passing his cultural heritage on to his children, there are happier ways of looking at what will become of Kathleen and Jat's intercultural family. Perhaps the Aluwalias' children will be world citizens, as Jat and Kathleen are themselves world citizens in different ways, as are the members of both Kathleen and Jat's extended family. Despite Jat's earlier comments about a sense of rootlessness that borders on displacement, he has come to love this spot in the Midwest and has made friends with many of his neighbors, whom he has taught to pronounce his last name by saying, "It's kind of like,

Hallelujah!'" One particularly bitter winter with record snowfalls, the Aluwalias were touched to find that a neighbor had come and plowed out their long driveway for them, despite the time it took in the freezing cold and deep drifts. "This almost moved Jat to tears," Kathleen tells us. "I thought I was going to have to carry him back inside!"

Kathleen's Iowa-based family, too — despite all the trappings of an insular Midwestern life, complete with livestock in the backyard and a dirt road out front — is about as multicultural as an American family gets. Kathleen's siblings have married people from Taiwan and Iran, for example, and a neighbor we met cheerfully described their family reunions as a "small United Nations." Kathleen and Jat are both citizens of the world, and their children will be shaped by this international perspective.

.

In the course of talking to Kathleen and Jat we heard one story in particular that moves us, that we feel illustrates something of what such a multicultural family might be about. Kathleen tells us that her younger sister, Maureen, married an African American man in 1989, and they had a son, Alexander. Though the marriage didn't last much beyond Alexander's birth, Maureen's relationship with her in-laws has remained strong and loving, and she felt so good about the home she was able to provide Alexander that she decided there was room in her life for another child.

The history of one little girl, a ten-year-old African American child named Tanya, caught Maureen's attention. On the video that introduced Tanya to prospective foster parents, she was vivacious and intelligent, but she had been in the foster-care system for too long. At the end of the tape, Tanya, convinced that she would still be looking for a family when the new year and new set of videos came around, addressed the cameraperson with a piquant mixture of sarcasm, sadness, and resignation: "See you next year," she said. Maureen was determined to adopt Tanya and to provide her with a home.

The adoption process, however, presented difficulties. Social workers at the agency were skeptical about a white woman's ability to care for an African American child in the Eurocentric world of tiny North English, Iowa. Maureen endured a series of grueling evaluations and worked tirelessly to convince the social workers that her home would be a healthy and loving environment for Tanya. Finally, as a last effort, Maureen made a video portrait of her multicultural and multiracial extended family. Although Tanya would have a white mother, Maureen tried to suggest, she would also be part of a family that embraced differences of many varieties — religious, racial, and national — and her extended family would be neither black nor white, but a colorful "other" of European, Asian, and African descent. The video persuaded the adoption agency, and Tanya is now a part — and by all accounts a happy one — of Kathleen and Jat's family.

Maureen's home with Alexander and Tanya is sewn into Barb's quilt beside Kathleen and Jat's house. It is ironic, in some ways, that Barb has chosen the art of quilting to depict her family's neighborhood, since that art tends to be interpreted as a beautifully parochial and particularly American form of expression. And the quilt's little rows of houses do suggest a tranquility and uniformity that belies the more complicated reality of Kathleen, Jat, and their extended family.

Yet in another way, Barb's quilt honors her intercultural family and portrays the Aluwalias' home quite aptly. The quilt is pieced together from different fabrics that, traditionally, would have come from a variety of garments and that might now originate almost anywhere on the planet, and the quilter brings together a diversity of colors, patterns, and textures to create one beautiful whole.

Like minds

CLARA & GEORGE

Clara & George. Photo by Lauren Smith.

eorge and Clara Kamats live in a housing development in Ypsilanti, Michigan, between Detroit and Ann Arbor. Theirs is a family-oriented area, built in the leafy Michigan countryside — people on bikes and handmade garage-sale signs everywhere. The couple's home is relatively new, everything fresh and unsullied. A cathedral living room opens onto a kitchen and den, which in turn looks out on a back porch and a vivid expanse of green grass. Clara, we are told, is in charge of interior design, and she has arranged the house with the precision of a professional, all the furniture coordinated, the colors understated. Though six months pregnant herself, Clara helps us settle into the den, gets paper towels for our sticky baby, and assures us that she is not worried about the pristine white carpet the baby is eyeing with drooly enthusiasm.

Our favorite spot in the house is a set of shelves in the den populated with dozens of framed photographs — friends, relatives, and a few shots of Clara and George at various stages of their romance. "We have at least one picture," Clara tells us proudly, "of every member of the family."

The faces in these photographs come from very different family histories and backgrounds — half of them Cuban and the other half thoroughly Anglo — though you cannot see this by looking at the pictures. George was born in Miami, but his father worked for the airlines as George does now, and he grew up moving from state to state, rarely staying anywhere for more than a year. "Pack your bag. Don't leave nothin' out," he says by way of summary. Then he adds, more seriously, "I liked moving everywhere." He got to see lots of different cities and parts of the country, but, more important, the frequent moves helped foster in

George a hard-edged independence that is a central part of his identity. For George, friendship is not a priority.

"I probably have about five really close friends from all the different places I've lived. I just don't like living in the past. Here, we are in the present. We're looking at our future, and that's where I'd like to stay. I told Clara when we moved away from Florida, 'You know it's nice that you're writing to all your friends, but you're going to send all these letters and make all these phone calls, but they're never going to call you back.' Whenever we do see our friends from Florida, they say 'Come by and see me! Come by and see me!'"

"'When you comin' to Miami? When you comin' to Miami?'" Clara interrupts with an imitation of those Florida friends.

"But few of them have come here to see us."

"I have a couple of really close friends, just a couple, who have come," affirms Clara.

"That's the way I've always been," says George returning to his focus on the present. "People think I have Alzheimer's, you know, they say 'remember two years ago when this happened,' and I'm like, 'I don't know.'"

"I remember everything," says Clara.

.

Among other things, Clara remembers parts of her childhood in Cuba before the revolution. Her grandparents had a dirt-floor farmhouse within walking distance of her home that Clara describes with particular fondness. "I used to visit my grandparents' farm, sit under a tree eating mangoes. We would pick the mangoes and then stop under the last tree with our buckets full of them. It was so hot sometimes that we would sit there in nothing but our underwear," she continues, as though surprised that she can still picture those summer days so vividly. Her grandparents' farm was situated on beautiful land, bordering a river and several smaller creeks. "We used to bathe in those creeks and play there. The government took the farm after the revolution. Eventually, the river flooded and washed the whole house away."

Clara is wistful when she tells us how her mother gave birth to Clara and her siblings in that farmhouse, returning home to stay there with Clara's grandmother during each child's first weeks of infancy. That sadness, however, is marked by a sharp clarity about the unfairness of her family's loss — of land, of family history, of heritage — in the wake of the Cuban Revolution. Clara and her family do not like what has happened to Cuba, and it is partly because of their dislike of Communist Cuba that they have embraced many elements of American culture — including the man who would become Clara's husband.

In fact, Clara believes that her mother, on some level, foresaw Clara's future with George. Her mother had always felt sure that she would eventually marry an American, rather than a Cuban, despite Clara's marked preference for the latter. "My mom said, 'You need to find yourself an American man,' and I said, 'Oh no, why?'" She looks over at her husband and smiles, "I thought they were bland-looking, boring, couldn't dance."

"'Because you don't do well with Latin men,' my mother said, and I didn't. Lots of relationships broken up, on again off again." Clara's mother felt that Latin men didn't give Clara the freedom she needed, but Clara had no intention of listening to her mother. She dated American men only occasionally and quickly lost interest.

{ *Like Minds* }

Ironically, George had a similar disinclination for Cuban women and wouldn't, he tells us, have been interested in Clara if he'd known when he first met her that she was Cuban. Clara explains her husband's disinterest, "Cuban women have to have the best clothes, and they have to have the best figure, the best hair."

"There aren't enough mirrors in Miami, let's put it that way," quips George.

Despite their mutual prejudices, on April 23, 1989, George and Clara met on a beach in Miami that both frequented — a quiet, family-oriented beach away from the crowded, touristy shorelines for which Miami is famous. George tells the story in his typically straightforward, almost telegraphic style. "I used to get there at eight in the morning when no one else was around. I saw her one time, and then I watched her for about four or five weekends. I just liked the way she looked."

Clara had seen George before, but she was not initially attracted to him. For one thing, he was a white American man, with much more body hair than she was used to seeing. In addition, he went to the beach with a Cuban friend, who wore a tight and fluorescent bathing suit. Together, they made something of a spectacle. "I'd seen George before — because you couldn't miss 'em — this big guy and this other one in an orange Speedo. My first reaction to George was 'Eww, he's got a hairy back.'" But Clara liked George's self-confidence, which bordered on arrogance. "He carried himself in a certain way, and somehow he intrigued me. I'm like, '*pleeease*, who is this guy?'"

The day the two finally met, after Clara had unpacked the car and gotten her sister, Lanie, settled ("she couldn't have any sand on her towel *at all*"), Clara and her sister started a game of paddleball. "So here's me, here's my sister, and George is over here," Clara explains, drawing a map of the beach in the air for us. "He was already sitting in his chair relaxing when we got there. He was asleep, supposedly." Clara's sister insisted on stationing herself, despite vociferous objections on Clara's part, in such a way that the ball was bound to land near George. "It happened three times," says Clara shaking her head in remembered exasperation. Finally, George spoke. "He goes, I forget what he said, 'Here's your ball,' or something. Then he asked me, 'Is that your daughter?' and I said, 'Oh, no.' Everything went on from there." The couple talked, in rapt attention, for three hours, Clara ignoring Lanie, who was used to getting Clara's complete attention. "Poor Lanie was like, 'I want to go in the water, I want to go in the water, now,'" Clara speaks in a falsetto, imitating Lanie's pleading, "and I'm like, 'Be quiet.' 'I'm thirsty'; 'there's your drink, get it yourself.'"

In those three hours, Clara says, she found out that George was divorced, that his grandmother's name was also Clara, that he was Catholic, that he went to church, and that he worked for the airlines. "It was a lot of fun," Clara says, and when George got ready to leave, the two decided to exchange telephone numbers. Unfortunately, George couldn't find a pen in his car and Clara didn't have one either. George asked a woman who was waiting for his parking space, but her pen, she said, was in her trunk — by which she meant to say that it was inaccessible. "'Well, could you get it for me?' 'No,'" Clara says, imitating the woman's irritation. "So he said, 'Well, you're not getting this parking space until I get a pen.'" The woman got out of the car and retrieved her pen from the trunk. George wrote down the number and said thank you.

George phoned Clara after that, and the two set their first date for the following weekend. But about midweek, Clara remembers, George called and said, "I can't wait to see you. I have to see you, and besides I want your mom to meet the guy you're going out with." Clara's mother was delighted with this respectful treatment. "She bought that hook, line, and sinker." After that, Clara's mother was convinced that George was the right man for Clara. "The minute my mom saw George — I could just tell — she fell in love immediately. My mom's about five foot one, and here's this handsome, big guy, who doesn't look like your typical American."

Clara was not as immediately certain. After four weeks of seeing George several times a week, she broke up with him. "He knew he wanted to be with me for the rest of his life, and I was like — eeee — how do you know? So I broke up. For a week, and then we got back together."

Despite his avowed devotion to the present, George remembers this episode in their romance with clarity. He'd been surprised by Clara's decision and, at first, didn't understand what she meant. "Does this mean we're not going to the movies on Wednesday?" he asked mildly. When he did understand, though, and realized that she was serious, his response was more emphatic: "What? I'm the first guy to treat you right. You're the one who's going to lose out. You're going to regret this, I'm a nice guy."

"I was, like, what is wrong with you? You're so full of yourself," says Clara, "though really, he was right."

"I told her," George says with a dismissive wave of his hand, "not to call me. There weren't any second chances. That was my policy." She'd really hurt him, he tells us, and at that point he had no intention of ever talking to Clara or seeing her again.

Clara's family was truly shocked by her decision to stop seeing

George. "My mom never told me what to do, ever. She just said, 'I don't understand.' My brother said, 'Are you insane? The first nice man that cares about you?' They all saw his caring side, and I did, too, but . . ." She does not complete this thought. "My sister-in-law, my mother, they just shook their heads."

A week went by, and Clara missed George's telephone calls. "He's very black-and-white," says Clara, "there is no gray area," and once they were broken up, she didn't hear a word from him. Finally, she decided to call. For the first three days, George was not there, inspiring more than a little jealousy on Clara's part, and when she did reach him, he was completely unreceptive.

"I'm telling you," Clara reports, "he did not mince words with me." George absolutely refused to see Clara or discuss their relationship, saying, "There is no us; you ended that." And he concluded their brief conversation by telling Clara not to call him again. "No, I don't give second chances," he said. "You had your chance, you lost it. Okay?"

"And I'll never forget," adds Clara, "he said, '*Comprende?*' Oh, I hated that. To this day I hate it." On top of that, George informed Clara that he'd already met somebody else. "So I remember," Clara continues, "I was sitting on my bed, and I must have had a look on my face — I don't know — but my sister, who's not very expressive, not very touchy-feely, came over and just held me. I was devastated."

Two days later, Clara returned everything George had given her, including cards and letters, with a note that she quotes to us: "Enclosed you will find your letters, poems, etc. Give them to your new-found love because maybe to her they will be real — p.s. please return my Sade tapes to the enclosed address." We all hoot now at the youthfulness of the tone, but Clara says that she would never want to relive that time.

For his part, George was so furious when he received the note that, he says, he "put it through the shredder."

Nevertheless, he called her three days later, and the couple agreed to meet. George told Clara that she'd hurt him very badly, that he wanted to see her again but didn't feel that he could trust her. "I'm looking at this big guy, this manly man, telling me all this." It was a revelation for Clara. She was surprised at the depth of George's feelings of vulnerability, and at his willingness to express those feelings. "We started seeing each other again after that," Clara says, "and the rest is history." She laughs, her hands on her pregnant belly.

We inquire why George was willing to break the no-second-chances rule, and he is, as usual, to the point: "I liked being with Clara, talking with her, going out with her. Right when I first met her, I knew that I wanted to be with her."

After they had reconciled, the couple faced another obstacle — George's family, who at first did not accept Clara. "Because I knew I wanted to be with Clara, I never took her to the family functions in Miami," George tells us. His desire to be with Clara, that is, was not up for discussion, and George was not ready to open his relationship up for the family's scrutiny.

"He'd been through a divorce and they were very concerned," Clara explains. "I was the mysterious woman he would never bring to family functions. 'Who is this woman?' they were asking." Clara herself was getting impatient. She couldn't understand why George didn't want to introduce her to his family or why she wasn't invited to his grandmother's birthday and other family events. "Because of who he is," says Clara, "George just had to do it in his own time — which happened to be on the evening I got my wisdom teeth pulled. My face is like this — " she puffs up her cheeks. "So he says, 'Let's go visit my mom.' His poor mom wasn't expecting us. She was in her robe. In a way, it was very typical. There was no chance to prepare, no chance for anybody to be anything but themselves."

Shortly after Clara met his mother, George decided that she should meet his family in Pennsylvania too, particularly his Grandfather George and Grandma Clara. Getting this past her mother — taking an overnight trip with a man — was easier than Clara had expected, but George's family was a different matter. His father was especially disapproving. "What kind of girl goes away with a guy to meet his family? We don't even know her," he said, and the family was abuzz with doubtful speculation.

"We got up there and the first night was church," George picks up the story. "Clara sat next to my grandmother and I sat one row up. They opened up one epistle and shared it together. When we got outside the church, Grandma Clara said, 'Clara you're going to have to come over tomorrow and visit with us.' Grandma Clara," George explains, "was the matriarch. Whatever Grandma said went. The next day, my father called, offering to drive us to the airport and so forth. It went from one extreme to the other." Since then, things have remained loving between Clara and her in-laws.

When we ask George why he grew serious about Clara so quickly, what he liked about her, he immediately says, "I liked her independence. I can't have somebody calling me all day long saying, 'Where you at? What're you doing? When you coming home? Why didn't you call me at this time?'"

"I'm like that, too," says Clara, "and that was the big thing with the Cuban men I dated. They had to know where you were, who you were with, what you were wearing every moment of the day, and I just couldn't stand it."

George also appreciated the ease with which Clara made connections with other people. "She was somebody you could talk to," says George. "My thing is, in a party situation, I only talk to the people I know. She talks to everybody, so by the time we go, they're wanting to invite me back because I'm the life of the party — when maybe I talked to one person the whole time I was there. It was really her they wanted back, and I was part of that package."

"But, um, we would just sit and talk," says George getting back to more important things. "The communication was there from the beginning. I always thought a big part of relationships was to become friends first. If you're not friends, when you're seventy-five years old, what the hell you got? You got zero in common. You don't talk to each other, so what good is it? I was very heavy on the communication side — to become friends — to find out who you're with. We did a lot of talking," he says.

Clara appreciated George's emphasis on friendship, especially at that time in her life. There were some serious problems in her family, then, and she needed someone to confide in. "It was a time of personal turmoil," she says, "but George never judged that. He would listen; he understood. He would never say, 'Oh, I'm out of here.'"

George makes it clear that his feelings for Clara have little to do with her cultural identity. He appreciates and cares about her family, but when we ask him what he likes about Cuban culture, he says only, "I like the food." What he does not like is the music, or the loud Cuban get-togethers where everyone is laughing and talking at the top of their lungs in the kitchen, or that Cubans, as he says, "celebrate everything." He shakes his head, laughing. "Everything's a freakin' party."

Clara loves her Cuban music and likes rowdy parties with her friends. To some degree, though, she agrees with George about what she sees as a Cuban penchant for huge celebrations. In particular, she did not want to have one of the large, expensive weddings that are part of Cuban culture in Miami. Marriage for its own sake, she says, had never been important to her or her parents, and a fancy ceremony wasn't important either. "All I really wanted for my wedding was to wear a wedding dress, in a church, with my family. I didn't care about anything else." The couple decided to keep the ceremony small — forty people attended — and their reception was also small, with carrot cake and Spanish cider. Clara had refused to have Cuban cake at the wedding, which she doesn't like, but she "gave in" on the cider — which is what Cuban people generally drink instead of champagne at weddings. The most important bicultural element of the wedding, though, was that the service was performed in both Spanish and English.

George, for whom memories are relatively unimportant, nevertheless cherishes his memories of his wedding. "It was a perfect day," he tells us. "I remember everything about that day, saying our vows, being with our family and friends."

After the wedding and the reception, Clara and George retired with their closest friends and their family to a restaurant they had frequented each weekend during their courtship. They would always drink beer, they told us, and eat chicken wings and shrimp, watch sports on television. This informal party — attended only by their closest friends and family members — was their favorite part of the day. "George and I had Killian's Red, chicken wings, and shrimp, just like we always did. It was our own little happy hour."

.

At first Clara, with whom one might easily talk for an hour without realizing any time has passed, and George, who would be content to nod and chuckle from his lounger through the entire interview, seem like very different people. Anyone who met them only in the context, say, of a cocktail party might perceive them as near opposites. He is big and fair-skinned, thoughtful, gruff, and more than a little reserved. She, on the other hand, is dark-haired and small — especially in her prepregnancy pictures. Even now, at the end of a difficult pregnancy, her energy fills the room. She laughs, gestures, and talks as fast as an auctioneer, filling each story with details and commentary that draw us into her narratives.

Despite their apparent differences, however, George and Clara are more alike than otherwise. Though Clara is the one who narrates their wedding story and explains the choices they made, for example, George clearly agrees with her depiction of events and ideas. They made their decisions together and share the practical philosophy behind them. They both seem especially disapproving about excessive expenditures for big weddings and exotic honeymoons — something they find disturbing about the Cuban-style wedding. As an aside, at one point, Clara tells us about an acquaintance whose mother offered either to pay for her wedding or to give her ten thousand dollars to use as she pleased. "She picked the wedding. *She picked the wedding!*" says Clara with incredulity. "The wedding was over in a couple of hours. She could have paid off her car; she could have made a down payment on a house; she could have invested the money." George makes a face that reflects Clara's disbelief and shakes his head.

This, however, is part of a much larger spectrum of values that George and Clara share. "I think we're alike in a lot of ways — except for the fact that she's really outgoing," says George. "We're both very independent. We are strong-willed, focused on what we want to do. It's fine for her to go out and do her thing, and it's fine for me to go out and do mine — then we meet, we sit down to a nice dinner and talk to each other. Also, we're both really family-oriented. She likes my parents, and I like hers. My parents and I didn't always get along. But now we're doing better."

"His father?" says Clara, "they're just alike. We could be in Wyoming now. His father would be in the exact same position is *his* lounger. The arm behind the neck, the leg crossed over."

He and his father are getting along better, George tells us, primarily because of Clara. "They really like her. Even if I wasn't around, they'd still have Clara over."

"And his mom will tell you that, too," says Clara.

The two also share an ability to say what they think. This is more obvious with George, who tends to boil everything down to its most salient point and who has a reputation at work and among family and friends for bluntness. "I don't have any remorse for what I've got to say," he tells us. "I'm black or I'm white. There's no middle ground. I'm gonna tell you what I honestly think no matter if I hurt your feelings. There's no reason to tell a white lie. I just don't sugarcoat anything, and that's the way I've always been."

While what she calls George's "baseball bat of reality" is not Clara's style, she too, we discover, knows how to say what she thinks. We witness this quality when she talks about her wedding, but we also hear it in the stories she tells us about her family. George's current relatively healthy relationship with his family, for example, is due partly to Clara's honesty. "You've got to talk to each other," she told George, and she said the same thing to her mother-in-law. "He's your son. You've got to talk to him. I can't get into the middle of this," she says with a firmness that we would find difficult to use with our family members.

Clara and George are most in accord when they talk about how to raise the son they will have in only a few months, Peter Michael, whose name honors people on both sides of the family. Despite the antipathy George expressed earlier in our interview for many elements of Cuban culture, George and Clara both want to support and reinforce their son's connection to his Cuban family and identity. They both want their son to speak Spanish, as well as English, partly because the language is part of Clara's heritage and her family. Their son's Cuban roots are so important to them, in fact, that they are hoping to bring Clara's parents up to Michigan to live with them.

Some holidays, they have decided, will be celebrated Cuban-style and others will be celebrated American-style. "We established right away that Thanksgiving would be done the American way — typical turkey and stuffing, nothing Cuban," Clara tells us. "And we would have Christmas Eve, one of our big holidays, with the Cuban food, the music . . . the loudness." Clara laughs. "Also, I want Peter Michael to know my music. Sometimes I can picture myself dancing with my son and having — " she searches for words, "and having the coolest feeling in the world."

Clara also wants to pass on certain other values she has taken from her culture but finds difficult to explain. "Just stuff that my mom taught me throughout the years, and that her father taught her, like how to be self-reliant." Even more difficult for Clara to explain, and for George to understand, is the sense of community involvement and commitment she wants for her son. She tries to clarify her feelings by talking about funerals in the Miami Cuban community. "It's hard to explain," she starts. "For example, if somebody dies, we stay up all night . . . friends, neighbors, families. Even if it's somebody you don't know real well, you go."

"I've never been to so many funerals in my life," George interrupts.

"You go and you pay your respects," Clara remains serious.

"It got so that when I went to the funeral parlor, I'd just go from room to room, just to make sure I didn't miss anybody."

"Geooorge," complains Clara, before continuing. "I just want my son to know about Cuban values," she says, "and about what life was like there."

Many of the values they wish to pass on to Peter Michael, though, are values their families have in common. They hope that Peter Michael shares their religious devotion. They both want him to share the deep respect for family that they grew up with, and they want him to have the work ethic that was common to both of their backgrounds. "I was always taught," says George, "you work for what you get. That's the most important thing." Clara agrees. "That was something instilled in me by my grandparents. You take care of your land, you take care of your home, you take care of your livestock, and you help others at the same time. My mother's grandmother had twenty births. I don't know how many of them lived, but she adopted the twenty-first child. It had been abandoned on the farm somewhere. But she always had her arms open to everyone."

"You know, I'm not averse to a seventy-hour work week, I can stay eighteen hours a day at work if that's what needs to be done," contributes George. Part of this philosophy has to do with the practical need for an income, something they want their son to be aware of, to be able to negotiate. "Love doesn't pay the bills, it's all money," George notes. "You have to have money to survive. It's a fact of life. It's not so much the importance of money, but how to use common sense. Peter needs to understand this," says George.

Clara nods her agreement while her husband talks. "But you know," Clara addresses her husband, "he also needs to see that you can have a passion about other things, outside of the work world. That's what we have. We come home from work and we put on our shorts. We never lose sight of what the other person is doing."

"Yeah," says George at intervals, "yeah."

Clara and George agree that Michigan would be a good place to raise their son, and, professional lives permitting, they would be happy to stay where they are. George likes the climate: "I enjoy living up here because, the way I look at it, you get nine months of free air conditioning instead of twelve months of heat. I like having four seasons, seeing the leaves change. I like seeing snow on the ground."

Clara says that her friends were surprised when she moved to "the God-forsaken North," and many of them didn't even know where Michigan was. When she first arrived, she missed her family and elements of her own culture, but she downplays her feelings of loss. "As long as I'm with George," she says, "I could really care less. I love the weather here. I love the changes and what they bring out in people. The spring and fall when everybody's excited; the summer's all fun, everybody's out doing things; and the winter's very dreary, but it's also a very beautiful time of waiting for the next spring to come. In Miami, it's always hot and there's nothing to look forward to in your physical environment." Also, both George and Clara agree that the Midwest is safer and friendlier than Miami.

"People say hi to you," George comments.

"Yeah," says Clara. "In Miami, if someone says hi, you check to see if your wallet is missing!" They both laugh. "I think people in Miami live in a constant state of tension," she finishes. Clara had never lived anywhere else in the United States than Miami before she came to Michigan, and she says she's learned a lot from moving to the Midwest. She's learned, she says, about the kinds of industries and people that keep the United States financially strong. She's met steel mill workers from Detroit and farmers from more rural areas of the region — whom she calls, "real Americans." Also, Clara is comfortable here, as an individual, as a Cuban woman. The people she works with may not know much about her culture — they may not know what guavas and mangoes are, but they are open to her. At least, Clara feels, they do show a friendly interest in finding out. "It's not hard to be me in this area," Clara says.

"I love my life," says Clara with finality. George smiles from his lounger, sanguine.

Seven seas

PETER & HUEPING

Hueping & Peter with their son, Vernon. Photo by Christy Mock.

hen Peter Meidlinger left the United States for Brazil in 1985 after completing a master's in linguistics at the University of Iowa, he believed he was leaving the academic life altogether. "I'm getting out of this" he recalls thinking, "academia isn't the right route for me." So when he returned to Iowa City in 1987 after teaching in an international high school in Brazil, he was only intending to make some money before going on to do something else with his life. As he puts it, he planned "a surgical strike — make some money, get outta there." But that summer, teaching in an ESL orientation program for international graduate students, Peter met Hueping Chin, a Taiwanese graduate student in the history department, and his plans for a quick departure were dramatically altered.

"Hueping has a way of looking at people," Peter tells us. "She is not fooled by appearances, and the look in her eyes can make superficial or phony people just a little uncomfortable. I noticed that in class." As Peter had glanced around the class of international students, he recalls that most reverently nodded and smiled and otherwise indicated their willingness to trust him, to give him the benefit of the doubt. "Not Hueping. She was reserving judgment. I was going to have to show her that I had something to offer her as a teacher, and I found that quality very attractive." Peter was impressed with Hueping's sensitivity and intelligence, and admired her sense of humor. "Soon I started having those giddy moments that indicate love is involved. As a teacher, I had to deny those feelings, but I looked forward to seeing her in the morning, took extra delight in her 'good mornings' to me. I had to remind myself that I was her teacher, that

I might never see her again after August, and that I might as well forget about it — what was I thinking?"

But instead of forgetting about it, Peter decided to stay in Iowa City in hopes of asking Hueping out. "So I went to one of my teachers, Jim Marshall, and I said, 'It's the end of July, I'm broke, I have no job prospects, and I'm madly in love with a woman who's stuck here for the next five years.' And Jim said, 'You're perfect for graduate school!'"

We all laugh at the story, but when Peter continues, he is serious, still marveling at the twist his life took. "I would not have gotten my degree, I would not have started the Ph.D. program at all, if Hueping hadn't been stuck in Iowa City and if I hadn't been committed to finding out what this relationship was about. The relationship *was* the commitment — not the degree. And I hadn't even asked her out yet. She still did not know I was interested in her! She claims to this day she didn't know."

"Well, I *didn't* know; I wasn't presumptuous," Hueping remarks mildly.

So Peter stayed on in Iowa City, entering the Ph.D. program but, more important, plotting how to approach Hueping. The summer course was over, and he didn't have her phone number. In any case, he wanted to be more casual than that, to bump into Hueping as though unintentionally. He waited for that chance encounter for weeks. "Finally, I ran into her at the corner of the library. I knew from the class that she liked films, so I said, '*Citizen Kane*'s playing tonight, do you want to go?' And we went together. Then *I* think we're dating." Peter sits back with folded hands as though in satisfaction, before leaning forward to add, "But *she* thinks we just ran into each other."

So sweet! we comment during this natural pause in the story, touched by Peter's plan and his persistence.

"See?" Peter says, in mock triumph to his wife.

But now Hueping wants to explain her view of things. She wants our opinion, what *should* she have thought? "There I was, just checking books out from the library, and we ran into each other. Just talked a little; exchanged news about the break, 'Did you see that the movie calendar is out — *Citizen Kane* is on — want to go see it? OK.' So, no, I don't consider it a date. We just happened to go see a movie together, that's all," she says reasonably.

Yes, we nod. We understand her point of view, too.

"See?" Hueping says back serenely to her husband.

Gradually, as Peter and Hueping continued to do things together, attending films and plays, Peter began to doubt that Hueping knew of his attraction to her. "It was really difficult to know what was going on in her mind," he admits. A couple of months later, after they had seen another film, Peter decided to clear things up, to tell Hueping that he regarded her as more than a friend; he chose as his setting the Great Midwestern Ice Cream Company. As longtime Iowa City residents ourselves, we can picture the scene for this romantic confession exactly: the Great Midwestern's brick walls and wooden floors, cheerfully lit and pleasantly full, the after-movie crowd mixing with the perpetual knots of students huddled at small wooden tables stacked with books and papers. "I said to her over our ice cream, 'Look, I really like you.' And I was met with" — here Peter pauses for emphasis — "silence."

Didn't she say anything at all? we ask, feeling Peter's discomfort with him.

Peter responds, "I don't think so," and shifts slightly as though still embarrassed by the memory these twelve years later. "I don't remember how we got out of there. It was uncomfortable."

"I was just trying to register this," Hueping explains. "I was trying to figure out, what's the rule here, this is a new game. I don't know what's really going on. It was still only my second year in the U.S. — I don't know about the love game — I'd never played that before in the States."

"That was something she taught me," Peter adds appreciatively. "I learned from that moment that a possible response to being confused is silence. From her I learned the power of understatement. Or no statement!"

For a while, as Peter remembers it, the two didn't talk. Hueping murmurs a dissent on this point, thinks they remained in touch, but both agree that some time shortly after this encounter Hueping began to call Peter. In any case, the matter was resolved one evening when Peter invited Hueping to dinner at his house.

The evening did not begin auspiciously because of a difference of opinion about the evening's plan. "I called her and said, 'Come watch baseball with me — it's a really good game, in the fourth inning. We'll watch it and then have dinner.'" While Peter thought he'd emphasized watching the game, however, Hueping heard an invitation to dinner, and when some time had passed without dinner prospects, Hueping got up to leave.

"It was 10:30 already," she exclaims, the hint of an old complaint in her voice.

"Actually it was 8:30," Peter counters. "It was still pretty early."

"No, wait, this is a different version," Hueping insists, laughing. "Actually, I got there pretty late and we had dinner pretty late.

When I got there, there was no dinner. Right?" She backtracks with Peter, seeking consensus.

"Right," Peter agrees. "Because I didn't know then that when Chinese went somewhere to eat, dinner had to be ready right away. I thought she was comfortable with the American way — "

"At least there should be something there. You know there's a smell of food that makes you feel hopeful," Hueping interrupts, eager, even a decade later, to pinpoint the source of her confusion. "Especially because he said he was going to make Brazilian chicken. Oooh! I love food! So when I got there I was expecting if it's chicken either it has to bake or roast or stew, at least there should be some kind of aroma there. And there was nothing. So I thought, what's happening here? Are we going to eat?"

"So when she was getting ready to leave I said 'wait,' and I turned off the TV. And she said, 'What's your story?' I thought, 'This is good, this is progress.' Then we told each other what we were up to, what our lives were like. We had a really long heart to heart about where we'd been and where we were going. Thought about where we were at that point."

When we ask Hueping what made her decide to call Peter back, she tells us that she liked him but had simply needed time to think. "At first I wasn't sure how to respond, but later I thought, 'Well, I can figure it out!'" In retrospect, Hueping notes, "the love game" is not played much differently in Taiwan than in the United States. Courtship is similar, although in Taiwan the custom of arranged marriage is still practiced, with an emphasis more on parental approval rather than permission. "In Taiwan, most people choose their own mates now, and actually, a lot of women choose *not* to get married these days. A lot of women who get higher education tend to be single because they cannot find the right ones and also because men still want traditional wives, a woman who is pretty, to take care of them. They don't want a wife who is smarter than they are, who has a higher degree."

Hueping's silence in the Great Midwestern that day was a complicated one. To begin with, she was not in a hurry to become seriously involved with anyone. "I was one of those women who would rather be single and happy — not just get into a bad relationship for marriage's sake or for my parents' sake." Also, she knew that if a serious relationship developed between them, someone would be losing a country and a culture. "That was also why I was hesitating for a while, I had expected to get my degree and go home, go back and get a teaching job."

We enjoy the couple's story partly for its irony — Peter was so sure he was leaving academia and Hueping was so ready to remain single. And yet here they are, presenting scholarly papers together at a conference in Chicago. The ending of their story also pleases us. The risks Peter and Hueping speak of were taken long ago and seem to have paid off for each happily. Both have found full-time teaching positions at Drury College in Springfield, Missouri, a feat many academic couples never manage; they have a son whom they obviously adore; and they just as clearly take great pleasure in one another's company.

•

Although we meet Hueping and Peter in the downtown Chicago Hyatt only minutes after they have arrived from the airport, they already seem settled enough to make even their hotel room feel somehow welcoming. Hueping and Peter kindly offer us the room's only chairs and sit companionably together at the end of a double bed while their son, Vernon, who is eight, leaps acrobatically from bed to bed behind them, before retiring under a lamp with some Calvin and Hobbes cartoons and a book, *Tintin Goes to Tibet*.

Peter has wavy blonde hair and is slender, with a sometimes droll, ready-to-laugh voice and large, dark-rimmed glasses that seem to slightly magnify his attentive blue eyes. When he is telling a story, he speaks quickly, at one point describing himself as gregarious, "excessive," though for much of our conversation he sits quietly thinking and listening. He has offered to hold the baby we have brought with us, and they are a happy duo — he bouncing her gently from time to time, she gnawing contentedly on his knuckle.

Hueping is a trim woman, with dark chin-length hair and kind but discerning brown eyes. She responds to our questions more slowly than Peter does, with a considered precision, but also with an understated levity. She knows how to appreciate a joke and seems to enjoy the opportunity to tease her husband that their reminiscences provide. Hueping sometimes answers our questions with a question of her own. She strikes us as a sort of anthropologist at heart, a quality that we suspect is linked to her parents' departure from China to Taiwan. This transplanting put the family on the outside of things, spurring what was Hueping's natural curiosity into a lifelong interest in traditions and rituals that are foreign to her.

Her parents moved from China to Taiwan when they were very young, after the civil war in 1948. "So we didn't have grandparents. I know I must have a lot of relatives, but they are not in Taiwan, but in mainland China. Actually, we did not have tradition in my family. My friends, our neighbors, many of them had lived in Taiwan for several centuries. Every time, on certain holidays, I saw them set a table outside worshipping spirits and gods and I was fascinated. I would observe them, ask them questions. Or whenever we went to a village and we saw little shrines and temples, I would like to talk to people, to learn what this is about."

From childhood on, Hueping tells us, this sense of being outside of the culture in which she found herself prompted in her a certain cosmopolitan quality, an awareness that there were many different lifestyles and cultures. At the same time, ironically, as a teenager she felt suspicious of any foreign presence and considered herself an "anti-imperialist." "I was just learning modern Chinese history, about all this hardship that came from the outside. I had an antiforeign kind of sentiment, I sometimes would joke, 'I think I am a Boxer, from the Boxer Rebellion.' So my friends were surprised that I married an American — 'isn't he an imperialist too?' they teased me."

Peter also depicts himself as an outsider, a quality that he feels resulted from frequent uprootings as a child. "By eighth grade, we'd moved seven times. My father was a gambler, and he tried to get away from gambling, so we moved to Salt Lake City where it was illegal. We'd live in one house, then we'd keep getting kids — eight altogether — so we'd need another. I remember my dad telling me that we moved whenever the rent was due, and I think," Peter adds wryly, "there was a certain amount of truth to that. Whenever the rent went up — everybody shifted." He pauses, head tipped to one side, as though trying to gather together memories of a childhood spent in many places. "I remember identifying with the underdog. I wasn't unpopular, just never rooted. I do remember when I got to college that I always went out of my way to talk to international students because I think I understood how they felt."

.

After their heart-to-heart on the Brazilian chicken night, which occurred in early October, Peter and Hueping saw each other regularly — eating, studying, and relaxing together on the weekends. At the end of that month, Peter recalls, the two had a "temporary falling out" and although the subject of it is hard to recall these many years later, their reconciliation persuaded him that they were meant for one another. "From that mending, I was convinced that there would never be a conflict that we couldn't work through. Shortly after that, I proposed to Hueping and she said she'd think about it only after finishing her comps in April."

Meanwhile, the two discovered that they had much in common: "We liked the same music, books, movies, food, friends," Peter tells us, his face brightening at the list as though rediscovering each new area of agreement. "We were committed to harmony and equality in our relationship, and we agreed on how to raise children." And, Peter notes, "We kept discovering things about one another — what it was like to learn to write Chinese as a child, to live in Taiwan, to have lived in the oldest world of them all. I realized that I would never run out of questions for her, never tire of hearing her experiences, never think of everything to ask. That's one treasure of an intercultural marriage."

Peter and Hueping married in November 1988 at St. Wenceslaus, a Catholic church in Iowa City, though neither Peter nor Hueping is a practicing member of that religion. "I was not Catholic when we got married," Peter tells us, "I was just raised Catholic. It was the tradition I was closest to."

Hueping adds, "I don't belong to any religious organization," and Vernon chimes in from the background, "I thought your religion was Buddhism."

"No, not really," she says to him tolerantly, turning toward him to explain. "You know, as a Chinese, the Confucian, the Buddhism, the Taoism, they are just all there. It's part of the culture, the way of life. My family never really observed any specific rituals, specific religious things. My mother, however, was baptized as Catholic, but she left China when she was very young, so she never really practiced Catholicism either."

She turns back to us. "The reason that we went to the Catholic church to have a religious ceremony is because we think we would rather do something ritualistic, something linked with spirituality. Some people think that a marriage should be 'go to the city hall and get a license,' but we think that's just too casual."

Their wedding was very small, just immediate family and closest friends. Peter's seven brothers and sisters sat on one side of the church along with their families, and on the other side were Hueping's friends, primarily from the Chinese community. "It was really divided," Peter comments, and Hueping nods.

Instead of having Hueping's parents attend the Iowa City wedding, Peter and Hueping decided to host a Chinese traditional banquet in Taiwan. "Which is more important than a ceremony," Hueping smiles.

"Because you eat," quips Peter.

"A feast is always important," Hueping agrees. "We went to a seafood restaurant, and my parents invited their friends, some of my friends. It's a kind of public announcement, 'Here are my daughter and son-in-law,' as well as a chance for people to get together and drink and eat."

Peter recalls the drinking more than the eating — the guests kept up an almost constant toasting of the bride and groom — and he still seems surprised, even all these years later, at the unusual sight of Hueping's family drinking alcohol. "Nobody in her family drinks at all. I've never even seen them touch a beer, except on those occasions when they celebrate. Then they drink a lot and have a good time. They loosen up and say things they ordinarily wouldn't say."

"Nice things," he adds quickly, and we all laugh. "They get gregarious and say something in Chinese that means 'You're the man,' and you say back, 'No, *you're* the man,' and then you say, 'Let's both drink, what the hell.' Then the next day, everybody's back to normal."

Peter and Hueping remember receiving only support from their families when they decided to marry. Hueping's parents, she tells us, respected her decision, and if they felt concern, they didn't show it. In fact, Hueping told her parents about her plans in a letter, and her mother wrote back, quoting a Confucian saying, which Hueping repeats to us softly in Chinese before translating: "'We are all brothers within the seven seas.'"

"Actually, I think my mother likes Peter better than me!" Hueping says, smiling. The patriarchy of Chinese culture, Hueping theorizes, made it simpler for her parents to be understanding about her choice to marry an American. The family didn't have as much at stake in her decision. She doubts whether her two younger brothers would have met with the same level of acceptance if they had chosen a similar path. "Chinese parents love their daughters, but the most important thing is their sons. So in a way I feel sorry for my brothers. They were under a lot of pressure, high expectations. But for me, they — my mother especially — said 'Do what you can do; if you want to pursue a higher education, go ahead, but if not, it's fine.' So the expectations weren't that high. Actually, the expectation is learning to be a good wife. Under that kind of a system the pressure is not that big."

Peter remembers that his family was glad he had found someone to share his life with. That his marriage would be intercultural and interracial did not concern them at all. In fact, one of Peter's sisters toasted this international element of their lives, complimenting Peter on embracing the world and bringing a global perspective to the family. It was only Peter's mother who expressed a reservation — she didn't want her son to move to faraway Taiwan.

.

The first time Peter went to Taiwan, he couldn't speak the language and people left him alone, but on the second trip he had learned more Chinese, and he saw more deeply into what was going on around him. "People sort of meddle in your life in Taiwan more than what I'm used to. It may be a family thing. For example, I was waiting with Vernon on the street and a woman came up to me and said 'He shouldn't be in diapers.' Or — 'Why are you teaching in college? You could make a lot more money if you invested in stock.' Or — 'Come back to Taiwan; you could make a lot more money here.'"

"That really is the Chinese way," Hueping agrees. "We offer advice — free advice to people all the time. More than you could need."

Peter remembers with particular amusement his honored status as son-in-law. "Yes, when we went there, I went out to do the laundry, and when I came back Hueping's mother was there scolding her. 'You know, he's likely to leave you if you make him do laundry.'"

"No," Hueping laughs, modifying the story, scaling it back. "She just came to me and asked if I knew that Peter was doing the laundry. And I said, yes, he was, because I was busy doing something else. Then two weeks later my cousin told me, 'I heard Peter did laundry for you.' Then I said, 'My God! If my cousin knows, it must be a really big deal for my mother.'"

"It makes me want to go back to Taiwan and tattle on her," teases Peter. "She's just not always doing the kind of things that a man likes!"

To a certain extent, Peter likes the attention of being the number-one son-in-law and has enjoyed getting to know Hueping's mother, who came to stay for a long visit when Vernon was born. "My Chinese isn't really good enough for us to talk well, but she and I can get along together, we know how to play cards. She's really good at cards — can pick up a card game like that — gin, hearts, backgammon, too." But when in Taiwan, he finds the extra attention harder to swallow. "There her mother waits on me hand and foot. She's really anxious to do everything for her son-in-law. I didn't really like that very much."

He remembers another kind of attention as disturbing, too. "People *look* at Hueping when we are walking down the street, an Anglo with an Asian woman. Not at me, at her."

Hueping explains, "It's curiosity from the younger people because they don't see that very often. And from older people — especially men — there usually is a kind of contempt. They think I am probably a loose woman. 'Why do you go with that foreign man?'"

Despite these difficulties, Peter liked Taiwan, and the couple seriously considered living there. Deciding where to live was, in fact, one of the most difficult decisions that they faced. Would they look for jobs in Taiwan? In the United States? What if they both found jobs in different places? Finally, their future clarified itself in unexpected ways. In the spring of 1990, while both Hueping and Peter were working on their dissertations, Hueping learned that she was pregnant. The couple decided that Peter would focus on finishing his degree and searching for a job. "Vernon was born on January 4, 1991," Peter says, "and I applied for the position at Drury then. When I got the job, we thought, 'OK, let's do this.'"

"It opened itself up to us," Hueping agrees.

So in 1992 the family moved to Springfield, Missouri. They had decided to prioritize family over jobs, even if that meant some career sacrifices — Hueping knew she could not get a job in Drury's history department, which is very small. But this part of the story, too, has a happy ending. After working in part-time positions at the college, Hueping now has a full-time job in the college's Center for Interdisciplinary Studies.

Although Springfield, Missouri, is not exactly a small town, Peter describes it as very homogeneous. "The black population is probably only two or three per cent. There was a public lynching in 1908," he tells us somberly. "Three black men were hanged, and after that, as in many other Midwest cities, the blacks left. It's a legacy you can still see."

Peter and Hueping's deliberate choice to settle on the older, more colorful north side of Springfield reflects their desire to live in as diverse a neighborhood as the city can provide. They chose to make their home there despite nearly everyone's assumption that they would move to the newer, south side of Springfield. "Ours is an older neighborhood and more diversified, integrated — but also poorer than the south side," Peter explains. "Many people come in and want only to buy a new house in one of the developments on the south side. We live where there is a good mixture of blacks, whites, and Latinos. In fact, we couldn't even get some real estate agents to show us property on the north side — because it is so integrated. They kept telling us, 'You don't want to live there, you don't want to live there.' But we did."

·

Peter, Hueping, and Vernon's home in Springfield reflects their intercultural lives. Hueping has taken the main role in decorating their home with artwork from China and Taiwan, which Peter jokes has as much to do with her being the eldest and him the next to youngest as it does with any conscious effort to bring an Asian influence to their home. "That's why we get along so well," Peter tells us. "This may be too glib a way of thinking about it, but she was used to being in charge, making decisions, and I'm used to just following the pack. 'How about this painting?' / 'Yeah, yeah!' Sometimes I'm in the car and we're going somewhere and I'm not even sure where — we're just going! I'll know when we get there. Even now, when we go to eat, I'll just say, 'You decide.'"

"Especially I care about food," Hueping explains. "If he makes the decision, I tend to veto it."

Though the couple still has some differences of opinion about culinary matters, it is Peter who has become the keeper of those family rituals that revolve around food and meals, especially since he is currently on sabbatical and Hueping has been working full-time. "I do well cooking when I have time, but if not, I'm happy with tuna sandwiches or spaghetti. But the problem is even when she's as busy as I am, that's not acceptable to Hueping."

"I am much more American now," Hueping says with regret. "I really compromise a lot; I don't cook much Chinese food now, since I'm working full-time. It's almost impossible."

"If it's up to me," Peter volunteers, "I'll just buy chicken or pork chops and just bread everything, because everybody likes breaded things. Stir fry broccoli, make some rice. I made Indian soup the other day."

But more important to Peter than the Asian influence on the menu are the rituals that the family has developed around meal-times. "How we organize our time is very Asian," he volunteers. "We have breakfast together each morning and we have dinner to-gether each night. If we don't see each other at any other time dur-ing the day, we *know* that we are going to have dinner together be-tween 5:30 and 7:00. And I think that's really a lot of your doing," he compliments Hueping. "Actually, I sometimes think that I'm becoming more Chinese than Hueping," Peter muses, "because I insist on small bowls of rice with chopsticks more often than she does. Hey, where's the Chinese food?"

"And tea," Hueping laughs, agreeing.

"Yes, I'll come home and say 'Where's the tea? You're making dinner tonight and you haven't even boiled the water yet; what are you *thinking* about?'" Peter pretends to scold. "And I say, 'When I cook dinner, the tea is ready when you come home, isn't it?'" The couple laughs together, probably thinking, as we are, of the Brazil-ian chicken blunder and of the many lessons learned since then.

"In the morning, the first thing is to boil water and make tea, and he does that," Hueping concedes graciously.

"It's such a great tradition — I love this ritual. There are things, for example, some Chinese dishes that I hated when I first had them, that now I've begun to crave. I've begun to demand the rituals she's introduced me to."

Both pause for a moment, as though reflecting on their efforts over the years to create bicultural harmony in their Missouri home. "We feel as though we've come to terms with this place," Peter offers. "We've made our peace with it, and right now I'd say we're as peaceful as we've ever been."

There are also, however, those days when Peter and Hueping "wish for a real college town or a big city." Drury is very small, and its international community is small, too. On such days, it is often a lack of cultural, and specifically racial, diversity that Hueping misses, partly because Springfield's homogeneity makes her so visible. Hueping admits that it is hard to always be different, and she sometimes longs for big city life where you can "find the people of your kind more easily." On a recent trip to San Francisco, for example, she remembers reveling in that atmosphere of visible diversity and thinking, "This is great, this is so nice — everybody's not *looking* at me."

Or sometimes, as Peter notes sadly, people in Springfield pointedly do *not* look at or speak to Hueping. "It's mostly ignorance, but some people will never look at Hueping when we are in a restaurant."

"I don't want to jump to a conclusion," says Hueping carefully with a wry smile. "It can also be sexism. But," and here she imitates a waiter who swivels his head away from her and toward Peter, "'What would you like to order? How is the food? Here is the check.' He will never talk to the woman, to me. It can be sexism or racism. One time we even went into a woman's clothing store, and that guy asked *you* if he could help you," Hueping reminds Peter.

"And Hueping will sometimes initiate the conversation with someone, and they'll still turn to me," Peter agrees. "And — I did this once — I'll say, 'Look, *she* was asking you the question.'"

Now Peter addresses Hueping: "I remember more than one occasion where you got pretty frustrated by people's ignorance. We were in a restaurant, and someone asked you whether people in Taiwan had cars or something. You just became very aloof, sort of short with them."

She nods to him before turning back to us. "Sometimes people ask me, 'Do they have highways there?'"

When Peter and Hueping describe such comments, they wear matching expressions of irritation with identically lifted eyebrows, as though they have agreed on the exact scale of the infraction: not worth getting too upset about, but certainly worth addressing. They also work as a team on their response. "It's not a big deal. But whenever it happens, we will look at each other and Peter will make a point of then saying to the waiter or waitress, 'Oh, it's her turn to pay.' So — " Hueping finishes with a determined smile, "a little education in the Midwest."

•

Peter and Hueping's desire to feel at home in their community has no doubt become increasingly important as their son, Vernon, has grown older and entered school. Hueping tells us that two of Vernon's best friends are also intercultural children and that the teachers at Vernon's school are open to multiculturalism — at least in theory. "In reality, there is still a lot to do. I would like them to do more, but I don't worry. I think the effort has to come from the community, and the community is doing better and better. It's really changing a lot since we moved here seven years ago. We have a new discovery center, a hands-on science center, and to-morrow they are going to have a Chinese culture festival — so they introduce lots of other cultures. There are activities like that, and we try to attend as many as we can."

Hueping has herself assumed most of the responsibility for making Chinese culture accessible to Vernon, perhaps most importantly by teaching him Chinese, but also by introducing him to Chinese games such as Go, Chinese chess, and Chinese checkers. She has also surrounded her son with Chinese stories. "Every time, when I go to Taiwan, I try to bring back tapes for him, buy him books, comic books. Even if he doesn't read them sometimes, they are there when he wants them. We do origami together, and I like Chinese calligraphy, so sometimes he will do it with me. And he loves Chinese character writing. He has a very good visual memory, and he can recognize a lot of Chinese characters. For a while we did practice it, though now we don't do it every day. In Chinatown we bought an abacus, and I want to teach him how to use it. We just have to wait for summer."

Hueping does notice with regret that, as Vernon gets older, speaking exclusively in Chinese has become more and more difficult. "I really try hard to speak in Chinese to him. But he doesn't have the vocabulary — his vocabulary is not expanding in Chinese. A lot of things we cannot explain very well to each other. For example, 'How does the space shuttle work?' — I find that hard to explain to him in Chinese."

Still, Vernon expresses great enthusiasm about his visits to Taiwan. He met his cousins who helped him with his Chinese and wanted him to help with their English. "They wanted to know how to say 'shoe' and 'fish,'" he tells us. "They said it in Chinese, and I said it in English." At first Vernon has difficulty finding words to describe his impressions of Taiwan — except to point out that the people there "wrote stuff in a different language." His parents wait respectfully and with interest to hear his descriptions and do not speak for him. Finally, he says of Taipei, "Even though I've never been to New York, it reminded me of New York."

"We went to the mountains, too," Vernon adds, now warming to his subject. "I liked it because it was so high up. It was nice and cool because it rained every evening."

"We saw a bamboo forest," his mother contributes, her hand on his head.

"And leaves *that* big," Vernon finishes, showing us their size with his hands.

By now Vernon has fully joined the conversation. He lies on his stomach between his parents, arms crossed under his chin, listening, watching the tape recorder as its tape turns round and round. We are struck by how delicately he balances the features of his parents: his hair is light brown and straight, his eyes a lighter brown than those of his mother. The playful smile is his father's, but it brings out lines and shapes in his face that belong to Hueping. It would be hard not to like this child who sparkles with energy but can be thoughtful and attentive, too.

Vernon sees himself as both Chinese and American. We ask Vernon what this means to him, and he cites his knowledge of two cultures, two kinds of food, two languages. His full name, Vernon John Weileong Meidlinger, reflects this double identity. His Chinese name, Weileong, means "precious dragon," he tells us proudly.

"And, just recently in school, he has started to write his name as Vernon Chin Meidlinger," Peter adds.

"Vernon Meidlinger *Chin*," he corrects his father. Over his head, his parents exchange a smile, pleased.

The world in the family room
DON & MARILVA

Don & Marilva. Photo by Christy Mock.

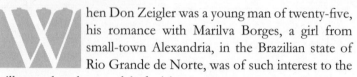hen Don Zeigler was a young man of twenty-five, his romance with Marilva Borges, a girl from small-town Alexandria, in the Brazilian state of Rio Grande de Norte, was of such interest to the villagers that the couple's decision — to marry, not to marry — was the talk of the town. In fact, though nearly thirty years have passed, the people of Alexandria are *still* talking about Don and Marilva, as the Zeiglers recently found out from their daughter, Lara, who is now studying in Brazil.

Lara, Marilva tells us, had bumped into another American in a washroom in the University of São Paulo, where she is attending school. It was one of those chance meetings that happens to Americans abroad, and the two were comparing their travels and studies when Lara mentioned that her mother was from northeast Brazil. "Oh really, where is your mom from?" the student wanted to know. She had just transferred from a school in the northeast herself, and her boyfriend was from that region, too. "Oh, you wouldn't know it — it's way in the boondocks somewhere," Lara replied. But when the young woman persisted, they discovered to Lara's amazement that her boyfriend was also from the same tiny, faraway town of Alexandria.

Marilva concludes the story triumphantly: "'Wait a minute!' the young woman asked. 'Is your mother the one carried off, along with her whole family, by that American guy?'"

"You see, we are a legend over there," Don smiles.

·

Almost thirty years have passed since the Zeiglers' story began, and we can feel the history of those years with us, an accumulation of events, discussions, and translations. Their stories are told in dialogue: sometimes they are a team, one finishing a thought for the other, and sometimes they are on opposite sides, wrangling with each other's accounts, qualifying each other's statements.

We first meet the Zeiglers in the kitchen of their Evanston home, where we sit at a small table flooded with spring sunlight. The two complement each other: Don is tall with long limbs that spill out of the small kitchen chair he sits in; with his midlength brown hair, horn-rimmed glasses, engrossed and energetic air, he could be a professor at nearby Northwestern. His hands are never still, alternately flying in the air to describe a scene or resting, rubbing circles on the table as though sanding it smooth. Marilva (pronounced Mari-ilva) is shorter, more compact, intense, deliberate.

At first we think perhaps she is shy, more of a witness to our conversation than a participant in it. But she is, it turns out, only listening, getting an angle on us and our conversation while she finishes making a vegetarian lasagna, fixes coffee for everyone. She enters the conversation with authority when she is ready, responding to our question about how the two became a couple.

"I think our friendship started mostly because I was the only person who could understand him," she explains. "I just had a knack to understand his Portuguese."

That Don found himself in Brazil, that he was in the Peace Corps at all was "something of a miracle." He came from a blue-collar family that had been affected deeply by the Depression, and he was the first in his family to graduate from college. Don's parents questioned his need to spend money on education, especially to get what seemed to them a "worthless" degree in history. "If you're going to spend all that time and money," he remembers them saying, "why not be a lawyer, and *make* some money? But I just followed my dream all the time. I didn't know where it would take me and I didn't care." So Don went on to do graduate work at Indiana University, where he indulged his special love of Latin American history by taking a summer intensive course on Brazilian history with — as it happened — the most famous living Brazilian historian, Sergio Buarque de Hollanda. "To be able to study with this man, to sit and have a beer with him — it was just wonderful," Don recalls.

Partly because of his objections to the Vietnam War and partly because he had just broken off an engagement, Don decided to enter the Peace Corps, something he had always wanted to do. He requested that he be sent to Latin America, and in 1967 he got his first choice — Brazil — for a two-year stint.

Don was hardly the typical sixties radical when he left for Brazil. On the one hand, he was deeply affected by the ideals of the liberal culture of the sixties, and, on the other, he was a conservative Christian who simply "tuned out" the drug culture and the rock-and-roll tunes of the era, listening instead to classical music. He was a radical in a crew cut ("I looked more like a marine than a hippie") who wanted to go into the Peace Corps to "make things better."

He remembers being critical of a United States foreign policy that was then supporting dictatorships all over the world, particularly in Latin America. "There was a terrible U.S.-supported dictatorship in Brazil at the time," Don tells us, a fact that made him all the more determined not to try to "convert" Brazilians by teaching them English "so they could become more American." However, his reluctance to teach English put him at a loss when he first arrived, given his inability to speak much Portuguese. "What could I do? These days, it's different in the Peace Corps, you have a specific role — maybe you work as an accountant or an architect or a nurse. But those days in Latin America you were just in 'community development,' whatever that meant. Well, the community didn't even know I was coming — it was only at the state level that the contact was made." So, in October, Don turned up in the small town of Alexandria, population 3,000, barely able to speak Portuguese. "When I actually knew the word I wanted, they couldn't understand me. I was almost deselected by the program because they thought, 'This guy's never going to communicate.'"

We get out our *Baedeker Brazil* travel guide and look together at page 29, where Don finds for us the little brown state of Rio Grande de Norte ("great river of the north") with its capital city of Natal. The state is far from the economic hub of Brazil — in the south near São Paulo. The area around the small city of Alexandria is the drought area, the hinterland, or *sertão*, not unlike Appalachia in its rural, sometimes impoverished nature. "It was four or five degrees south of the equator, so it was very warm, but once the sun went down it cooled off, just like Arizona. It had these dramatic mountains off in the distance. When it rains, it's beautiful, but sometimes it can go almost a year without rain. It's rich with culture but poor economically." Don admits feeling culture shock and some homesickness, which hit especially at Christmas. In Brazil, the seasons are opposite those in the United States, so Christmas occurs in summer and is anything but white, Don says. "But I tried to look around and think, Christ was probably born in an area like this."

His sense of disconnection eased as Don began getting involved with the community. When a German priest who had been teaching English heard that Don was in town, he moved out saying, "Let the American teach." His predecessor's English was so horrible that Don took heart, and teaching high school English gave him something to do while he learned the language. "I taught in two schools there, and who should be one of my students but — Marilva."

At the time, Marilva was studying to be a teacher herself, so we ask her what she thought of Don, as a person and as an instructor. She turns to Don, laughing. "You were a different type of Peace Corps volunteer — most of them were into Bob Dylan or the Beatles, but you were the one in the crew cut holding the books under your arm, very intellectual! And smoking a pipe. Always a pipe in those days."

"And you were the homecoming queen!" Don offers back, a characterization that Marilva promptly dismisses, saying, "We don't have homecoming queens."

"Equivalents!" Don protests, "I am looking for equivalents."

"Well, I used to do some modeling for school fund-raisers," Marilva relents. "Maybe that's what he is thinking of. Of course, I weighed about ninety pounds at the time!" Marilva laughs as she says this, but with her delicate features and lovely smile, it is easy for us to see the high school glamour Don attributes to her.

"He was a good teacher," Marilva finishes, smiling again briefly.

As a student of Portuguese, however, Don was still struggling, and Marilva began to accompany him as his unofficial translator, his spokesperson. "When I would go around to meet with the school officials and the mayor — she understood me, so she would come along," Don tells us.

"Yes. I would try to make them understand what his point was. I would jump right in before he would finish — "

"Before I made a fool of myself," Don clarifies.

Don and Marilva began attending social events together,

though the Zeiglers are quick to emphasize that the nature of dating in Brazil is quite different than that in America, less exclusive and more open, social, and group-oriented. Dating meant attending dances together, or walking round and round evenings with the rest of the village in the town square.

Marilva describes herself as different from her friends in Alexandria because she planned to escape the traditional expectations that awaited most of that region's citizens. Without hesitation, she credits her mother as the one who instilled in her a deep respect for the value of education, or, as she says, "a desire to do better than your parents." It was also her mother's love of travel, despite a life that had afforded little of it, that helped shape Marilva's plans for the future. "I was going to get educated, become a teacher, then travel," she tells us. Marriage didn't enter into her picture of the future at all.

But it was not long before Marilva modified her plans. The Zeiglers agree that Marilva's departure to continue her education helped clarify the nature of their relationship. "We broke up before I left for Natal. I think it was mainly because he wasn't sure and I wasn't sure what we thought it would be. So we just — broke up," Marilva says lightly, with a lift of her hand and voice, as though it was no big deal to her. Marilva insists that neither she nor her family had big expectations of the relationship. "I don't think my family expected anything because — Brazilian culture is a little different from the rest of South America. People there are a little more avant-garde. 'Boyfriend' and 'girlfriend' are less serious there. Anyway, I thought I wouldn't get married, that I would finish school, get a job, save money, and travel. That was my intention."

But Don soon came to Natal for a visit. "And instead of us

talking about getting back together, he asked me if I would marry him. He was very drunk, and we were walking along the beach when he asked me. I looked at him, then he asked me again. I thought this guy is so drunk he doesn't know what he is saying."

"But you agreed," Don reminds her.

"I said yes, but I thought, 'Yeah, tomorrow, who will remember this?'"

But Don did remember, returning the next morning to ask, "'You said yes, do you still mean it?' And she said that she did."

When we ask Don what made him change his mind, Marilva laughs and says, "Yes, Don, let us know."

He struggles to explain what helped him overcome his uncertainty. "We missed each other. We were in love," he says after a while, and it seems to us that his love for Marilva took in not just her but her family, her town, her culture, her country's way of life. He lived on the same street as Marilva's family and would sit with them in the evenings under the stars when her relatives would pull their furniture out onto the sidewalks, all the neighbors coming by to laugh and chat and joke.

Don was free in Brazil in a way that he had never been before: he grew his hair long. "The Brazilian barbers didn't know what to make of it, and they certainly didn't know how to do a crew cut!" he tells us, and he learned to dance the samba, to be less physically reserved. "I wouldn't dance here because I was so embarrassed. I just couldn't. I didn't go to my own high school prom because I was a very conservative Christian and we just didn't do those things. But in Brazil, no matter what I did I was going to be different, and that gave me a lot of freedom."

After the two were engaged, Don traveled to Natal as often as he could, which was not very often, we discover. To us, Natal is an innocent distance on the map, a mere quarter inch. But in reality, the distance between Alexandria and Natal is one complicated by the terrain, bumpy roads, and infrequent bus schedules. It was quite a distance.

"The trip took about eight hours," Marilva says.

"Eleven," Don says with authority. He was, he reminds us, the one who made the journey.

Soon the couple began planning for their future. "Then the real questions began," Don comments. "Do we live here? Do we live there? Where should we get married?" In the end, Don canceled a request to extend his Peace Corps commitment and returned to America to work and save money.

Don returned to the United States — a history major, a Peace Corps volunteer, a self-described dreamer — to find a job. He had less than $500, a beat-up VW beetle, and deep anxiety about a future that he could not bring into sight. What kind of job should he get? Which city should they live in? He looked for work in New York and Washington before returning to Chicago, where he continued to search for a job from his sister's home, staying in a bunk bed above his nephew, dreaming and writing letters to Marilva. "You couldn't just call back then," he tells us. "When we talk to our daughter in Brazil now, it's like a local call, but back then it wasn't easy, and there was no Internet. So we wrote and wrote." Eventually, he found a job as a health educator and community organizer. "Who," he jokes about the reason he was hired, "would work cheaper than a Peace Corps volunteer?" Ten years later, Don founded one of the first wellness programs in the country.

His parents were unhappy about the couple's engagement. They had not understood Don's interest in the Peace Corps, which they considered "wasting time." "And then when they found out I was engaged to a Brazilian — well, weren't there enough Americans?"

"Don's mother was never accepting," Marilva agrees. "She had wanted him to marry a Swedish girl. His mother was the daughter of a Swedish immigrant herself, without much education. I wasn't very pleasing to them. I tried to understand them the best I could, but there wasn't anything I could do to make them like me." Eventually, Don's father relented, learned to appreciate Marilva, and one of her favorite wedding photographs is of Mr. Zeigler bending to kiss her cheek.

"I came from a blue-collar area on the west side of Chicago, a lot of stereotypes. People were judgmental, even though there were immigrants in the area and it was all these struggling people from Eastern Europe," Don explains. "I didn't have a lot of exposure to other places before I went to Brazil. But now it's so natural for me to interact with people from other cultures."

Don's experience in Brazil — and with the sixties — had changed him and had changed his relationship with his parents. "Do you remember Archie Bunker? *All in the Family*?" Don asks. "Well, we would all laugh at that show, but I could have been the son-in-law and my folks the parents. It was a very good program because it showed the change in culture between the different generations, the change in values, politics, and everything. All good people, hard working and honest, but they sure saw the world differently. I changed politically a LOT in the sixties, and my folks — they didn't."

Marilva's parents, in contrast, were much more receptive to their engagement, partly because Brazil itself is a country based on intercultural and interracial unions — Asians, Africans, Europeans, natives. "Intermarriage in Brazil is not unusual — there are

Brazilians married to people of different races and nationalities," Marilva tells us. "And my mother was proud, because she really liked Don, and was happy to have her daughter marrying this pleasant American with a college degree. Her pride was not because he was American — but this man, this distinct man, who had an education. Some townspeople did say to my mother, 'He's just a Peace Corps volunteer, he doesn't make any money.' But for her, the money was his education."

"In that area of Brazil they would call you 'Doctor' if you just went to college," Don adds appreciatively. "I've never been in a place where there is more reverence for education."

While Don was trying to establish himself in the United States, Marilva began to prepare by taking English classes. Marilva reports that she felt no fear or ambivalence in the months before her departure. She had calculated the risk and made up her mind, and she was not scared but excited, even impatient for her adventure to begin.

When Marilva describes the trip to us, she frowns. "I remember how poor the airport in Belem was — that was my first shock. Then Miami was shocking, too, because somehow I didn't feel like I was in America. It was so warm, and people didn't look European like I expected them to." But Marilva's arrival in Chicago was also jarring. It was July, hot, with a humidity Marilva had never experienced before. "I had to ask Don to stop the car and get something cold to drink because I thought I was going to pass out."

"And I thought, 'My God, what is going to happen to us now? This is July — what about January or February?'" Don tells us, remembering his alarm. He was not expecting his fiancée to react to the summer heat. If Marilva was uncomfortable already, how would she survive her first North American winter?

But after that, Marilva continues, Chicago didn't alarm her at all. "I was so curious to see everything. It was a beautiful experience, and of course, I got to be with him."

Marilva moved in with Don's great-aunt Helena ("Aunty Craig") who took the couple under her wing, supplying a warmth and understanding they hadn't found with Don's parents. "We used to sit and talk. I would tell her about my country, and she would tell me about Don's family, their history. We were always very close to her." Marilva stayed with Aunty Craig from July until the couple married in September.

"We got married broke," Don grins.

"I had my dress — a nice little white dress, very simple, above the knee — a little something on the head, and a bouquet of red flowers."

"One," Don corrects her. "One flower. You just carried a rose."

"That's right, and you wore the same suit you went to work with."

Despite their limited finances, the Zeiglers clearly remember this time in their life with great fondness and seem proud of the festive wedding party they hosted. "We had over 100 people and it cost us just $100," Don says proudly. His sister donated the cake, which she had decorated, and the couple married in the church where Don sang in the choir. "We didn't even send out invitations, just said, 'We're getting married on Thursday night, please come.' Afterwards, people said that's the way to get married, we didn't spend thousands. I didn't even get a haircut," says Don.

By then Don had found a minister from a congregation in Chicago who spoke Portuguese, so they decided to have half the ceremony in English and half in Portuguese. "We had two pastors and spoke half our vows in each language," explains Don.

"It was a very intercultural wedding. We were a little ahead of our time," offers Marilva.

.

Don was worried that Marilva, who was very sociable and enjoyed being with people, would feel isolated away from her family and friends, so they arranged for Marilva to teach Portuguese in the Berlitz language school soon after they were married. Marilva tells us that Don was much more worried than she herself was: "He was scared to death that I would come, not like, and decide to go back. But I was thinking, well, I always wanted to see different cultures and different countries, so now I'll see. And I wanted to experience everything. Really, I could be anywhere. I never had second thoughts." If she did have second thoughts, Don assured her, they could return to Brazil to live.

"I was willing to go back. In fact, I'm probably more willing to go back and live in Brazil now than she is," Don notes with irony.

Didn't you miss Brazil? we ask Marilva. We try out one of our few Portuguese vocabulary words on her, *saudade*. Don and Marilva both take the word in, murmuring it, passing it back and forth between them. "Homesickness," Don offers a fraction before Marilva says, "loneliness." They trade; try on each other's translations before agreeing on both as acceptable approximations of a very complex, difficult-to-translate word.

"In the beginning, I missed my family, my friends, I missed the weather sometimes — the beaches. Where we come from, we have beautiful beaches, the most beautiful in the whole country. I may be atypical, but I think I have a lot of my Portuguese ancestors in me, you know, the Portuguese have been all over the world, and that's in my background. I miss Brazil, but it's not like I have to be in Brazil."

Now much of Marilva's family lives in the United States anyway. They came one by one, all settling around the Chicago area, usually after extended stays with the Zeiglers. It was the beginning of what they refer to as their "revolving door policy," which began with family members but eventually included exchange students from all over the world. "We decided, because it was so expensive for us to travel to Brazil, that instead of spending this money on trips, why not just bring the whole family here? Immigration was easier then. Two of my sisters came first, then later on my mother with the three younger ones. I was the oldest, and I always felt responsible for the younger ones. I wanted to give them a chance."

Is that revolving door policy very Brazilian? we wonder.

It was not at all part of *his* family heritage, Don avers. "I don't know if it's Brazilian, but it's very Zeigler, very much *us*," Marilva laughs.

Meanwhile, the Zeiglers had begun their own family, with their son Karl arriving in the spring of 1972, followed by Dietrich in 1976, and their daughter, Lara, in 1977. In the beginning, the couple spoke only Portuguese to their children. "It was their first language," Don says proudly. "I had an advantage because I had lived in the culture and loved the language, so I could speak it with them. Speaking Portuguese trained their ears. Now, for example, Karl's Portuguese comes out with less of an accent because he learned to speak it when his brain was a sponge for language."

The Zeiglers have successfully encouraged their children to be at home with their mother's language and culture. Karl lived for a year in Brazil as an exchange student and is, his father says proudly, "Brazilian to the core. He could go and live in Brazil today and be completely happy."

Their son Dietrich, Don feels, takes after him in many ways. "Looks like a gringo, is language challenged." Even though Dietrich has the least aptitude for language, however, his parents agree that he may, with his fun-loving nature, be the most Brazilian one of them all.

And he did pick up a few expressions, Marilva adds. "We had some neighbors who spoke Spanish and French, and they would tell Dietrich, 'Say something to us in Portuguese.' So he'd say, 'orange juice' and 'apple juice' and 'bunda mucha' (soft butt). They would say, 'Oh we know that word; it's the same in French,' and they would laugh and laugh."

Lara, too, speaks Portuguese and communicates well with Portuguese speakers at her São Paulo university. She has found the transition sometimes difficult, but she is coping skillfully and gaining insight in the process. "Lara said to me today on the phone, 'Now I have more respect for foreigners coming to America than I did before.' Because now she's going through what they're going through. Right now she passes for Brazilian in most situations but people look at her differently when they learn she's American, mostly because of the global economy — 'Oh, a rich American with that dollar that is screwing up our economy.' But she understands that, she's very sympathetic to the Brazilians."

•

When their children were young, the Zeiglers tried hard to find cultural events for them to attend and were very active in a Brazilian organization that hosted holiday parties and carnivals. "It was partly for the children and partly for myself," Marilva explains. Marilva found that she grew to deeply value the diversity of her

Brazilian heritage. "Brazilian culture is very rich, very diverse, much more diverse than American culture. That was something that I came to appreciate when I came here. There are people with many different backgrounds, but even though there are German, Spanish, Portuguese, Japanese, we all manage to survive the same way. We eat the same things, and we all speak the same language even though it's a huge country."

In addition to speaking Portuguese with their children, the Zeiglers also tried to teach them some Brazilian customs and to incorporate Brazilian values into their family lives. "For example," Marilva tells us, "in my part of Brazil, we don't have fireplaces, so Santa comes through the window at Christmas instead of down the chimney. We would always put little boxes on the windowsill when Christmas morning came."

Don tried to bring the warmth he had witnessed in Brazilian families to his own parenting. "Going to Brazil really opened me a lot. I had changed so much in the sixties anyway, but I came from a very cold family that didn't touch or hug. But when I went to Brazil — there you touched! You were close to each other all the time, hugging and kissing, and I said, 'Wow, that's great!' We wanted to continue that with our kids. I tried to pick the best of what I saw there."

The children have had some difficulty with their bicultural identities. They sometimes felt embarrassed, for example, when their parents spoke to them in Portuguese in front of their school friends. Once, one of their children's friends mistook Marilva for a housekeeper. "Just because I had an accent," she notes wryly. For the most part, however, the Zeiglers' children have a healthy sense of themselves and a respect for others as part of an interest-

ing, multifaceted world. When we admire the results of their efforts in raising bicultural children, Marilva agrees. "The turnout
has been good," she says.

What the Zeiglers most wanted to give their children, however,
is not so much access to their Brazilian heritage as access to a variety of different cultures — an international rather than a strictly
bicultural identity. They wanted their children to be prepared for
different cultures, countries, situations; in the interest of helping
their children develop such capacities, the Zeiglers have hosted
many international guests and exchange students over the years,
people from Iran, Sweden, Venezuela, Brazil, France, Uruguay,
Mexico. "We have constantly imported culture," Don says with
satisfaction. Their most recent exchange student is a young
woman, Ana, from Brazil, and the Zeiglers are as enthusiastic
about her as if she were the first visitor they had ever hosted.
"She's teaching me how to cook Brazilian food," Marilva reports,
amused at the irony in this. As a result of the Zeiglers' revolving
door policy, they have not only a very international home but
places to stay in almost any country they might visit.

The Zeiglers' home itself exemplifies their intercultural philosophy. They live in the upstairs of an old Victorian house, and they
have worked hard to preserve as much of their home's original
beauty as possible. For instance, though the delicate radiator vents
no longer supply heat, the Zeiglers have left them uncovered by
the carpet, and Don has painstakingly replicated the fancy wood-
work in brackets around the windows on the upper level that previous owners ripped off when they installed siding. "There were
these gaping holes when we stripped off the siding. I left them
there for years while I worked on other things, including getting

my Ph.D. in public health. It took twenty-five pieces of wood to replicate each window bracket. I had to make stencils of the ones on the lower level to get the exact look."

"It was supposed to take six months," Marilva says wryly of their renovation. "So far, it's taken ten years."

"Well, I was a bit more realistic about how long things would take," says Don, "but I just said, 'OK, let's get started.'"

One of the first things the Zeiglers did when they began remodeling was to create a room with a cathedral ceiling and crisscrossing rafters by knocking down a wall that divided their dining room space. The dining room is not particularly Victorian now, but the Zeiglers have approached their renovations much as they've approached other parts of their lives. They've taken what is best in the Victorian house and combined it with some of what they like about modern architecture and design, creating an effect that — ironically — has prompted more than one visitor to say the space feels somehow Brazilian to them.

Don has done most of the renovations himself — though he claims that, when he began, he only knew how to screw in a light bulb — and Marilva has done the decorating, a challenging task in a house that has some of the small rooms of the original architecture as well as the large modernized spaces created in the renovation. We admire her success at bringing together the warmth of the home's Victorian elements and the airiness of the contemporary: the furniture is cozy and eclectic, and the artwork international. Prints by Kandinsky and Monet are placed near masks created by the Yanomami Indians of Brazil and tiny Italian and Czechoslovakian watercolors. Over the stairway hangs an intricate quilt made with gleaming, delicately embroidered sari borders from all over India — a gift from a Polish woman in the import business whom the Zeiglers had, at one time, "helped out."

We are drawn especially to the family room, where vases and statues are artfully placed in niches and on shelves. From a distance, we assume that the objects are all from Brazil, but moving closer we see a statue from Japan placed next to a ceramic jug from Mexico, a handwoven basket from Australia near a grouping of artifacts from Brazil. We are appropriately admiring.

"A little bit of the world in the family room," Marilva says, pleased that we have noticed.

Kai loma (half and half)

GEORGE & VIOLETTE

George & Violette. Photo by Christy Mock.

When the Peace Corps assigned George Ricketson, then of Fort Worth, Texas, to the country of Fiji, his first reaction was, "Where's that?" His second reaction, more characteristic of the person we are getting to know, was to promptly find out. Locating the archipelago of Fiji on a map, small bits of green land boxed off from the other islands sprinkled throughout the blue of the South Pacific, he remembers thinking, "Well, that might be nice."

In fact, the islands of Fiji *were* nice — so nice, his Fijian wife, Violette, tells us with some amusement, that it had the highest extension rate of any Peace Corps destination. Fiji is prized not only for the allure of its tropical setting but also for its kindhearted and easygoing people, and other volunteers who learned of George's destination would ask him enviously, "How did *you* get to go?"

Completely by chance, as it happens. George signed up for the Peace Corps because he had an extremely low draft number to fight in a war he didn't believe in; at the time, Peace Corps work was still considered an "occupational deferment." George had a degree in accounting, and Fiji needed business people to help develop marketing for agricultural cooperatives venturing into the fruit-processing trade. The match was made.

Fiji is a collection of islands, tropical and sometimes mountainous, with a great diversity of animal and plant life and a range of climates — even on the same island, a mountain may collect the cool moisture of the trade winds on one side and harbor a dry warmth on the other. The biggest Island, Viti Levu, where George lived, "looked something like a cross between Hawaii and California." Despite its many attractions, however, Fiji still took some getting used to, George tells us. "It was pretty difficult because I was in a rural setting working with agrarian villages. It was beautiful

country but a very hard life, a different standard of living —
bathing in cold water, only one dirt road out of the valley."

George also struggled with what he depicts as the Fijians' "laid-
back" attitude, "and with the sharing. In Fiji, it's hard to make
business decisions that are competitive in nature because it's not a
competitive environment," he says, his face reflecting a serious
concern for the project underway all those years ago. "But then,
when you get to the weekend — well, that's a nice time to be part
of the culture," he finishes, his face lightening. It was on a weekend, after all, that he met Violette.

.

We first make the acquaintance of George and Violette on the
square of a small Illinois town west of Terre Haute, Indiana, where
the Ricketsons have lived for the past ten years. It is one of those
early spring weekends when it is impossible not to be distracted,
not to stop midsentence struck by the familiar newness of things:
the drone of a lawn mower, a tree breaking into blossom, a bird
vivid against the foliage. So at first we miss the Ricketsons' arrival,
even though we have been looking for them. When George and
Violette Ricketson walk across the green of the town square toward us — their hands linked lightly, shoulders touching — they
could be any middle-aged Midwestern couple dressed in casual
spring clothing. But as they come closer, their differences begin to
suggest the story they will tell us over the course of our afternoon
together.

Violette is brown-skinned and wears her dark hair long; it is
streaked lighter red-brown in places by the sun. Her voice con-
tains a loose gathering of rhythms and accents acquired in the
many different places she has lived; sometimes it is soft, almost

Southern, at other times punctuated by more precise British syllables. She often raises a hand to her mouth when speaking, as though to cover a smile or soften the impact of her words. George, in contrast, is fair and green-eyed; with his glasses and short salt-and-pepper hair, cotton shirt, and khakis, he looks like a businessman relaxing on the weekend, which, in fact, he is. He is funny and smart and speaks in a matter-of-fact shorthand so brief that at first we don't catch the Southern accent that becomes more apparent when he is more expansive.

The Ricketsons' story is complicated by more than their twenty-year history or the distractions of the spring day, though. Theirs is a tale told in parentheticals, facts nested in stories requiring other stories to contextualize or qualify them. For example, early in our conversation, as though to set the record straight, Violette explains that some Fijians would not consider her a true Fijian, but *kai loma*, translated in one guidebook as "part-European" and by Violette herself as "half-caste" and "half and half" at different points in our conversation.

Who married whom that you are so international? we ask Violette, delighted that this is turning out to be a story of intercultural marriages from way back. The Ricketsons laugh, exchange a look — the answer is complicated, their expression suggests — but Violette takes a breath and attempts to explain. "My parents were already a mixture; they were half English and half — " here she stops, backtracks, continues. "My mother was Fijian-American and my dad was Polynesian-German. My dad — what generation was he — third? Fiji was a British colony in 1874, and many British men married local women. Miller was my maiden name — the Millers were Germans who came through Samoa."

She hesitates again and looks at George, who elaborates further. "Fiji is one of the larger and more central areas in the South Pacific, so there's not only the Indian population, originally brought in to work sugar plantations, but also other Polynesians. Fiji is very multiracial and multicultural in itself. You have Fijians, Indians, Europeans, and Chinese. Violette is part European with a lot of British in her background."

Not only is her family's history and identity complicated, but so is their relationship to language. "My family is bilingual and we would switch back and forth. If we were with someone who was an English-speaking person, we would switch to English, and if there was a Fijian person we'd switch to Fijian. And later, when my children visited, they would get lost. My son would say, 'English please, English.' Their cousins were so used to a bilingual family that they couldn't really understand why their two cousins couldn't speak Fijian, as well as English. My mom probably spoke more Fijian and my Dad spoke more English, but we understood both languages and the dialect of the area that we were in, which was different again from standard Fijian.

"Anyway, my children get very confused," Violette finishes, commenting on the complex tangle of linguistic and racial identities that her children must grapple with.

They would have a hard time checking off that box for race, we agree.

"Other," George and Violette say in one voice, and Violette continues. "Sometimes they'll check 'Pacific Islander.' But when we lived in Fort Wayne, Indiana, there was an elementary school where we had to check a box that had 'Other' and in brackets it said 'Unknown.' So we talked to the principal. We told him, 'Well, we *are* other, but we *aren't* unknown.'"

Sometimes their children will simply list Caucasian on these forms to avoid such situations, Violette tells us. "Marianna looks more like her dad, and she's always complained that she doesn't look ethnic enough. In my family, we come in different shades. My own mother had green eyes, my daughter does, too. But people often would say to her, '*That's* your mom?' And people would say to our son, '*That's* your dad?' People tend to think our son is Hispanic." Violette pauses, thinking. "I especially confuse people," she adds. "In the Midwest, people always seem to notice that you're browner round about spring because they're thinking 'tanning salon.'"

"She does confuse people," George agrees. "Once we were in Samoa, and a Samoan woman got irritated with Violette because she spoke Samoan to Violette, and Violette answered, 'I'm sorry, I don't speak Samoan, I speak English.' The woman was mad because she *thought* Violette should speak Samoan, just because of the way she looks."

"Also, Hispanic people come in the airports to talk to me, and I say 'I'm sorry, I don't speak Spanish,' and they look at me and say, 'Oh, sure.' And Native Americans," she continues, "they make a beeline for me, they come straight to me and ask, 'What tribe are you?'"

We must look confused, our pens poised but still, trying like the census takers, bureaucrats, to find a way to categorize all this information, stopped by the complexity of it. Violette takes pity on us, tells us another story to make us feel better. "I took my son when he was in high school to a family reunion — the Whippys — on my mother's side. They came from Salem, Massachusetts, in 1824. David Whippy was the first European — "

"American!" George interrupts to remind her.

"The first *American* to settle in Fiji, so there are all sorts of Whippys there. Anyway, my son was lost. I would introduce him to someone, and he would say to me, 'I'm just lost.'"

.

What becomes clear to us early in our conversation, however, is the central importance of family in Fiji. The very interconnectedness that makes it so hard to trace the branches of Violette's family tree is at the heart of the Fijian family's character. "It's a Polynesian culture, so we have more of an extended family than the United States does, and we're not as mobile. It's smaller. Fiji is not very big, only a little bigger than Hawaii, so extended family is very important. I am my nieces' and nephews' other mother, and the language reflects that. Either you are 'big mother' or 'small mother.' Because I am older than my sister, I am 'big mother.' When the families are together, I don't hesitate to discipline my nephew and my niece. And vice versa." Their son well remembers this aspect of the culture. He'd gone back to Fiji as a senior in high school, to attend a gathering honoring the one-year anniversary of his grandmother's death. At one point, when he was attempting to help with something, one of his great aunts reached over and smacked his hand in admonishment for a minor breach of custom. "At the time," Violette smiles, "he was seventeen and well over six feet tall, so he was rather taken aback by this."

This concept of extended families — in such contrast with the typically nuclear American family — increases the closeness of the family even while increasing its numbers. "So instead of a granduncle, that's another grandfather," Violette explains. To illustrate, she recounts a Lakota story about an encounter with Leif Eriksson. "He would ask the Native American children, 'Who is your mother?' and at four and five some of them didn't know because everybody was their mother and they were brothers and sisters together. Lief was shocked," she says with a mischievous smile. "But from the Native American view there was a sense of 'Poor white children — they only have one mother.'"

Fijians share property in much the same way they share family members; the Fijian system of land ownership is communal. "In Fiji, you do not own a piece of land or have a title to it." The combination of extended family and communal property, we learn, ensures a community-based identity, more "we" than "I," a system that emphasizes sharing and cooperation over competition, respect and love for family and friends far above individuality, independence, or personal achievement.

Violette makes this point, as she will make most others in our conversation together, through narrative rather than direct explication. Her explanations of Fijian culture and descriptions of her childhood tend to accumulate over the afternoon in bright fragments that form a collage, stories interrupted to make way for other stories. In any case, her dark eyes gleam when she thinks of her Fijian world, and her voice is so soft, imbued with such appreciation, even longing, that her sentiments are catching. We find ourselves feeling nostalgic for her people, for a past life where the boundaries between members of the family and community were less rigid.

Ironically, it was Violette's very community-oriented values that would launch her on the first of many trips away from home. Because schools in her own rural town were poor, Violette left her home at the age of six to live with her grandparents. "My father would take me in his boat to my grandparents' house, and I would come back for the holidays. It was difficult for a six-year-old. I remember my father having to disappear. He had to, because I would just cling to him." But Violette's schooling was not just for her own benefit. She was expected to use her education to help her family and community. Fijians, Violette tells us, value education as the means to empowerment, and Violette eventually embraced her culture's respect for education, too, and understood her parents' decision to send her away for school.

Fijians appreciate education so much, Violette tells us, partly because their opportunities and resources are more limited than those of Americans; for Fijians, education is less a burden than a privilege. "One thing that always amazed me in the United States is that there's so much around. You shouldn't have any illiterate people," she says in a tone as close to sternness as such a gentle person ever gets. "We just don't have the resources and the libraries, so for us education is a luxury. Most Fijians would go to a village school, but the ones who did well their families would try to send to better schools."

Violette, we infer, was one of those selected for better schooling, though she views this not as an individual achievement but as a responsibility. Primary and secondary education are taken much more seriously in Fiji than they are here, and even by junior high Violette felt the importance of doing well: "Even in the eighth grade, you sit in an exam and it's like college. You apply to good high schools, and you go to the one where you are accepted. I went to a school where my father had gone, and my grandfather in the Miller family."

Violette had received a scholarship for high school and was, upon graduating, offered another — this time to attend college in

New Zealand. It was her first trip abroad, and she vividly recalls her encounter with a new social world. "I was so surprised to see these white people in blue-collar jobs. They were servicing planes. There were two of us Fijians, and I remember us looking out that oval window and saying 'Look, there are white guys fixing the plane!' In Fiji, they were always in the white-collar jobs — judges, businessmen." Her scholarship required that Violette return to Fiji to work in education. "That was how I got to college in New Zealand. My family would not have been able to afford it."

Her view of education as a privilege to be shared has profoundly influenced Violette's recent work at Indiana State University, where she teaches early childhood education in a lab school. "In my work with college students, I pose the questions: Do you get educated to empower other people or to look down on people? Does education make you a member of an elite group, or do you share it with others? I tell my students that I'm very egalitarian — and that I'd like them to share the privilege of their education." Many of the people Violette teaches are first-generation college students themselves, from small towns all over Indiana. We can imagine Violette inspiring them to return to their families and communities, changed but not alienated by their educations. "We do go back and help others," she finishes, proud of her students.

When Violette returned from college in New Zealand, she began teaching sixth graders in the capital city of Suva; she had been there for a year when she met George. By now we have moved to the lounge of a lovely Victorian inn on the square where we met the Ricketsons. We lean forward in our chairs eagerly, asking for details of their love story. They begin haltingly, looking at each other with slight frowns. It is as though we have asked them to embark on an architectural dig. First, they stake off the general area of time, counting forward from George's arrival in 1969 and back from their marriage in 1973 to arrive, tentatively, at 1971. Then they locate other major facts: When? A weekend in the summer. Where? A Chinese restaurant in Suva, a local hangout for Peace Corps volunteers.

And? we prompt them, hoping for more detail.

They look back at us, mildly apologetic. George and Violette are busy people, busier than ever with an upcoming move from Indiana to New England, and George is now commuting each weekend from Connecticut. We get the impression that they don't often think about their lives in the way we are asking them to, that details from their twenty-year-old love story are not foremost in their minds. Remembering these details makes them laugh; more than once they lean their heads together in amusement at their own loss for words and the speed with which time has gone by.

Nevertheless, Violette begins, looking up at the ceiling, her statements often trailing off into a question. "I was there with my college friends visiting from New Zealand. We had gotten together for a reunion. You were there by yourself and met up with some other Peace Corps people? There must have been about fifteen of us there."

"I saw Violette, thought she was cute, and tracked her down. That was about it," George says briskly, cutting to the chase and rescuing Violette in one sentence.

"He did!" agrees Violette, sounding as freshly surprised as though George had just then appeared at her apartment door. "There was such a big group in the restaurant that I couldn't remember his name. I wasn't really paying attention because I was catching up with my friends.

"But," she turns back to George, still sounding a little apologetic, "the next day you just showed up at my door, and I couldn't remember your name. My New Zealand friends and I were all trying to remember: what's his name, what's his *name*?"

Violette attributes George's bold action to his American nature and explains how that was part of the attraction. "I had never dated an American guy. Americans were very different from New Zealanders or British guys, and that was one of the things I liked. He was more interesting, *and* more persistent. Americans are known for being go-getters, and that's true. Some of it is independence — if you're interested in something, there's nothing to hold you back. So he just came on over."

We turn to George, impressed. How did he find Violette's apartment? Suva is not New York, but it was then a city of 100,000, which seems to us a little daunting. This George brushes away as a small concern — he simply asked other Peace Corps volunteers. How else, he points out, could he have tracked her down? There weren't any telephones.

What George considered a more serious obstacle was the reactions of Violette's coworkers to their relationship. "She was one of the first locals to teach at this international school there in Suva. There were all these haughty English people there, and it was kind of embarrassing for her to date a Peace Corps volunteer in shorts and sandals, wearing glasses."

Violette agrees that Peace Corps volunteers were different. "They were — I shouldn't say hippielike — but they'd wear John Lennon glasses and a certain style of clothes that contrasted with that of the British civil servants, and the New Zealanders and

Australians, who tended to be businessmen." But she also explains that she admired these differences. The work that the Peace Corps volunteers were doing was "something that not a lot of overseas people did, they were going out to remote places. Many Fijian teachers did not want to go out and teach in these places, and here were these Peace Corps volunteers who did, and who spoke Fijian pretty well, too."

Soon George and Violette began to see each other regularly on the weekends. Violette recalls how she and George would walk by the markets in Suva "where there were these sword sellers who would see him and think, 'Here comes a European, let's try to sell him souvenirs' and then we'd get closer, and the merchants would say 'NAH — he's a Peace Corps volunteer.'"

"Once," George recalls, "we were in a nightclub when we were dating, and a friend came up to her and said in Fijian, 'Hey Violette, where'd you get the white guy,' a question which rankled George, who understood the man's words exactly. Before Violette could say anything, George answered the question himself. "I said to the guy, 'Sigatoka,' which was where I had been staying."

"My friend was so upset," Violette remembers. "He said, 'why didn't you *tell* me he knew Fijian?'" In fact, George had an ear for language and understood the regional dialect of his host family better than Violette herself did.

George and Violette tell us these stories lightly, amusing us and each other. They did not, they tell us, ever really feel uncomfortable as an intercultural couple in Fiji because the country is such a multicultural and multiracial place already. "There's a certain tradition of Europeans marrying natives," George tells us. And there was also a "hierarchy of desirables" on which Americans, who had access to better employment, rated fairly well.

Violette recalls a moment in their courtship when George distinguished himself from other boyfriends, and her feelings grew more serious. Violette was supposed to visit George on the side of the island where he lived at that point, but she came down with a terrible mosquito-borne illness. "One weekend I was very sick with dengue fever — it's very horrible to have — so I sent him a telegram saying, 'I'm sick, I can't come.' In those days, Peace Corps volunteers made maybe $70 a month? But he got in a taxi — sixty miles of dirt roads — and came and made sure that I went to see a doctor, which itself is very American. We Fijians refer to a hospital as 'house of death' — you basically go see a doctor in the hospital when there are no other options. So George came in a taxi and made sure I was all right, and that was when I thought, this guy really takes care of me."

This story, like many others the Ricketsons tell, highlights George's aggressive approach to life and contrasts it with Violette's more easygoing philosophy. It is a balance that works for George and Violette. Violette respects George's energy, organization, and focus; George appreciates Violette's flexibility, accommodation, and concern for others. At times, they strike us as the two halves of the yin-yang symbol — opposites that border and shape each other, together making one whole. On a more mundane level, they are deeply different people in a constant and loving conversation, one informed by a respectful, almost anthropological, understanding of each other's cultures.

.

George's conversation with other cultures extends beyond his relationship with Violette and her family and is presaged by a family history of interest in education and travel. George was born in North Carolina but moved from there to the Fort Worth area of

Texas when he was a child. "And we never had enough money to move back! So I grew up in Texas, went to school in Texas." When we inquire how George got from Fort Worth, Texas, to a life as an international businessman, he cites two factors that shaped his destiny. First, his grandparents valued education; his own grandmother had a university degree at a time when college-educated women were the exception. Also, two of George's uncles worked and traveled overseas and returned to tell stories about living and working in such far away places as Saudi Arabia, the Philippines, and China. "My uncle Robert was a missionary; he was extremely bilingual in both Filipino and Chinese dialects, and he had these very interesting stories to tell. In fact, both uncles spent more time overseas than they did in America. I always heard tales about those two abroad, and I used to love for my uncles to come and tell stories. Nobody else in Fort Worth had uncles who were coming back from the Philippines and Saudi Arabia."

Also, Violette gently points out, George did not enter the Peace Corps just for adventure or with a purely pragmatic spirit; he was an idealist. He believed in the work the Peace Corps was doing, wanted to help improve the Fijian economy, and is still proud of the difference he helped to make. He had a serious ethical objection to the Vietnam War, not just an antipathy to being drafted. "Remember how you and your father wrote and wrote those essays about how the war was wrong?" she reminds him.

Not surprisingly, the Ricketson family was supportive of George's engagement to Violette. In fact, because his father was seriously ill with cancer, George's family members "chipped in" and paid for Violette's fare to come to the United States to meet him. "It was a Christmas present," George tells us, one that touched Violette and made her feel welcome.

Violette's own family was very receptive to the match, too. "My mother really liked George. She particularly appreciated how he would eat anything. She used to say she had never met an American — "

"Your mother never called me an American!" George interrupts to remind Violette. "She always called me European." George's good-natured tone implies that this long-ago quirk was so constant, and so Fijian of her, that it has long since been transformed from an irritation into the pearl of a family joke.

"Well," Violette continues, "she'd never met a *European* who would eat anything."

•

George and Violette were married in a Methodist church on Suva in January 1973. Methodist, Violette explains, because Fiji is "ninety percent Methodist — since the Methodist missionaries got there first." George was raised Southern Baptist, but he tells us, "If you are going to get married on Fiji, you only have two choices, Methodist or Catholic."

Weddings in Fiji are big occasions where different branches of the family contribute the food for the celebration: "One branch does all the desserts, another the meat," Violette explains. George and Violette's reception banquet was held at the Hotel Suva. All the Peace Corps people came, as well as family and friends — a mixture of Europeans, part Europeans, and Fijians. "And I taught sixth grade, so my sixth graders came, too. It was an international school, so there were children at our wedding from all over the world."

"They were still calling you 'Miss Miller,'" George smiles, remembering.

In the first years of their marriage, the couple moved frequently around the South Pacific as George pursued jobs in a variety of places, not sure where they would settle. They first tried to move to Hawaii. "It was kind of halfway in between," George explains, "both American and Polynesian, the perfect compromise," but jobs were scarce in Hawaii. Soon the couple relocated to Guam, which was an American territory at the end of the Vietnam War. Guam was a big military base, dependent on American dollars, and the Guamanians had lost quite a bit of their culture because of that American influence. George and Violette, who did not fit into either the military group or that of the Guamanian locals, felt closed out of both communities. "There were a lot of restricted places where you needed passes to go, and we didn't have those passes since we weren't part of the military, which was like a little village unto itself. But the locals still treated us like part of the military." Despite some positive experiences, most notably the birth of their daughter, Marianna, in 1974, the couple was happy to leave the place. After Guam, the Ricketsons returned to Fiji, where they lived in Savusavu near Violette's family for several years, and where their son, Tsali, was born in 1976.

This was a golden time for George and Violette, and especially for their small son, who benefited from the extended family that surrounded him. The Ricketsons speculate that Tsali's outgoing nature may have its origins in a childhood where he was "handed around" as a baby from relative to relative. George tells us that he was out riding in a truck one day with his Australian boss, who was struck by the sight of a "little blonde kid" riding on a Fijian man's shoulders. "That's *my* kid," George said. "Who's he with?" George's boss asked. "I don't know," George replied, completely unconcerned.

But in 1978, when George faced another job change, the Ricketsons decided to move to the United States, a decision that was especially wrenching for Violette. "He was the one who wanted to go," she tells us. "It was always hard for me to leave, actually." George tries to reconstruct their thinking at the time; he begins and breaks off, his speech becoming uncharacteristically halting, as though he is picking his way over difficult terrain.

"The children were not yet school-age, but getting close to it. We were making a choice for them. We loved Fiji and thought it was a great place to live and, in some ways, raise children — but our kids would never have the chance to come back to the U.S. and be successful. You could always come from here and go to Fiji, but I thought we'd be making that choice for them if we decided to stay there."

"There are a lot of educational, developmental opportunities in this country that just aren't available in Fiji," George asserts, pauses. "Of course, there's a lot in Fiji, too, and so it's a tough choice."

Thinking about this long-ago decision still seems to make Violette sad; her face is, for a moment, closed to us, a little distant, and we imagine her thinking about a small blond child riding on the shoulders of one relative, reaching out to another, laughing. "It's the hardest part," she acknowledges. "Always having to choose one over the other."

The couple emigrated for the second time to the United States, entering again through Hawaii, where officials once again looked at Violette's Fijian passport ("I couldn't give that up") and then addressed all questions to George, assuming Violette did not speak English. Initially, the couple lived in the South with

George's mother. "Polynesia meets Southern Baptist," George jokes. Then to Colorado, "where Violette and the kids first saw snow," before settling in the Midwest. It would be almost ten years before Violette returned to Fiji, almost twenty-five before George would revisit the country.

Violette confesses that she did suffer initially from culture shock. What she recalls most clearly from that time was a deep homesickness for her family and a distress at the radical changes in Midwestern weather, where the mercury could drop forty degrees in one night. A more significant difference, one she has still not become accustomed to, was the competitiveness of American culture, a contrast that became painfully obvious to her during job interviews. In Fiji, she explains, "you had a job designated for you when you came back. Your government nominated you, which is very different from the American system, where you have to go after jobs."

"That's one thing she cannot do, when we move from place to place, is to go and ASK for a job," George agrees.

"In the Fijian system, the community decides who is the best person for the job — we designate our leaders this way as well. Whereas in the American system, it's whoever's the most aggressive. It's a very competitive culture. I would cringe when George would tell me, 'You have to sell yourself,' because we were taught you ought to be humble about your talents. I'd hear him say, 'Well, I'm good at this —' and that is so difficult for me. In Fiji, you cook enough food for a hundred people and then apologize because you are serving a small meal. We were taught to be inconspicuous. That humility makes you more part of the community."

Most Fijians, she goes on to point out, don't seek individual honors or engage in individual endeavors of any kind. "Fiji does not win Nobel Peace Prizes. We don't make very good business people because there's a certain individuality required that we just don't have culturally. Fijians tend to be more cooperative than competitive. Awards and monuments are not really part of that culture, either. Your reward is the memory of the people you lived with. People remember my mother as a very kind person, but I don't have to go and erect a monument in her memory."

Still, Violette feels that she adapted more easily to her life in the United States than many might have, in large part because of her background in British education. "It's probably been easier for me to adapt to the American system because of that. I knew a woman who got here, and all she could say was 'I have no money.'" English is also a point of commonality for the couple, as are certain elements of their schooling. "We both did Shakespeare," Violette says simply, summing up a variety of educational parallels.

George and Violette also share an appreciation of the Midwest as a "tolerant" place to raise a family — especially in contrast to the more racist South they deliberately chose to move away from. It is sort of laissez-faire tolerance they describe: the people are "easygoing" and, George says, "No one ever bothered us here." They felt safe from violence or overt racism, though subtler forms of racism, especially a frank disinterest in other cultures, were also a part of the Midwestern mindset. Violette has often been surprised over the years by the lack of geographical knowledge many Americans have demonstrated. When she told people who inquired that she was from the South Pacific, they might respond, "Oh, I had an uncle who served in Korea." George's depiction of American, particularly Midwestern insularity is more blunt: "OK. Fiji's not here. That's all we need to learn about Fiji."

Such apathy and ignorance is disappointing to them, something they have reared their own children to resist. Violette's openness to other cultures combined with her husband's determination that the children not miss opportunities have jointly created a family that challenged and changed its community in its own small ways. For example, their children have always been interested in and embraced other intercultural people. Tsali, they tell us, has always had friends of all kinds and colors; as a high school football player, he was a bridge between the black and white athletes and their families. "People used to say, 'I know you're from Jamaica,' and he'd say, 'Yes, mon,' or they'd say, 'You're from Samoa, right?' and he'd take on a Samoan accent. They didn't know how to classify him. He wasn't black, or white, he was the one kid in the middle, the *kai loma* — so they all adopted him. He was open to everyone, the kind of kid who hugged everyone's mom." Both parents see their son's adaptable, outgoing nature as very Fijian.

Marianna, too, thinks of herself now as half Fijian, wants to claim her Polynesian heritage. "At times I think she wanted to be more Polynesian looking," Violette tells us, showing us a picture of her daughter, who is striking with green eyes, light skin, thick brown hair. "She played on the soccer team in high school, and other parents were always wrongly assuming that the Italian girl — dark hair, dark skin — was my daughter. They wouldn't connect Marianna to me, and I think sometimes she would be sad." Violette brightens, tells us of Marianna's excitement when a Polynesian student at a "semester at sea" program asked her whether she had any Polynesian background. "She was so excited; it was the first time anyone had recognized her as part Polynesian."

The Ricketsons' kitchen has also always been a multicultural one. To have a Fijian kitchen is to have Indian, Chinese, Polynesian influences, Violette tells us, and when they were younger, the children were always bringing friends home, making them "part of the family." "We invited one of Tsali's friends home for dinner and he had never even eaten rice! We were just astounded — this was in junior high," she recalls, her astonishment even now clear on her face.

.

Both George and Violette are proud of their children's accomplishments, and both see their children's choices as influenced by Fijian values, from their appreciation of education (both intend to continue in graduate school) to their choice of community-oriented vocations. Marianna, a Purdue graduate who will be doing graduate work at Columbia in computers and education, plans, like her mother, to be a teacher. Tsali, a graduate of Yale and currently an Americorps volunteer, imagines himself becoming a lawyer specializing in child abuse and would like to be a judge in a juvenile court someday.

Despite the deep pride and pleasure Violette takes in her children, she acknowledges certain regrets, and one is that she did not teach them to speak Fijian. George comments, practically, that they would have had no one to speak the language with. "Fijians like to live in Fiji," she concedes a little sadly. "They love their country, and they like to stay there." Violette insists on the pain of losing so much of her culture, not just language, but also ways of relating to her children, cultural assumptions she'd expected to share with them. In fact, she tells us, such losses become more recognizable over time. "We don't share that same background, and that's something I've struggled with. In some ways, my children are very Americanized. They've lived here for two decades, and I have to remember that."

Of particular difficulty for Violette is her children's independence from her. "American children have to go away from their parents, have to be independent," she tells us. Partly, American offspring are more materially able to distance themselves from their parents. "American children can afford more transportation than Fijian children. There's a big difference between my sister and her kids and the relationship between my kids and me because of this." But American children also have an intellectual independence from their parents that sometimes translates into a lack of the kind of respect Violette expects. "Sometimes I will find in Asian students a certain respect for the teacher or the elder or the mother. My children are very considerate of others, but they are American in that they talk back to me. I would never talk back to my mother, and I find that hard." Violette struggles to balance her own feelings and upbringing against her desire to be fair. "I know it's part of their being American, but it's just so in-your-face."

But if Violette has lost some elements of her culture since coming to the United States, she has also learned to assert the value of Fijian culture in her work. Part of the Fijian influence on her teaching is an openness to others. "So whoever comes into your classroom becomes part of your family," Violette tells us. In fact, Violette mothers more than just her own two children. With each new wave of four- and five-year-olds, Violette's quiet conviction grows that her cooperative, collaborative, respectful culture has something to teach — to the children who inhabit her classroom as well as the teachers who come to observe it for its intercultural qualities.

Violette models respectful behavior to her young students, especially toward mothers. "I sometimes will say to them, 'I want you to help your mother by putting on your coat,' or 'your mother needs your help right now and I want you to be the one to carry your bag.' Or 'ask your mother nicely.' Sometimes I stand up for the mother!" In keeping with Polynesian values, Violette also emphasizes treating children with the same respect, valuing each of them as unique. "That's something I run into a lot with my American colleagues, that they mistake kindness for weakness. I'll say to American teachers, 'Why do you think American kids need to stand up for their rights? Because people step on them more here!'"

The Polynesian values of flexibility and accommodation are particularly well suited to working with young children, for whom serendipity often organizes the day. "To work with young children you have to be very flexible. I think Polynesian ways are very suited to small children, because there isn't an agenda, there isn't any sense of time. If four-year-olds decide they want to go out and dig worms, then off you go to dig worms!" Violette has noticed that the spontaneity so ideal for young children and so simple for her to offer them is sometimes difficult for Violette's more super-organized American counterparts.

She also feels that Fijian children have advanced social skills because of their life within extended families, a network few American children have access to. Blue-collar families, Violette says, who have less mobility than other Americans and often depend on one another for childcare, come closest to the Fijian model, and their children have the social skills to prove it. "They know how to share, they're not as egocentric, they have excellent skills in conversation, and an ability to negotiate that gives them high marks on the social skills checklist," Violette comments.

The parents and children must be sad that you are moving to New England, we observe.

"Yes, well, they're not too happy with George," Violette says, deflecting the compliment with a characteristic modesty.

We have caught Violette in a moment of looking back. Getting older, she tells us, has prompted her to reflect on what she has lost by leaving Fiji, especially since her mother passed away not long ago. She has been returning home, she tells us, with greater and greater frequency, taking advantage of her summers off to volunteer in Fiji's early childhood programs. Her trips back teach her just how American she has become after so many years here. "I miss *Good Morning America*!" she tells us, "and I have a greater appreciation for central heating, for how well everything runs here." More often, however, these visits illuminate the advantages of life in Fiji.

In particular, it is better to age in Fiji, an issue that the couple is facing at this midpoint in their lives. "America is a very youth-oriented culture, and that's something we struggle with as we get older. It's one of the things I accept more peacefully: this is where you are in life, this is part of life. But George, being the American, wants to change things. He thinks if he just works harder, organizes it better, he can get the outcome he wants."

"And it's usually true, he does make things happen — almost everything but eternal life," she finishes gently, touching George's arm in companionship or comfort.

"I've lost both my father and mother. Somehow I never worried about them, though, in their old age. I always knew that the family would take care of them. My mother died in an accident, but, by the time I got to Fiji, my brothers had arranged the funeral; the family just came in and took over. Basically, I just had to be there. I worry more about George's mother in that way because she is part of a nuclear family. I have said to my children, 'I'm not going to grow old in the U.S. and go to a nursing home.' That's not in my cultural background. Whereas George's mother, being a very organized American, has planned everything out. She remarried, and they have this retirement home all selected."

Will Fiji be the next move on your horizon? we ask, and the Ricketsons respond with uncertainty. They won't have to worry about their children's education any longer, Violette points out. "We're back to being just us." On the other hand, there may be grandchildren to consider.

"From Connecticut to Fiji," George chuckles. "That's going to be an interesting decision for us." After their upcoming move to New England, the source, ironically, of the Whippy branch in Violette's complicated family tree, a final move to Fiji seems right.

Perfect, we say.

The Ricketsons nod thoughtfully. "The circle would be complete."

Alterations

JANET & ANDY

Janet & Andy. Photo by Christy Mock.

W hen we first open the door of Janet Ingle's dress shop in Wauwautosa, Wisconsin, just outside of Milwaukee, we are confused about whom to greet. There are several women who have turned to look at us as the door jingles open. One, an elegant black woman with white hair and a confident air, wears a beautiful mud-cloth coat that we immediately recognize as African. This, we think smiling in her direction, must be Janet. But it is another woman, sitting unselfconsciously on the floor pinning a hem, who invites us in. This quiet, unpretentious person in black stretch pants and turtleneck is the woman we have come to see.

Janet can't talk to us right away, so we chat with the clients and examine the merchandise in her store. One wall displays some "Mama Africa" posters and is fronted by a glass case filled with African beaded jewelry. Another is covered in traditional West African clothing hanging in colorful tiers: most are garments called *grands boubous* — very long shirts over loose-fitting pants, both in a solid-colored, heavy cotton and beautifully embroidered. Nearby racks display dozens of children's dresses, done in the most elaborate of Western styles with pleated yokes, puffy sleeves, lace pinafores, and underskirts.

We watch as the women in the store try on the bags of new clothes they have brought for alterations and a few garments from Janet's selection, teasing and prodding each other. Joyce, the tall woman we spotted earlier, looks good in everything she tries on and tries on more than anyone else, twirling and dancing lightly before the mirror. "She comes alive when she wears clothes," one friend says admiringly.

Janet sits on the floor with her legs splayed at a right angle and a yellow tape measure around her neck, the tools of her trade scattered about within reach. Something about the humility of Janet's posture, her quiet, brief remarks, the concentration she gives her work make her a sympathetic character, especially in relation to the boisterous, self-confident women she is assisting. She is completely unassuming in this moment, concerned with everyone else's needs and appearance, and not at all with her own.

Finally, Janet pins her last hem. The women surge out in a noisy wave, leaving a heap of clothes for Janet to alter and little time, apparently, for her to do the work. Other customers call or stop by during our interview and add to the pile. Janet apologizes but says she must work while we talk. And work she does — on an ordinary sewing machine without special appendages or fancy stitches, while we pull our chairs up close and arrange our tape recorders so that they are as unobtrusive as possible. Janet takes clothing from the pile that has accumulated behind her and tells us a story that is moving in ways we did not anticipate.

Janet grew up in Ghana, West Africa. She laughs at one of our first questions — about how many people were in her family. "When you ask an African for family, you're asking for trouble. What do you mean, 'family'?" We narrow our question, ask how many sisters and brothers she had, and Janet tells us that her father had eight children, that she was the eldest one. Her father was highly educated — "He attended graduate school in Halifax, Canada, had a master's degree, and he wanted every one of us to go to school to do something. I wanted to be a doctor, but after a while my dad was not paying my school fees, so I had to take care of myself." It was the Salvation Army in Ghana that rescued her in the last instant; they needed nurses and paid Janet, who had settled on a career in nursing, to work for them while she finished training.

Janet met Andy Ingle, who was a Peace Corps volunteer, while she was working for the Salvation Army. "When he came to the hospital where I was working," Janet remembers, "I was the first one he saw. He was speaking the language, and that was fascinating to me — a white man speaking the language. In the Peace Corps, they teach you how to get by, get around." But Andy wanted to do more than just get by in the culture where he found himself. In particular, he liked Ghanaian food but didn't know how to buy or cook it, so he asked Janet to help him.

When we inquire of Janet whether she thinks, looking back, that Andy was asking her on a date or whether he was really hungry, Janet tells us quite definitely that it was the latter. "He was hungry because, compared with the other British doctors and nurses in the Peace Corps, Americans really like their food." As she recalls, Andy found the portion sizes woefully small. "In the morning, he'll want two eggs for breakfast, and the British will want him to eat half an egg! 'No, no, no, I'm from America, eggs are nothing!'" Janet imitates her husband. "He worked too hard," she continues in his defense, still disapproving of that long ago rationing. "He needed the energy. So I would cook. He would give me money for the market and then come and eat. Later, he'd ask me to go places with him, help him get around."

Janet and Andy became friends quickly and were soon spending time together every day, sometimes strolling through town to the market, turning mundane errands into friendly outings. People in town teased Janet about this friendship — sometimes with a certain sharpness — referring to Andy as her boyfriend and making occasional suggestions about what might be going on between the two of them. Janet thought Andy was a good man, but she did not think of him as a romantic interest because she was acutely aware of the barriers between white American men and

African women. She knew that few members of the community were prepared to perceive a relationship of mutual regard between them, so she was surprised when Andy told her he cared for her, and even more surprised when he proposed.

What could he see, she wondered, in an ordinary African girl, a black girl from a poor country and a struggling family? It was not that Janet lacked a sense of pride. She had an education, she was a nurse, and these things represented significant accomplishments. Janet did not, however, see herself as different from the women around her, certainly not as an unusually attractive or desirable woman, but Andy thought otherwise.

He thought she was kind-hearted and intelligent, and he told her so. "He was the first person to tell me I'm beautiful," Janet recalls. Even after Andy had persuaded Janet of the sincerity of his love for her, however, Janet was unwilling to consent to marriage. She could see the tension between blacks and whites in her own country, and she had heard the situation was much worse in the United States. More than anything else, Janet was afraid of how racist feelings and ideas might affect her relationship with Andy's family. She did not believe the Ingles would be able to accept her, and she could not be part of a family in which she was unappreciated or unwelcome. Janet's concerns were shared by her parents: "What my parents feared was him takin' me to the other side of the ocean and his parents not acceptin' me."

Despairing of another way to convince Janet that she could live happily as his wife, Andy invited his mother, father, and two brothers to Ghana to meet her. When Janet describes this meeting, she puts down her sewing for a few minutes. The family touched her, she tells us, with their warmth and open-mindedness. "If Andy loved me, they said, I must be a good person." They hugged her, asked her lots of questions about herself, welcomed her into their family.

We find the generosity of this gesture on the part of Andy's family remarkable. We are not under the impression that the Ingles are possessed of a vast fortune, and plane tickets to West Africa are expensive now. They must have been even more expensive in the seventies, when such trips would have been rare. For a Milwaukee family to make this long trip during that era, all to convince one young woman that she would be safe marrying their son, and that she could count on their help and loving presence in her life, strikes us as more than a little unusual.

Wow, we say, for want of more perspicacious comment. He must have really loved you to bring his whole family over like that.

"Yes," she says, smiling and picking up her sewing again.

Andy and Janet finally did marry, quietly, before a justice of the peace, and the couple made their home together in Ghana for the next five years. "The living there was good. We had a beautiful house, four people who came every day to help us clean it. Andy even had a bodyguard." They had no particular desire or reason to move. Janet continued working as a nurse, and Andy took a job with a nongovernmental organization.

They brought two children into the world in Ghana, both easy births for Janet. In fact, Janet delivered her first baby herself. "That day I scrubbed everywhere. It was Christmas Eve, and I wanted to eat corned beef so bad. My husband said he'd get some for me while he was out getting cash for Christmas." In Africa, money for Christmas is distributed to children on Christmas Eve like candy on Halloween is in the United States. "I got all ready and when I was in the shower I felt the first pain. 'Geez, if this is the start,' I thought, 'how many hours of this am I gonna get?' But then I just went into the living room and had the baby. They had to go find Andy and tell him the news," Janet laughs, remembering her husband's surprise at being called home from the bank to meet his baby before he had even finished his errands. The Ingles' son was named Benjamin Yaw ("Yaw" for male born on Thursday). Their daughter, Yaa-Joy ("Yaa" for female born on Thursday), arrived with similar ease two years later.

Janet's social identity changed after she married Andy. She tells us that many people in Ghana who did not know them assumed that Janet was a prostitute when they saw her in public with her white husband. She just shakes her head when she remembers this. Most people, she tells us, had a friendly curiosity about her, as if her marriage had transformed her from the ordinary African woman she perceived herself to be into something else. We are amused to hear that the children called her "the white woman" and that they considered it a special treat to get cookies and other goodies from her house during the holidays. She was a novelty, and the children liked to visit her.

Finally, the project Andy was working on in Ghana was over, and well-paying jobs like his were few and far between. When another job failed to materialize, Andy and Janet decided to move to the United States, much to the delight and relief of Andy's parents who, hearing about wars in other parts of Africa, feared for their son and his family.

Though Janet expresses no regret about the choice, it was obviously a difficult move for her. She was leaving behind her country, family, friends, and job for Milwaukee — a city full of snow and white faces. Initially, the couple moved in with Andy's parents and the Ingles lived up to their promise to nurture and support Janet and Andy's marriage. "When I first came, I was tryin' to be careful, but they were right there helping me out, helping me adjust." The Ingles left no room for Janet to be shy or standoffish. "In fact," she marvels, "my mother-in-law was so great, so understanding to me. Now we share clothes, even underclothes! We taste each other's food, 'Take a bite, try this,' a real closeness. But back then it was a shock to me. I had thought, 'You don't know what these white folks think, be careful.' But then I see with them that it's a different kind of love they have for each other."

The Ingles would buy her presents, she tells us, especially clothes they had seen black models wearing in catalogs — colors they thought would look good with her skin tone. They appreciated her food and tried to make food she would like. They told her she was beautiful and, in a lingo that must have been foreign to them, that "black is beautiful." Far from feeling this attention as awkward or strained, Janet appreciated it, still appreciates it. If she needs something, she tells us, all she has to do is call Andy's father or one of his brothers, who will drop everything and come to help her.

Nevertheless, the first couple of years were difficult. It was cold, Janet's nursing certificate was not valid in the United States, and she knew nobody except the Ingles — nobody else from Ghana — to talk to. Despite her in-laws' warmth, she experienced the neighborhood as very isolated, especially in winter, especially compared with the African community she had left behind. "Before, you asked me about family?" she reminds us. "There, we have extended family that comes and goes all the time. Even your neighbors have to say hi. There, if you don't go say 'Good morning, neighbor' every day, they're wonderin' if you're sick or if you've gone somewhere."

"I was depressed," Janet admits, "coming from a different

culture. I was home with the kids, and it hit me right there, so I decided to do something." Facing her depression with the stalwart ingenuity and self-confidence that we are beginning to see as one of her most remarkable traits, Janet decided to teach herself to sew. At first, she made clothes only for her own children, but soon it was evident that she had a serious talent for working with fabric, a talent others began to notice. As Janet's creations appeared on her nieces and nephews as well as her own children, other parents and friends began inquiring where these wonderful outfits came from. Janet's clothes made a reputation for her. "I decided, 'I like it,'" Janet says in her understated way. "Sewing got me out from depression."

It was the beginning of a new business, new connections, and new friendships. Ten years after Janet first picked up a needle, it is our impression that she has barely paused between that day and now. She still makes children's dresses, samples of which are displayed in one corner of the shop, but she also does a booming business in alterations. In addition, she makes beautiful clothing for adults and has just begun a serious effort at marketing imported clothing, *grands boubous*, West African mudcloth, and southern African tie-dyes.

For the Ingles' children, the transition to their new home was easier, though in the beginning, Janet's two-and-a-half-year-old son refused to speak English, "because," Janet tells us, "he says he's not a white man. But he learned English." And, Janet adds ruefully, "he don't even know one word of my language now."

She pauses to reflect. "I wish we could've kept it going, speaking my language, but when we first came, the family used to take the kids, to help out, and to get them used to being with the family. They were the first grandkids, so they were very special. And I didn't want to reject their kindness." Andy and Janet's light-skinned children adapted well, and soon Janet became a cultural and racial minority in her own house, as well as in the city. Her daughter, who had seen black faces exchanged for white in every part of their lives and who had herself grown lighter away from the hot sun of Ghana, expressed concern about her mother.

"'Mama, how come you're not turning white? Grandpa is white, Grandma is white, Papa is white, we're turnin' white. You're not turnin', how come?'" Janet reports Joy asking.

"And I said, 'Well Joy, I don't think . . . you see, God baked me too long in the oven, so it would take me a long time for me to be that white.'"

"Don't worry," Joy reassured her. "You'll be all right."

Also, and not surprisingly, the American racism Janet had feared when Andy first asked her to marry him made its presence felt in Janet's new Milwaukee life. When the Ingles arrived at a Milwaukee hospital to have their third child (Ursula Adjoa, female born on Monday), the nurses asked Janet, "Where's your husband?"

"My husband was standing right next to me," Janet tells us.

"*Oh*," the nurses said. Janet says that "oh" again, the second time drawing it out, making us laugh at all the implied meaning that one word contained.

Janet also tells us the story of a man she saw frequently when she was waiting for the bus at a particular stop in Milwaukee.

"Hi, nigger," the man would say to her whenever he saw her.

"Hello, white man," she would always say in reply, showing neither fear nor anger. Apparently, Janet's self-possession impressed the man as much as it impresses us now as we sit listening to her story because eventually the man began to greet her with more courtesy — simply nodding, saying "hello," moving on. Despite her early feelings of isolation and her experiences with racism in Milwaukee, Janet is reluctant to draw broad conclusions about the city as monocultural. At first, she tells us, she was too involved with her new family to seek out other Africans in Milwaukee, and later she was too occupied with her new business. And, she notes with pleasure, she now has a friend with whom she speaks her native language.

Janet does not feel the same universal distrust of whites that some African American people do — perhaps for obvious reasons. In fact, while white racism has been an undeniable part of Janet's life in Milwaukee, so has the prejudice of African Americans who do not approve of her marriage. "To be honest," she reports, "sometimes I felt white people liked me more and that I even felt prejudice from black people. White people seemed more interested in me and were often more kind to help me out. Even a black once called me, 'African monkey.'"

Janet tells us a story to illustrate this point. "Last week, two black ladies came here. One buys stuff here a lot, brings her friends with her. She asked me about my husband. 'Is your husband African?'

"'No, he's American,' I told her.

"'Black American?' I said 'No, he's white.' She got so mad! 'I hate that — niggers married to white folks — what are you, a nigger, doing with a white man?'

"And I said, 'You know what? You're the first person who make me think my husband is a different person with a different color. Other than that, I don't see a color. I see a good husband and father. That's all what it is to me. So don't worry about me, I'm ok.'"

Still, Janet tells us, the woman persisted. "'Is he a *good* white man?'

"And so I say, 'No, he's not. He's a *good person.* He's just a good human being.'"

Then, Janet says, the woman took a different tack. "'What about your kids? Your kids are gonna suffer.'

"'You know what? In my house, we don't call color.'

"She got mad and walked out. So I realize I'm gonna face all that, but the kids are happy. They're proud to say that they're from Africa, 'I'm African.' My husband jokes with them, 'Wait until you go there.' Because my kids are afraid of bugs! 'Then you may want to stay an American!'" Janet laughs with us before becoming serious again.

"I tell them, you should be proud to be both. And I teach them how pretty they are, that they have a beautiful color. Even the pure white people want to stay in the sun to be like them. So they have that in mind. I told them they have both sides to learn from. They've got African minds, and they've got white minds. So they're gonna be the best. That gives them energy about being themselves."

The phone rings; it's Andy. "He's just calling to tell me he's gotta go to three schools," Janet smiles woefully at her husband's schedule, is silent for a moment, thinking of him.

"You know, I don't see him as white until I see other people looking at us. Then it clicks. He's — Andy. Other than that, it's nothing." She pauses, looking down at her hands as though they hold a picture she's trying to describe. "I see a man," she repeats. "A good man. A good husband."

{ *Janet & Andy* }   217

Janet recounts this story just before she tells us that Andy is dying. We have asked whether she and Andy plan ever to return to Ghana to live. "No," she tells us with such finality that we ask if that is because they are so established here.

"No, because he's sick. He has colon cancer," Janet replies. Into our stunned silence, she speaks quietly. "Two years ago, we found out that he had colon cancer that he almost died from. So he's still working now, because he had treatments of chemotherapy for one whole year. They took his colon out. But it would be hard to live anywhere else now. He has to be close to a doctor."

Oh, we say, feeling stricken. We are so sorry.

"That's — life," Janet says softly, without a trace of self-pity or irony. In fact, her voice lingers over these words acceptingly, almost reverently. Suddenly, she's the one comforting us. "We take it one day at a time. At the moment, we don't think about it."

We are experiencing Andy as something of a revelation. We had been put off, just a bit, by his apparent unwillingness to meet with us. Not unwillingness, Janet had steadfastly explained, inability, due to his schedule that kept him busy even on evenings or weekends. Andy teaches science and technology at a nearby public school, and while we have a healthy respect for the hectic life teachers live, we were still surprised to hear that Andy had literally no time to spare. What Janet has told us illuminates, suddenly, a completely different reason for Andy's frenetic work pace. He is neither resistant to meeting us nor an American workaholic. Instead, we see a man trying his hardest to provide for a family during what may be the end of his life.

It is a terrible, fast journey we have taken this afternoon from indifference to appreciation to sadness. Despite Janet's own composure, we feel overwhelmed by the unfairness of Andy's illness as a possible ending for this particular love story.

Trying to recover, we look down at our dwindling list of questions. We have forgotten, we see, to ask about the wedding ceremony. "At first, I didn't want no wedding," Janet remembers. "I didn't want publicity. Sometimes you think about it in the beginning — you got a little feeling about what people think and how people look at you. What they're gonna say. All that. So back then I said, 'Ah, let's just go to the courthouse.' But now I want a big wedding!" she adds with a mixture of humor and wistfulness. "As it grows — we've been married for eighteen years — you don't care anymore what people think."

Not long after this, we leave, though not before putting our arms around Janet, who comes out from behind the sewing machine to see us off. The afternoon traffic has begun to pick up outside her shop, and we are conscious, suddenly, of the precious hours Janet has given us. She has given us more than time, of course, and we feel all that we are taking as we step into the sunshine that seems almost painfully bright.

Despite our need to get on the road, we are reluctant to give up the gifts of the afternoon to the everyday business of filling the gas tank, checking route signs, merging with impatient highway travelers. So we linger for some time in the Burger King across the street from Janet's shop, trying to digest what we have heard. We want to make a few notes, write down our impressions. We watch silently as long shafts of sunlight stream through the smoky air, catch in the dust motes above our cups of decaf, but we cannot find words for what we are feeling. In a little while, we put away our notebooks, call our own families who are waiting for us, tell them we are on the way home.

Black is black

MURTIS & NANA

Nana & Murtis. Photo by Christy Mock.

One day, many years ago, Murtis Grant-Acquah was chatting with a white couple, strangers, at a YMCA near her suburban Milwaukee home. They were joking about mundane things, the noise the children in the building made or the hassles of family life. It was the sort of casual camaraderie that can sometimes lead to a real connection — when you find you are nearly neighbors or have children in the same school. To Murtis it seemed like just that sort of conversation: she'd learn their names, maybe, wave to them across the grocery store parking lot. So she was more than a little surprised when the couple's four-year-old child walked over to her, kicked her in the shoe, and said, "I don't like niggers." The parents said nothing, just picked up their child and walked away.

"What could they say?" asks Murtis. That child did not come up with those feelings on her own, Murtis points out, "She got that from her family" — the very family Murtis had been joking and laughing with moments before. That moment, for Murtis, was paradigmatic. If behind the smiling faces of that YMCA family lurked such blatant race hatred, who could say that every other smiling white face didn't likewise cover some ugly, unexpressed feeling.

Murtis was born in Forest, Mississippi, and grew up in Milwaukee, but it was her early experiences in Mississippi that have marked her thinking about race, convincing her of the pervasive nature of white American racism. "I guess growing up in America, being from the South," she says, "I always strongly felt the differences between the races. Black is black and white is white." In the world of her childhood, people were either white or black, and any other differences were irrelevant or invisible. White people, across class and religious difference, were to be avoided; and black people, despite any possible differences, felt a certain solidarity.

It is not surprising, then, that when Murtis met her African husband, Nana, she did not think of him as a cultural other because he wasn't *the* other — he wasn't white. When we ask her in the interview about meeting Nana for the first time, about time they spent together early in their relationship and how their differences of nationality manifested themselves then, Murtis comments only on the minor difference of Nana's accent.

"He just spoke funny. That's probably the only thing that I noticed," says Murtis.

"I didn't speak funny, I just spoke in a way that was probably different," Nana objects.

"Okay, okay," Murtis agrees, laughing.

Except for the sound of his voice, she didn't feel any barrier between them at all. The ease of their understanding she wraps up in one neat package. "He's black," she says simply. Likewise, about the African college students who were his colleagues at the time she says, "Black is black. We're black folks, we're just different, that's all." They were all, therefore, in the same boat; according to Murtis, there were no relevant differences.

.

Nana and Murtis met in a genetics class in Platteville, Wisconsin, in 1971. Nana had a strong background in the material and he tutored Murtis that semester. They prepared for exams and did homework together, and eventually Murtis included Nana in the circle of friends who came to talk and eat, party and study in her dormitory. It didn't occur to her to make a distinction between African and African American blacks, and she thought her friends felt the same. The campus was so small, only 9,000 students, and

{ *Black Is Black* }

the number of black students, African or African American, tiny. She moved among the African and African American students with an easy, assumed camaraderie and soon included Nana's African friends among the network of people who came and went in her dormitory room. The African students "were people," Murtis says emphatically, "they were black people."

Nana remembers things a little differently.

"In Africa," he says, "we didn't think about the separation of the races." He was much less likely to see other black people as certain allies. He did not, in fact, always experience them as allies. He agrees that Murtis made no distinction between the African and African American students, but he says that other African American students were less open to befriending their peers from the motherland.

"From my perspective, they made me feel there was a difference," he tells us. In particular, he recalls, people responded ambivalently to the different accents and mannerisms of the African students. "Every time I thought I was speaking clearly came 'Eh? Eh? Huh? What did you say?'" Nana says. "It turned me into an introvert. I felt rejected, felt that I didn't need to talk that much anymore." We are saddened by the idea that Nana, always vibrant and enthusiastic when we see him, a natural extrovert, should have had his spirits so dampened even for a little while.

While he was struggling hard to understand American culture, neither black nor white students could even say his name. He finally changed it, for professional purposes, from Grant-Acquah to Grant, despite his name's cultural and historical meaning and his father's puzzled disappointment over the change. In fact, nobody he met knew much of anything about his homeland, Ghana, and few people seemed particularly interested in knowing more.

Though the African students eventually developed relationships with the other black students, the social groups were separate, Nana says. African students often felt isolated, lonely, and foreign — and they relied on and identified largely with each other.

Still, the connection between Nana and Murtis grew stronger, though the exact nature of that connection, we gather as we listen, was pleasantly unclear.

"We were just very good friends," says Murtis, but Nana responds to this with a certain irony.

"There were men around all the time," he says, remembering an old frustration. "She had a lot of guys after her."

"Awww," says Murtis, "they were all friends. You know, we were young people, in college." Now she is looking at us to agree with her, and we laugh, imagining her small room full of people smoking cigarettes, laughing, and wet cans of beer or pop on the floor. Nana, we imagine, is looking at Murtis, who is first talking to someone on the other side of the room, then greeting another friend at the door, answering the phone, getting someone a drink, or handing someone a cigarette.

"Back then," Murtis says, by way of explanation, "I was just a hippie. I enjoyed Nana, I enjoyed everybody. I just loved people."

"I don't know how our marriage came about," Murtis continues after a moment, and Nana shrugs wryly. "Maybe it was the Mustang."

"My cousin gave me that car," Nana offers. "It was a very nice car. Maybe that was what attracted her! Maybe she thought I was a rich African prince." Nana is joking, of course, but there *is* something regal about him — his sense of humor, for one thing, which is always expansive, including and welcoming everyone in the room.

"It must have been hanging around in that old Mustang,"

Murtis decides finally, bringing us back to the subject of their courtship. They flash each other a private smile.

"We were really tight friends," Murtis adds, but Nana is more emphatic.

"She was my best friend, my very best friend," he says with an earnestness more powerful in contrast to the levity he brings to other parts of the conversation.

When Nana was ready to leave town, headed for medical school, they decided that Murtis should go with him. From the way they talk now, it was a decision made without a lot of fuss. They eloped. No ceremony, no honeymoon, no special dress, no flowers.

"It was just you and me and a couple of little white people we didn't even know," Murtis says to Nana. He nods.

Murtis's family was surprised by her marriage, and at first they were frightened about what would happen to her.

"My parents had never met an African until they met Nana," Murtis explains.

"Initially, I think their greatest fear was that I was going to take their daughter to Africa," says Nana.

"And put me in a pot and cook me," Murtis adds. Nana laughs good-naturedly. He had already become accustomed to Americans' lack of knowledge about his homeland, a small country on the southern coast of West Africa, most famous for its Gold Coast and its first president, Kwame Nkrumah. Her family had never learned anything about Africa, Murtis tells us, so they believed stories about what it was like. "They just didn't know," she says, "but after they became better acquainted with Nana, after they understood what he was all about, they didn't have any more problems. They liked him."

Nana's family accepted Murtis with even more ease and expressed happiness about her marriage to Nana. Cape Coast, where Nana's family is from, is bigger than Forest, Mississippi, and, as a trade center in Ghana, is naturally international. Like many gifted children in West Africa, Nana and his siblings dreamed of going away to school, somewhere in Europe, Australia, or especially the United States. Several of Nana's sisters and brothers have succeeded in finding schools and jobs abroad and have settled all around the world. Practically from the beginning, then, the international world was on the horizon for Nana and his family, so it was relatively easy for them to take Nana's new American wife in stride.

When she visited Ghana for the first time, Murtis tells us, she liked his family, too, right away. It was a dangerous journey in a way Murtis's parents could not have foreseen, however, because Murtis made this first trip during the 1982 coup, perhaps the worst time ever for an American to travel to Ghana. It was frightening, Murtis recalls. "You could see the army people with their guns. Basic things — bread and rice — were hard to come by." Murtis remembers the tension vividly and was glad, maybe lucky, to get back to the States alive and uninjured.

.

Ten years and two children later, Murtis and Nana married again, but they underplay this ceremony, too, don't offer to show us pictures, and are not inclined to wax sentimental. It was a traditional American ceremony, they say, except no white dress. It was big, they tell us, with lots of food and lots of friends, a band, champagne, dancing. We push to know more: Was it intercultural? Did you serve African food? Was there African music? Was Nana's family able to attend? No, they tell us, the food was catered and

226   { *Black Is Black* }

American; the band was local and American; only those African friends and family members already living in the United States could afford to come.

Sitting in Nana and Murtis's living room now, big-screen TV on mute in front of us, stereo remote at hand, VCR remote on the table, everything nicely decorated and in perfect order, it is hard to imagine the days before marriage and medical school when Murtis was a high-spirited young "hippie" and Nana uncertain, a stranger to this country. Almost everything around us now speaks of a perfectly American comfort and well-being. In fact, our first impression is that there is little difference between the upper-middle-class world of this household and that of every other household in this well-manicured, riverside neighborhood. Their home is on a quiet road that curves along the Wauwautosa River; houses set back from the road on big lots are private and secure. The Grant-Acquahs' own house has large windows overlooking the river, a neat secluded garden out back, a three-car garage, and easy access to the suburban village of Wauwautosa, which is replete with coffee shops, antique stores, and small, river-view restaurants.

The Grant-Acquahs, of course, make no apologies for this hard-won material well-being. Nana is an anesthesiologist who works at Community Memorial Hospital, and Murtis is a small-businesswoman in Wauwautosa. By their own account, they live a hectic life. Murtis sometimes works from seven in the morning until midnight for weeks on end. Nana has the typical life of a doctor: long hours, plenty of on-call evenings and weekends, lots of anxiety. We conduct the interview on a Sunday afternoon, which slips into an evening. Even though it is Sunday, however, Nana carries a pager with him and takes one long call during our interview. Murtis, too, cannot get through the afternoon without having to do business over the phone. Murtis and Nana tell us that there are many weeks when eating dinner together is an anomaly, and some when neither has time to cook anything at all. They make us tired just by telling us about a typical workweek in their household.

The couple's teenage sons, Kwesi and Kweku, seem to be on the high-activity, high-achievement path of their parents. Kwesi attends the University of Wisconsin at Madison, where he takes science courses in hopes of going on to medical school. During our interview, he is busy packing to go back to school after a weekend home. Kweku, still in high school, is constantly out with his friends or involved in some school activity. He already thinks a lot about what he wants to do with his life and is making plans. In the room where we are conducting the interview, there are pictures of Kwesi and Kweku in tennis shorts and jackets, rackets in hand, looking confident and ready for adulthood, the linear world of the tennis courts behind them.

In many ways this seems like an archetypal upper-middle-class American home. The frenetic activity, certainly, strikes us as familiar and American—as does a push to succeed at sports and academics that begins in childhood. The children we see in the pictures, glaring sun out of sight above them, standing on the hot cement that surrounds the tennis clay, are American if they are anything. In their very short, sporty haircuts and matching sport clothes, they would be recognized the world over. They dress like Americans, speak like Americans, and have gone to American schools all their lives. Later, when we are driving around Milwaukee after the interview, Kweku calls Murtis on her cell phone. He is going to the mall, he tells her. He needs money. Since we have been talking about what it means to be African and what it means to be American, this makes us laugh. Malls and cell phones seem so utterly, so undebatably, American.

Still, when we ask Murtis and Nana whether their children think of themselves as partly African, they answer in the affirmative. Yes, they say, the children have spent time in Africa, and they know who they are. At first, it is very hard to see the African aspects of their identities. Describing their visits to Ghana, Kwesi and Kweku say that they did not particularly like being there. To begin with, they are not big fans of the African foods that Nana's family prepared for them, and American food was difficult to find. Also, they tell us, Ghana is "kind of primitive," you can't get many channels on television, there are no malls or video games, and there isn't very much to do.

Because of Kwesi and Kweku's responses to our questions, we push harder to understand what Murtis means when she says that the boys have African identities. Are there particular elements of African culture that they have been taught? Certain ideas or ways of doing things Nana and Murtis have made sure to transmit to them? Nana shakes his head, as though expressing a little regret at what may have been lost. But Murtis has a more positive take on things. "I think Nana brings elements of his African life into ours without being aware of it. He'll say, 'Back home, we didn't do this,' or 'My dad didn't teach me this.' He's not giving explicit lessons on African values, and it's not name-the-country-capitals, but he does do it."

"We have taught them by example," Murtis concludes, after a long pause. There was no need to make a special point of this or that way of looking at the world being African. They simply lived and taught the boys their own values, which are, Murtis insists,

African values. What this means to Murtis is, in part, what she has been saying all along. The Grant-Acquahs, including Kwesi and Kweku, are an African family partly because Nana is Ghanaian, but also because they are a black family, part of a history in which black people have had to defend themselves on every front from white people.

Despite Murtis and Nana's different perception of race issues when they met, American racism has turned out to be something they understand similarly and fight against together. The Grant-Acquahs are especially animated when we talk about white American attitudes toward people of African descent. There are those things that Nana experiences because he was born in Africa: the continued discomfort of Americans, especially his patients now, with his name and his accent, the absolute ignorance of the vast majority of Americans about his home country. Once, he tells us, a teacher at a supposedly top-notch private school where the Grant-Acquahs sent their children for a time asked Nana, "Is it true that people in your country live in trees?"

More often, though, he talks about things he and his family have experienced because they are black. Nana tells the story, for example, of having police stake out his home, watching for drug deals, based on no other evidence of such goings on, apparently, than the Grant-Acquahs' expensive appurtenances, Nana's occasional late-night trips to the hospital, and his race. In short, Nana tells us, you can't have money if you're black without being suspected of dealing drugs.

.

Nana tells us that he didn't know, at first, how much this country was divided over race. He was too distant from the culture to understand the full meaning of the things he saw around him. He didn't understand the division into white and black because people in Ghana identify themselves according to language, ethnic group, or hometown, and Nana identified himself that way, too. What Nana doesn't say directly but which becomes clearer and clearer as we talk is that his perspective has changed somewhat. As a younger and less experienced man, Nana was not inclined to see the world as Murtis does — he did not perceive black people as certain allies. However, if the distinctions between Africans that Nana grew up with, the lines that separate black people across the globe by ethnicity, place of birth, and language, have not disappeared for Nana now, they have blurred a little. In the meantime, the line between white and black has emerged as one that has serious bearing on his life and the lives of his children and his wife.

If Nana seems Americanized, with his collection of cars and high-tech equipment, with his comfort in suburban America, he has become Americanized in this way, too: he perceives himself as living inside of the black-white dichotomy that monopolizes American thinking about race.

.

Despite what feels so distinctly American about the Grant-Aquahs' life, our reception at their house is categorically African. Even in the face of their busy schedule, the Grant-Acquahs give us not just their afternoon, it turns out, but their whole evening. During our interview, they are friendly, though sometimes reserved. The questions we ask are personal, and it is not particularly African or African American, they tell us, to divulge such information. Once we turn off the tape recorder, however, the conversation grows warmer and easier. They cook an elaborate and delicious meal for us, including chicken and fish and a Ghanaian corn porridge called Ka'Kay.

The house, too, we realize once the official interview is over and we have had the full tour, is more African than it seemed from the vantage point of the den. The living room, besides having large windows facing the river, is separated from the den and back hallway only by white latticework, and the ceiling is high. The openness created by this design recalls that built into the homes of many West African families who can afford the luxuries of space and thoughtful architecture. Walls in such homes are often white and the ceilings are as high as possible so that the hot air can rise to the top. Latticework, like that in the Grant-Acquahs' living room, is everywhere in West Africa, though not often made with wood. Lattices are an attractive way to give people privacy without restricting the air flow necessary for comfort. Standing in the couple's living room, we flash back to such open rooms we have visited in much hotter parts of the world than Milwaukee.

More important, there is beautiful African artwork everywhere in the house, on the walls, in corners, on shelves and tables. When we go out, Nana wears a jacket of handwoven and hand-dyed Malian cloth. Vibrant African batiks in reds, oranges, yellows, and browns adorn the walls, most of them depicting traditional aspects of African village life — the baobab tree, mother and infant, round West African houses.

We are impressed to learn that the Grant-Acquahs, and Murtis in particular, have a whole shop full of such pieces at the other end of Wauwautosa. Their store is located in a lovely building, a medium-sized late Victorian that the Grant-Acquahs have worked hard to restore. The outside is painted a dark cream with rose

{ *Black Is Black* }

trimmings and rails. The walls inside are all freshly painted, too, some of them with small leopard spots for accent.

We only notice the house itself, however, after our third or fourth inspection. At first, all we can see are the colors and shapes and textures filling every available space. One window seat spills over with colorful baskets, which are also stacked along the walls and hanging from the ceiling on either side of the window. In a corner we see musical instruments of every West African variety we know — from ballophones to percussive gourds and carved flutes. There are paintings, masks, carved tables, chairs, and walking sticks — mostly from Kenya — and carvings from all over West Africa.

The pieces in Murtis's store are both traditional and markedly creative, and all bear witness to a skillfully selective eye. Almost to an item, the pieces are without stray threads, paint smears, or slips of a tool made into awkward, last minute flourishes. We have also shopped in international marketplaces, trailed by persistent merchants whose wares we have passed by, faced by a wall of new merchants who have already begun the bargaining process before we have even registered what it is they are selling. Such markets contain an abundance of everyday beauty, but the kind of craftsmanship represented here is hard to find. The store has clearly been a labor of love for Murtis, and she has named it after her husband: Nana's Imported Arts and Textiles, LLC.

The Grant-Acquahs, as it happens, have invested quite a bit in Milwaukee. Their sons have grown up here. Their home, Nana's practice, and now this remarkable enterprise, Nana's boutique, are all here. Does this mean that Milwaukee is a particularly good place for their family to be? we ask them. Is it a good place to be an intercultural family? Murtis's answer to this question is unequivocal. Despite the different reputations of Mississippi and Wisconsin, Milwaukee is at least as hostile to people of color as any of its Southern counterparts, at least as ignorant about race. If Mississippi opened Murtis's eyes to racism, Wisconsin, she tells us, "made it a reality."

Besides, she adds, "It's boring." Murtis compares Milwaukee unfavorably to Miami, where the couple lived previously, and where the range of international people is much broader, the international communities more active and more visible. In Milwaukee, Murtis tells us, "You're missing out on so much. I don't think this city has much of an international community." There are some Germans, some Polish people, she tells us, but not many Africans at all.

"To me," she says, "when you have to go look for these races, I don't call it international."

Murtis misses the diversity of Miami, where she had "daily contact with people from China, Cuba, and India. Even if I never talk to the woman from India, let me see her, the way she's dressed, the way she carries herself. She's showing me her culture." Murtis also misses being in a multiracial city where she could sometimes escape a society divided, otherwise, so persistently into black and white.

Nana agrees with Murtis that Milwaukee is a less interesting place for an intercultural and international family to live. He doesn't suffer from the difference as much as Murtis does, however, because he is more "self-sufficient," but he definitely notices and is trying to do something to make Milwaukee life more interesting. He supports Murtis's business, which does its part to enrich the Milwaukee area, and he and Murtis are trying to make African music more available. They sell some African music at their

shop and hope to expand their collection, but they have also begun to discuss ways of bringing African singers and musicians to
Milwaukee for performances.

Nana and Murtis work to develop American interest in African
art and music as a natural expression of who they are, not as a way
of bolstering the African element of their identities. This is part of
what Murtis is telling us when she says, "Black is black." According to Murtis's way of thinking about things, their family does not
have to do anything to be African, they simply *are* African — tennis rackets, cell phones, and all — even while they are also American. After we have turned off the tape recorder and returned from
our tour of Milwaukee, Murtis tells us something about her philosophy. We all came from Africa originally, she reminds us, and
so, "We are all Africans."

Furthermore, she believes that the continent of Africa has
shaped world cultures much more than it is given credit for doing,
that a significant portion of what we value as Western culture actually made its way from ancient black Africa, through Egypt, to
early Europe. African spirituality, too, has a fundamental, universal nature, according to Murtis, capable of embracing, if not already a part of, spiritual practices from many different cultures.
On a second visit to Murtis, we see a flyer advertising a talk about
the connections between African and Celtic religions. Such a talk
is perfectly in keeping with Murtis's own spirituality, which is si-
multaneously hybrid — always considering what is best in the religions she encounters — and fundamentally African.

We talk about African spirituality for a long time during the
evening after our interview, our stomachs full and our tape recorders packed away. We also talk about the ancient empires of Ghana
and Songhay, about the impressive libraries and universities in the

ancient kingdom of Mali. We try to imagine the gold-laden camels of Mansa Musa crossing the desert from Timbuktu to Mecca, to picture the Timbuktu from which he started, the object of so much fascination on the part of Europeans and guarded so fiercely by Africans. Sitting here in suburban Milwaukee, where a teacher can ask if Africans live in trees, where people learn almost nothing about the continent of Africa in school, and almost no one has even heard of the great Mansa Musa, it is difficult to bring that place into view.

Threaded through all of our discussions are Kwesi and Kweku's phone calls or trips through the house. At some point in the evening we ask the young men if they think they will ever go back to Ghana.

"Oh yes," they both tell us despite the negative reports they had given us earlier. Kwesi says he would like to spend a year studying in Ghana, and he would like to learn at least one West African language. He's sure he could appreciate West Africa better now — because, he says, "I wasn't as open-minded three years ago." His goal is to be a physician like his father, and West Africa is one of the places he sees in his future.

Convergence

VILMA & TOM

Tom, Vilma, & Zoe. Photo by Jessie Grearson.

When we ask Vilma Seeberg what was most difficult about moving, at twelve, from her childhood home of Hamburg, West Germany, to Washington, D.C., we are not surprised that she tells us it was culture shock, but we are interested to learn that the source of her discomfort had little to do with the challenges people typically name — like language or climate. "The first thing that registered with me was that girls here were wearing bras. I was a girl, not a woman in any sense of the word, but I had to make a real quick shift from being a person who happens to be a girl, to being a young woman with boys around and dating — all that creepy stuff. Everyone had autograph books at the time, and I remember making a million *faux pas* because everything had a connotation I wasn't aware of." She shakes her head at the memory and turns to look at her own baby daughter. "Germans wouldn't think of turning preadolescent girls into Barbie-doll types."

We can't imagine Vilma ever trying to fit in with the Barbie and Ken crowd, but we are meeting her some thirty-odd years later, and the distance between the little German girl looking with dismay at her American counterparts and the woman who sits across from us now is vast. This Vilma lives with her partner, Tom Jacobs, and their recently adopted daughter, Zoe, at their home in historic Shaker Heights, just outside of Cleveland. This woman — with her short, slightly funky hairstyle and lively, intelligent eyes — radiates a peaceful self-confidence that puts those around her at ease.

We sit on a comfortable leather couch in the couple's living room, a haven from the hubbub of airports and hotel lobbies. The room is long, and the pleasantly worn furniture in it is arranged in enclaves that encourage conversation. Books on art and music are stacked on the coffee table; on a nearby mantelpiece, contemporary authors compete for space with colorful children's stories — and even the air seems scented with books and the smell of smoke from an old fire. The bay window area where we sit is ringed with the living green of plants. While she talks with us, Vilma reaches back and deftly trims a drying leaf from a bamboo tree.

Vilma is at once relaxed and poised; she answers our questions so quickly and precisely that it seems she's been expecting them, and is equally ready to laugh at a joke or to make a playful quip of her own. In contrast, Tom's long pauses before he answers our questions are disconcerting at first, but he responds thoughtfully, and his voice is pleasing and sophisticated. He looks sophisticated too, we think, with his graying hair and glasses, introspective eyes, eloquent piano player's hands. His worldliness is amicable, as though he has met and befriended many people from different places and is prepared to like us as well. Vilma and Tom seem particularly in tune with one another and deeply compatible, although we rarely talk to them at the same time and our conversation occurs in shifts.

In fact, it took Vilma and Tom many years following different but parallel paths to arrive at this peaceful place together. Vilma came to the United States in 1960 when her father, who worked in the film industry, took a job in Washington, D.C., and the family followed him. It wasn't necessarily easy for a German family to move to the postwar United States — Americans were openly hostile to Germans, all Germans, regardless of the role their families had played in World War II. "Oh, there were all the jokes about Germans wearing boots and the Nazis, not seriously mean stuff, just high school ignorance." Vilma is dismissive of these early difficulties, has to think hard to remember them at all. She focuses instead on the excitement of a new life in a country poised for change. Vilma remembers Martin Luther King's 1963 March on Washington; the excitement of the sixties was one her whole family participated in. "Kennedy had just been elected, which was for my family . . . well, maybe there's hope for the world. Postwar Germany was rather a depressing place."

By the time she was in high school, Vilma had already become active in the politics of her new country. She'd worked hard to perfect her English, to banish her German accent, and was eventually elected to the student government, aided by a self-confidence she credits to growing up a girl in Germany. Inspired by King and the Civil Rights movement, as well as some supportive faculty members, Vilma helped to integrate her school government with that of a nearby black high school. That was just the beginning of a long career of political activism.

Vilma traces her attraction to the politics afoot in the sixties back to her childhood in postwar Germany. Vilma's grandmother was Jewish, and her husband's family, which had needed to pull together to protect her during the Nazi regime, had been deeply politicized by the war. She remembers hearing story after story about Jewish family friends — who survived and who didn't. Her grandmother was "hidden on paper," a feat the family managed partly by moving from place to place. "Sooner or later, the paperwork would catch up to them, so they were always on the run." Though Vilma thinks her grandfather's war stories, in which he often played the part of the hero, were sometimes exaggerated, he nevertheless served as an important role model for her. "He showed me, from small on, that I could do something just in ordinary life."

While Vilma's family remained in Hamburg, furthermore, they

lived as refugees — sharing a house with distant relatives and friends of the family, most of whom were living in similar circumstances. "It was a big house, and every bedroom had refugees in it. They all told stories, and they all pulled together. Then the Iron Curtain came down, and some people who escaped across were put up for awhile. So I got that whole sense of family — as keeping together and bringing in friends and helping each other out." These relationships and experiences, Vilma tells us, helped her appreciate the historical changes taking place in the United States. Her memories from this refugee household also laid the foundation for some of Vilma's most basic values, particularly her belief in "the necessity of acting in the world for some kind of moral purpose."

When the company Mr. Seeberg worked for relocated in 1966 and the family moved back to Germany, Vilma was already in college at the University of Wisconsin at Madison and decided to stay behind to act on those beliefs. "It was too exciting a time to leave," she says. Although Vilma stops short of describing herself as a hippie, she was involved in campus politics in a variety of ways. She was, for example, part of Students for a Democratic Society, attending meetings and protests. She believed in the politics of SDS, but says she is "not a joiner" and also objected from the beginning to "the men preening up front, handing each other the microphones back and forth. When even the lefties kept going with that crap, I just thought 'ehhh,'" she says, making a gagging sound.

"It was about getting girls," adds Tom, cynically. "It wasn't always about a cause, it was about getting over."

"Yeah, that was part of it, too," Vilma agrees. Though somewhat disillusioned about SDS, Vilma nevertheless remained committed to the social activism of the decade. After graduating from college in 1970, in fact, Vilma went on to give the next eight years of her life to an alternative community called Freedom House. Freedom House, one of many community-based cooperatives, began as a drop-in education center for runaways. Vilma began teaching in the drop-in center, though she had not initially intended to go into education at all, and her first attempt — "I went from a college rebel to student teacher at a suburban high school" — made her question the vocation.

But Vilma was attracted to Freedom House, began working there, and "pretty much took over the place." Her vision and hard work transformed the drop-in center, though she is too modest to tell us this, and we wouldn't have known at all if Tom had not prompted us to ask the right questions. From the beginning, Vilma wanted to make the center, which had served a primarily white community, more multiracial, and she wanted to transform it from a drop-in center to a school. "And that's pretty much what we did," she says succinctly. "We bought an old Baptist church. It was wonderful." By the end of Vilma's years at Freedom House, however, she was spending all her time writing grants to keep the school afloat, an already difficult task that became more so at the dawn of the Reagan era, when many poverty programs were cut. Finally, Vilma decided to move on, though not before she felt she had brought Freedom House to a place that ensured its longevity. "It just wasn't fun anymore," she says, but this statement covers over the exhaustion that keeping the school running had caused her. "I went through my twenties at a pretty rigorous pace," she finally admits. "I burned up a whole lot of gray cells I wish I had now."

In part, her burnout was caused by working so intensely with the students who called themselves "throwaway kids," many of

whom were all but doomed from the start. One family she remembers as emblematic of the pain these young people went
through, and the pain of working with them. "There were three
kids, two of them with us, and the mother was on drugs. The
youngest one was twelve. He was a pyromaniac — wild and very
smart. Finally, he died in a car crash. Life was an accident, for him,
and he made a lot of them happen." She is silent for a moment,
remembering.

"It was so rough just keeping those children alive," she continues, but Freedom House had its successes, too. "Another family
had five sons, two or three of which were always involved in petty
thefts. There was alcoholism in the family — that was their problem. One of them I'm still in touch with today. We dragged David
through the school and made him graduate. He joined AA and got
off alcohol ten or fifteen years later, and he's living in California as
an insurance salesman. One of his brothers became a monk in
some order that is delivering wheelchairs to Honduras." When we
ask Vilma if she thinks that Freedom House was the reason for
this boy's success, she says yes without hesitation.

·

Tom Jacobs grew up an outsider to mainstream American culture
for an entirely different reason. He was raised in an African American community in Columbus, Ohio, a community so complete
unto itself that Tom had little experience with white people before
he graduated from high school. Tom's father, on the other hand,
Thomas Jacobs, Sr., was one of a very few African American professionals of the time who managed to succeed and advance in a
white world. "My father was the first African American — or, at
the time, 'colored person' — hired in a white-collar job in the city
of Columbus. This was 1949. He was a draftsman and worked for

the city planning commission." Tom admires his father for surviving in his profession when all the cards were stacked against him. "One of my regrets is that by the time I understood how special my father was, and really wanted to sit down and talk to him, I had lost him. It would have been such a tremendous benefit to me to talk with him as I began my career. He was the only black professional I knew who worked in an integrated world — the black professionals that you found at that time dealt with black clientele only. My father worked with both."

His father was handsome and tall, well-spoken, "someone you noticed when he came in the room." He was also shrewd — well and practically educated. "My father was in city planning before it was even a discipline. Took courses in Montreal, Boston, all over, because you couldn't just get those courses anywhere." But it is his father's honesty that Tom most credits for his remarkable success. "As the city planner, every building in the city of Columbus came across his desk. He would tell me the story of how often envelopes were laid on his desk because it was just assumed that he'd take the money. I think that was one of the reasons he did survive. Because he was so ethical."

Success did not distance Tom, Sr., from the black community. Instead, he moved between the two worlds he inhabited with grace. "He never forgot where he came from — he could talk to the guys on the block as though he still lived there, and he never viewed himself as being above anybody." In fact, the African American world that Tom, Sr., knew was vital, exciting, and he had an appreciation for it that he passed on to his son. "You have to understand about black America at that time," Tom explains. It had its own culture, and there were thriving businesses and pubs and activities. "When entertainers came, when Duke Ellington came to Columbus, for example, he couldn't stay in downtown. It wasn't allowed, even in the midfifties, because of segregation. He had to stay out in the neighborhood, so consequently there was a much tighter community." And Tom's father knew many luminaries. In particular, he was close friends with Lionel Hampton, who stayed, with his wife, Gladys, in the Jacobs' home whenever he was in town.

Even though the Civil Rights movement was still in its most nascent phases, Tom never considered his options limited or his life circumscribed by racism — or anything else. "I don't think I even had a sense of being different until the early sixties." Part of Tom's feelings of security and possibility had to do with growing up in Columbus, Ohio — in the Midwest — rather than in one of the more oppressive Southern states; when he first experienced the most blatant kind of racism, it was on a trip South. "Segregation certainly existed in some parts — but I don't remember not being able to go places when I was growing up. My first conscious memory of segregation was in the early sixties. We were in Cincinnati and we went over into Kentucky. There was some place we stopped, and they wouldn't serve us. That was very strange to me. And because the Civil Rights movement really picked up in '61–'62, I did not suffer like folks did in the South."

Tom was also protected from the embattled life of many of his peers partly by his community, which lived out its separation from white society with a vitality that belied the disadvantages of segregation. Tom's mostly black high school was, he says, "wonderful," the site of some of his best memories. "East High instilled a tremendous amount of pride in its students," and was well known for producing brilliant athletes, though it also counted many formidable scholars among its student body.

Not until Tom went away to college at Denison University, a small, competitive private school about thirty-five minutes away from Columbus, he tells us, did he really feel like a minority. Attending Denison was a difficult choice for many reasons, not least of which were financial. The entire sum that his parents had saved for his schooling, enough for four years at a public institution, would only get him through a year at Denison. Nevertheless, Tom felt that he would get a better education there, have better opportunities with a degree from the private school — and so he managed, on work-study scholarships and loans, which it took him ten years to repay.

Tom and his best friend were the first two blacks from Columbus ever to be admitted to Denison, and they were two out of only thirteen on the entire campus. "It was culture shock," says Tom, echoing Vilma. "I went from a very comfortable community where I basically didn't have any problems to a town that had three thousand white people." He corrects himself. "No, it had 2,996 white people, of which 2,990 were conservative Republicans. We were oddities, more than anything else." It wasn't easy; all eyes were on him and the other twelve black students — sometimes quite literally. The first time Tom took a shower in the dormitory, he tells us, he had an audience. "All of a sudden there's like ten guys in there. They're dressed! I thought, what the hell is this? I think they wanted to see if the myth was true. I'm sure they were sadly disappointed," he finishes, laughing.

"No comment!" Vilma calls from across the room, where she is playing with their daughter and listening to Tom tell his story.

On another occasion, Tom's roommate confessed to him that he'd "never seen another black person" other than his maid. This sort of thing Tom talks about tolerantly. As surprising and irritating as such incidents may have been, they felt benign to him, just curiosity or benevolent ignorance. Another incident Tom remembers from his freshman year, however, was less benevolent, its effects longer lasting. He had been working in the cafeteria, as most work-study students did, when a fraternity boy called him over to his table, saying "Hey boy, come over here and clean my table." Tom took the tray, dumped it in the young man's lap, and said, "Bus your own damn table." Tom was enraged, and he has never forgotten that moment; his voice rises as he talks. "I turned around and walked out, never went back. And I never bused another damn table in my life after that. I view myself in a certain way, and I act accordingly. You will treat me the way I want to be treated. I demand that," says Tom, his anger pulling him off topic, "and my ego and my arrogance — "

"He's getting better, though," Vilma interrupts him, and when Tom continues, his voice is quieter, returning to its easygoing, conversational pitch.

"In my old age, I've mellowed out," he agrees. "But I think that attitude helped me in my television career, though, a very tough and competitive area — in which I was often the first or the only black person doing what I did."

His experience at Denison also launched him into political activism. "I was there doing it all, black power, the whole ball of wax." Although he was not part of any of the better-known Civil Rights or Black Power organizations of the sixties — "I'm like Vilma; I'm not a joiner" — he helped organize a black student union and several strikes. He and the other black students at Denison also decided that the university's black student population should be increased, so they started a student-run minority recruiting program, which Tom designed and operated — a first of its kind. "When I was nineteen years old, I had my own office and was in charge of a program that had sixty students working with it. We traveled all over the country going to high schools, recruiting for our university." He laughs, "It was great being black in the sixties because white folks felt real guilty."

"And had money," Vilma adds from her station across the room.

"And they'd give it to you to do anything," Tom finishes. Despite the support his activism received from the university, Tom too eventually "burned out." It was partly the frenetic pace he'd been keeping up during his college years. Also, however, the deaths of Martin Luther King, Malcolm X, and the Kennedy brothers disillusioned and disheartened him. "Everybody remembers where they were when JFK was killed. I remember where I was when Martin Luther King was killed. I was home on spring break, driving down Broad Street in Columbus to pick my brother up from music lessons, and I remember pulling over — " here he breaks off, looks out the window before resuming. "It was not a good time. When Bobby Kennedy was killed, I was very much into politics, but the death of King and Kennedy resolved the problem of political involvement. I decided I would express myself through — well, *not* through politics."

Tom's career in television began almost by accident, as he tells it. His father had died during Tom's final year at college, and he felt he needed to start looking for work, someplace close to home, near his mother, who was deeply mourning the loss of her husband. He thought he would be a history teacher, but in the early seventies "there were plane tickets to Vietnam, but no jobs for history teachers." A Denison connection encouraged him to apply for an opening as floor director at a local television station, a job he would not have obtained, he thinks, without the clout of being a Denison student. In any case, he was hired on the spot to work from four o'clock to midnight. "It just seemed right," Tom reflects.

Once Tom knew that he wanted to be in television, he began a steady ascent that found him, eventually, anchoring a news program. This ambition satisfied, Tom set his cap for a management position, even though blacks had only just made it in the door as journalists at the end of the sixties, and such assignments were made primarily to investigate riots white journalists were afraid to cover. Tom was successful as a manager, too, and by the late eighties he was at the top of his profession, with the reputation, the paycheck, and the lifestyle to go along with it.

•

In the summer of 1974, when the demands of Freedom House threatened to engulf her, Vilma decided to learn Chinese as a kind of diversion. When we laugh at Vilma's idea of a break, she explains, "It gave me something I could sink my teeth into, distance from the everyday harshness of trying to solve those kids' problems." But after leaving Freedom House at the end of 1978, Vilma was at a loss for what to do, so she returned to Germany where her parents busied themselves trying to "line up a reputable career" for her.

She enrolled in graduate school in Hamburg — a compromise, she explains, between her parents' desire to find her a career and her own intention to eventually go to China. "We'd all suffered from a great infusion of propaganda about how great China was at educating the masses — one of their big headlines over there was 'Mass Literacy,'" she says, explaining the attraction. Only a few weeks later, in the first days of the new year, Vilma received a call from her "old Freedom House buddies," who told her that the Chinese embassy had called in response to an application she'd sent years earlier. Vilma was offered a job teaching in Hefei, Anhui Province, and she accepted it, making her one of the first Americans to live in China after the border opened up in the late seventies.

Unfortunately, Vilma's experience in China was, in many ways, tremendously disappointing. Sixties leftists in the United States had idealized Maoist socialism, looking to China for a viable alternative to Russian socialism on the one hand and a voraciously expansionist American capitalism on the other. Vilma had been especially looking forward to seeing Chinese education in action. Instead of an exciting, egalitarian society, however, she found poverty and stories about the abuses of state government. At Freedom House, Vilma had worked with poor families, but the poverty she saw there was never as pervasive and unmitigated as what she saw in China. "I learned how bitter poverty can be, how bitter it makes people, how it isn't something quaint or anything to romanticize. The monotony of daily life there was just outrageous. I read *Scientific American* from cover to cover — just for something different. Never done it since."

Perhaps even more disillusioning were the secrecy and paranoia that came in the wake of the Cultural Revolution. "I think the first moment when I realized things were not as they had seemed was when one of the older faculty members in the department took me aside and said, 'You have to be very careful about what you say around here.'" When Vilma expressed her confusion, that she had no idea what might or might not be appropriate to say, her colleague simply replied, "Just don't say anything beyond the absolutely necessary." She also encountered a rigid adherence to rules that was sometimes ludicrous in practice. Vilma tells us how she — a petite woman of medium height — had to be taken to the tailor's "because I couldn't buy anything in the right size since I was too big. And even at the tailor's you had a choice of three pant sizes — that's it! They didn't measure, they had only three lengths. I was told that Madame Mao had personally set the length of pants."

Worst of all were the families torn apart by the Cultural Revolution. One couple that Vilma worked with had been denounced by their daughter and spent years in a labor camp, separated from their child, whom they saw as a victim of the situation. The parents were hurt and chronically ill because of their experience at the labor camp, but for Vilma the most wrenching part of the story was their uncertainty about how their daughter would cope with what had happened, whether or not she "would be friendly with them" when they saw her again.

Despite her disillusionment, there is much about Vilma's experience in China that has shaped her life in valuable ways. When we ask her about this, Vilma makes an eloquent, encircling sweep with her arms, referring to the Chinese wall-hangings and artwork she has everywhere in her house, the books on Chinese education — before closing them around her small daughter, who stands between her knees. "This little one — I don't think I would have adopted a baby from China if it hadn't been for the time I spent there. I don't think it would have occurred to me." Vilma, who is fluent in Chinese, speaks the language with Zoe as often as possible.

Her way of seeing the world changed, too. For one thing, the culture shock she experienced as an immigrant to the United States was just a fraction of what she experienced when she went to China. "I didn't *know* culture shock until I tried China. I remember driving down a street and thinking, now, I know that's a building. I can tell it's a building — but I have no clue what its function is." That cultures could be so different from each other, that people could be so different, was a revelation to Vilma — though again, not always bad news. She deeply appreciates the Chinese vision of loyalty and friendship, for example. "If you are a friend, you are a lifelong friend and there's no doubt about that." What's more, even in that context of deprivation, friendship meant "an exchange of resources — it could mean something material, or it could be whatever you need."

Also, Vilma's vision of the world, particularly her political vision, was transformed by her stay in China. Before China, Vilma had been more impressed, more influenced, by political ideas and philosophies. She describes herself as having had a penchant for "lefty political discourse" that she lost her taste for after her trip to China. "I had all kinds of things to explain to people, but I stopped. Because the reality was so overwhelming. So you talk about imperialism, but how can one word express what the people are going through — people who don't have anything to burn to heat their food with?" After a while, Vilma, who finished her dissertation on literacy in China and eventually became a professor specializing in international education at Kent State University, began to talk, to teach again. "But," she tells us, "after China, I stopped proclaiming."

.

After Vilma returned from China, Vilma and Tom's lives resumed their parallel courses. Over the span of the next five years, Vilma finished her Ph.D., worked for the World Bank, fell in love, married, gained stepchildren. Tom moved from place to place and position to position to arrive, finally, at the top of his profession, able to pick and choose between jobs and locations. Tom, too, had fallen in love, married, and adopted a daughter.

Vilma does not talk about her marriage at great length, and when she does, she looks and sounds uncharacteristically spent, both physically and emotionally. Her former husband, she tells us, an African American man who had worked in the sales end of the television industry, had been fired in 1987. He filed suit against the company with the Equal Employment Opportunities Commission, a suit that he eventually won. When Vilma tells us this, she uses her hands to make quotes around the word "won," however, to show how much was really lost, since the money did not come through until her former husband's life had fallen apart. "He got involved with some less desirable elements, mixed up in a money-laundering scheme that was an FBI sting operation — just once — but he had a court trial and went to jail," Vilma says simply, though of course the story is more complicated than that. The company against which he had filed suit slandered him, filed countersuits against the company he created after losing his job, essentially denied him his livelihood, and drove him to desperation. "He just couldn't stand up under the pressure," says Vilma. She stayed with her former husband through the trial and some years of jail time ("that's what families do," she tells us steadily) but because his desperation turned violent, she finally left him.

In the early nineties, Tom met with a remarkably similar series of calamities. A floundering station had hired him to pull it out of trouble, and he did the job with such success that he became interested in staying there long-term. When the news director's job came open, Tom applied, lost the position to a less-qualified candidate, and filed a complaint with the EEOC. Tom also eventually "won" his case, but not until after a series of anguishing losses. The station he had sued slandered him and pushed the bank to recall his loans, cutting him off from his profession, ruining his credit, souring his view of the world, and undermining his self-confidence. Tom's own marriage, already stressed by extreme changes in lifestyle, could not survive the bitterness, however understandable, that came in the wake of the suit. "Let's just say I wasn't exactly easy to live with during this time in my life," he tells us. As if all this were not enough, Tom lost his mother and was struggling with an unacknowledged depression. "I had reached a personal and professional low. I was so far down I had to look up to see the bottom."

·

Vilma saw Tom for the first time over the New Year holiday in 1995. He was walking across a parking lot in Tampa, Florida, and in retrospect Vilma thinks of it as a portentous moment, the background "like a movie setting," with sailboat masts and Tom's beautiful apartment building — an old Moorish-style Spanish hotel that had been converted into permanent dwellings. At one point during our visit, when we are touring the house, Tom pauses on the landing, shows us a photograph of this view, sailboats resting in a harbor, a sunset, all that he gave up to be with Vilma. "If that isn't love," he tells us, "I don't know what is." Later, when we refer to this sacrifice of "Tom's boats," Vilma gently corrects us. "Well, he gave up his *view* of the boats, let's be clear about this. Still, it was love, I think."

Tom was the friend of a friend Vilma was visiting over the holidays. The three went to a party together, but Vilma found herself focusing on Tom. She liked his demeanor and was taken with his straightforward kindness. The next day, the two had lunch together, and Vilma remembers being pleasantly struck by the way Tom ordered his meal. "We went to a Cuban vegetarian restaurant and what got me was how, when I ordered, he said, 'I'll have the same thing she's having.' First, that he listened, and second that he wasn't afraid to admit it."

Later, they attended a New Year's Eve party together. "We mostly talked," says Vilma. "The rest of the party was all big hairs and people in chic dresses and high heels. You started talking about your work and telling me about the black circus," she turns to address Tom, remembering. "Then we started talking about seventies music, and that was it, that sealed the pact."

"We're Otis Redding fans, Motown, Aretha Franklin, Temptations, Isaac Hayes," says Tom, running through a list of the music they bonded over.

"No," says Vilma when Tom gets to Isaac Hayes. "That's your music."

"We both like jazz, too," Tom adds, "though she's more into the saxophone and I'm more into the piano, because I played."

But both were still healing from their broken marriages, and neither was ready for a new relationship, as far as they knew. "Bayshore Boulevard in Tampa Bay is the longest continuous sidewalk in the country, twelve miles," says Tom. "To tell you where my head was at, Christmas Day I walked it from one end to the other and back. People were not where I wanted to be."

"And I was still pretty injured, too," Vilma adds. "We had both been in relationships that weren't too happy. We had that in common."

Despite their mutual wariness, Vilma and Tom ended up spending most of the next few days together, and their weeklong fling quickly developed into something else. They visited each other, and Tom often phoned Vilma first thing in the morning. She is not an early riser, he says emphatically. "I'd go out for a walk at sunrise, and then I'd call her — 'arrgh,'" he says, imitating Vilma's voice at dawn. "To this day I have no idea what she was saying. I'm surprised she even remembers me calling, because she was out of it most of the time."

Although the connection was strong and loving from the beginning, the couple didn't know exactly what to do about it for a while. Vilma wanted a family life, not just a work life, and was unsure whether Tom, who was so consumed by his work, was sufficiently "balanced" in his perspective to be the kind of partner she sought. For his part, Tom didn't feel ready to make a commitment, particularly one that involved leaving his beautiful Florida apartment. "When I came to visit, the house just felt very comfortable. The dogs were terrific — I took to them, they took to me. But the relationship was still just . . . we had a good time, I was comfortable, but I lived in Florida. She heard this a lot. 'I live in Florida.'"

The matter was resolved in 1996, when Vilma went to China on sabbatical. While continuing to insist that he "lived in Florida," Tom volunteered to house-sit for Vilma while she was away, since a project he'd been planning to work on had fallen through. He also came up a week early to help her get ready for her trip.

"I'd never experienced anything like that," says Vilma about the care he took helping her. "I was just basking in it. Even my mother hadn't been that helpful."

Still, Tom didn't admit the depth of his feelings for Vilma until she had left for China. "She was gone less than a week, and I really missed her. I was not used to missing anybody. I'd gotten myself to the point where I was used to being alone without being lonely. All of a sudden, she was gone, and I was really lonely. I gotta tell you, if the dogs hadn't been there I'da probly — "

"Cried everyday," Vilma finishes for him, jauntily, though when Tom continues, his voice is serious.

"I believe things happen for a reason, and I don't really question what those reasons are. I've learned that if it's working, don't screw around with it. I reconnected with my faith. I was never terribly religious, but there's a faith I have in the higher power, and I knew that since I had been with her my life was better," says Tom. "In my previous relationship there were some real good highs, but there were some real lows — and suddenly I'm in the kind of relationship I always wanted."

Finally, Vilma had to come home early from China, sick. Tom took charge of the transportation, complicated when it involves China. One important flight had been canceled and Vilma, already suffering, got caught first in Europe and then in Pittsburgh, where a flight was canceled. "I said, 'fine, I will drive there and pick you up.' So I drove from Columbus to Pittsburgh — it was 12:30 in the morning when I got there, and the terminal was empty. I got to the gate and she's not there. Finally I saw her; she'd been in the bathroom. At that point, I knew I would stay in Cleveland and work." And so he did, picking up freelance writing for newspapers and media journals with a surprising ease, keeping his beautiful Florida apartment for nine more months, and then, finally, letting that go, too.

.

At one point, Vilma is talking with us about Tom's EEOC case, about the vicious maneuver of recalling Tom's loans, and the train wreck that made of his life. We are shaking our heads, feeling glum about Tom's suffering, then about the prospects of our own loved ones should they face similar discrimination. It is at this moment that Tom appears in our range of vision. He is returning from a walk with the dogs on one side and Zoe, dragging two empty leashes, on the other, the whole party moving along the sidewalk in front of the house with a happy energy. Zoe is the center point of the picture they make — the sun shining on her glossy cap of black hair, her cheeks pink with exercise, round face tilted up toward Tom, and then back toward the house.

This panorama would not be complete without Zoe, of whom Vilma has been dreaming, for whom she has been working and planning for many years. During her first marriage, Vilma says, she wanted a child but her husband resisted. "*He* wanted to be the child," Vilma says briefly. That the hoped-for baby had never come was one of the sources of her deep sadness when the marriage ended. In 1994, Vilma began trying for an American adoption, but most possibilities would have been cross-racial, a match the county welfare agencies strenuously resisted. In 1995, Vilma filled out adoption papers for a Chinese baby, and in the fall of 1998, she received a picture of Zoe.

Once he'd committed to his relationship with Vilma, Tom was equally committed to Zoe. In October 1998, he accompanied Vilma to China to pick Zoe up. It was not an easy trip. The travel to China was itself exhausting, but after that, there was paperwork and obfuscation. The time for meeting the children, furthermore, was put off by a day, a long time for anxious parents. Finally, they were bused from their hotels in Nanjing to the provincial welfare department where they would pick up the children. Though a terribly important event for the semicircle of adoptive parents waiting to receive a child, the moment was utterly inauspicious. The children were carried by their social workers to the dreary parking lot where their parents had been told to wait, handed over without ceremony, and, after interminable paperwork, bused with their parents to a hotel in yet another city.

Zoe (whose Chinese name is Su Guan-lan) wailed during the transfer. "A good sign," says Vilma. A baby who did not wail probably had nothing to lose, a potential inability to bond, and likely emotional disabilities to overcome. Zoe, who cried for three days, clearly did not have such disabilities; interestingly, it was only Tom who could calm her.

Even Tom's first few days with Zoe, however, were not without incident. Once, Tom tells us, Vilma had left their Beijing hotel to take a break from the difficult adjustment mother and daughter were still making. Tom had put Zoe safely, he presumed, in her crib, but when he went to check on her, he found an open window and a missing baby. He laughs now at his own terror, but we can imagine his horrified surprise. Tom looked everywhere, even out the window, but saw no sign of Zoe. "All the while I'm panicking and thinking, 'How'm I gonna tell Vilma I lost her baby?'" It turned out that the crib had been designed with a kind of false bottom and that Zoe, in her thrashing and crying, had gotten underneath the mattress and fallen soundly asleep.

Tom and Vilma stayed in China for two weeks, and, by the time they left, Zoe had made a qualified adjustment to Vilma, but there was still a difficult journey ahead. On the way from Hong Kong to Seoul, Seoul to Chicago, in an airplane crammed full of passengers, Vilma became violently ill. She made her way, as quickly as possible, toward the bathroom, but there was a long line. Instead of making room for her at the head of it, however, the Korean passengers simply turned their heads away — so Vilma could "save face" while she vomited in the aisle.

We have not, Vilma says, gotten to see the best of Zoe, who has been ill during our visit, and less energetic and talkative than she would normally be. She is quiet, but we can see how loving she is, how she turns to her each of her parents with arms outstretched. Her toys and books she has happily carried to every quarter of the house. In fact, it is hard for us to believe that this child — so obviously at home, so rooted here — joined the family only months before. But then it is equally hard for us to imagine, with the dogs snoring on the hearth next to us, that even Tom and Vilma's paths converged somewhat recently. She is lucky to have you, we tell Vilma and Tom. "We are the lucky ones," says Vilma.

Unveiled

SHIRLEE

Shirlee. Photo by Christy Mock.

Our first impression of Shirlee Taraki is one of energy: a petite woman with light brown eyes below a fringe of straight gray bangs, Shirlee swings open the door of her apartment immediately on our arrival and welcomes us in briskly, as though there is little time to waste. She begins telling us important stories long before we have had time to unpack our tape recorders. Our tour begins with a wall covered in a mosaic of art and photographs of or by women — some artists we recognize, some Shirlee introduces us to. "This is my wall of women," she states, with a sweep of her arm. It is a tribute that we will come to appreciate more fully as we learn about Shirlee's life.

Just by being in this apartment, which is also full of books, photographs, and international objects that Shirlee has collected or received as gifts, we learn something about her vitality and internationalism. We turn from paintings to admire handwoven rugs, draw a finger across Shirlee's collection of boxes from different countries, before we finally stop at a series of sepia photographs in wooden frames on her bedroom wall. In these pictures we glimpse Shirlee's own face in the angle of a relative's cheekbone, the distinctive shape of someone's dark eyes.

Shirlee's parents were the children of Jewish immigrants in Chicago, her father from a German-speaking Hungarian family that perceived itself to be part of a very different class, and world, from that of Shirlee's mother's family, who were Yiddish-speaking eastern Europeans. It is difficult for us to see past the yellow tint of the family photographs, the old-fashioned clothes, and solemn poses to any differences between them. Shirlee, however, can see more than we can about the divergent histories and cultures recorded in those photographs, things that would have appeared as even starker contrasts to her parents. Shirlee, in short, was the product of differences from the very beginning.

And she grew up in Chicago, a city pieced together from immigrant groups. It was a time before life in the city necessarily meant dangers a family wouldn't find elsewhere, when people did not sequester themselves in their own homes and neighborhoods out of fear, and Shirlee and her siblings had the freedom to explore the city, including all the different neighborhoods with their various cultures and peoples. "We could take the train here and there — we went to the Chicago World's Fair alone when I was only twelve! When I think of all the things we got to see and do, well it was a wonderful time for us."

Chicago's internationalism affected Shirlee's life even more deeply when she attended college at the University of Chicago. It wasn't necessarily the norm for families of Shirlee's generation to send their daughters off for serious university educations, but education was important to Shirlee's family, and to Shirlee herself. She enrolled at the University of Chicago, majoring in psychology, and she was drawn, almost immediately, to the exciting world of the university's international community. Part of Shirlee's attraction to this world had to do with her own membership in an immigrant community with distinctly international concerns and loyalties. Another part of her interest was intellectual. Her studies in anthropology and psychology deepened her interest in other cultures, and listening to the international students' stories and descriptions of their homes gave her firsthand information, the kind she could not get from textbooks. Many of the international students were freethinkers, some of them serious intellectuals with big dreams about what they might do when they returned to their homelands. They formed a vibrant and intelligent group, and Shirlee enjoyed her conversations with them.

In her last quarter at the university, Shirlee took a room on campus at the University of Chicago. It became the high point of her college life, giving her a freedom that must have been sweet to her. "I wanted to do my comps, but I also really wanted to feel what it was like to live on campus. I'd been living at home and commuting all those years." Now Shirlee was able to be part of the thriving extracurricular life on campus. It was during this time that she met two men from Afghanistan in a graduate-level statistics class, Abdul and Mir. The men were two of five chosen by their country to come to the United States to obtain degrees in education. Shirlee became friends with these men and began attending Sunday afternoon teas with them at a place called the International House, where people from all over the world came to discuss world events.

When we see the pictures and hear the stories about this time in Shirlee's life, we can understand the excitement she must have felt. It is 1943, and the black-and-white photos — partly because of what Shirlee tells us — are imbued with romantic overtones. There are pictures of Shirlee's college friends in clothes and hairstyles we recognize from old movies we love. The young people we see are attractive and confident-looking in their gray suits and dresses with sharply padded shoulders. Shirlee tells us a little of each person's story, and we are surprised at what we hear — about late-night dinner parties and candlelit dances held after the clubs have closed, about couples who lived together before marriage or without ever marrying at all. We are surprised that students of that time — especially women students — would be so adventurous. "Oh, it was an atmosphere of so much freedom, very bohemian, with the men and women coming and going."

Shirlee found herself particularly drawn to one of the young men from Afghanistan: Mohamed Taraki. "I was studying psychology, and I remember that when I met him we had a little argument about Freud at the tea table at the International House. It was October 1943; we met on Halloween, or the day after. Later on we did a lot of stuff together. We'd go to dances — we won a prize for the waltz because he was a great dancer! Oh, he was great at the tango, too."

When we ask Shirlee when she knew for sure that their friendship had turned into romance, she smiles indulgently at us. "OK, all right, you want to know about the courtship. I think it started at Paul's house. Paul was an older man from Algeria who was always floating around that campus. Anyway, he had an apartment under a popular restaurant, the Tropical Hut. He was always inviting people to come to his house; he'd put on music and candles and make it very romantic there. That kind of cemented the thing."

Their courtship occurred mostly on weekends, since Mohamed was in Evanston and Shirlee in Chicago, though he did finally move closer, to Hyde Park. "Unlike some of the other girls, I did not move in with him, though," she states firmly. "That would have killed my parents. I went back home, and I took a job at the University of Chicago. And somewhere along the way, I decided to marry him. He wanted me to go back to Afghanistan with him. So I changed my field from psychology to education in preparation. I knew I was going to be teaching English, and they had no classes in ESL at that time, so I did my work in reading."

Shirlee talks about her decision to marry Mohamed in the context of their conversations, their weekend visits, the urbane social life they shared. She speaks in practical terms of the preparations she made, as well as the ways Mohamed tried to prepare her for, even warn her about, the life she was choosing. "He kept telling me how primitive life was for them, and he was even painting a picture for me of what kind of a house I would have with a hole in the ceiling where the smoke would go through. He told me that women had to stay at home and wear a veil called a *chadari* when they went out, that this veil was a kind of tent with small openings for the eyes. That by 'modernizing' they meant the holes in the veils getting bigger."

She also talks about that long-ago choice from a great distance, like some ancient gamble she cannot entirely explain. "We just knew kind of mutually that we wanted to marry. The more he told me about it, the more interested I became. There was a certain love element, OK? But more than being in love with this person was the challenge. Going to another country — they're not Jewish, they're not white, they're from an altogether different culture, their ways are different." Shirlee wanted, she tells us, to see the Afghanistan Mohamed described, to see the world. She wanted to have an adventurous life, and to marry Mohamed was to marry that adventure. Such a choice makes sense to us.

You sound like you were ready for excitement, we suggest.

"Excitement — that's it — I was ready for excitement!" When Shirlee recounts this part of her story, she is alive and energetic, her eyes sparkle and her hands dance with a restless energy over the table, tracing out an intricate pattern on its surface.

It is not surprising that Shirlee's family was upset about her choice. Not only was Shirlee choosing to marry outside the Jewish faith, but she was marrying a man from a very different religion and an entirely different culture. Still, Shirlee characterizes them as being "a little bit supportive," which is to say they did not disown her, a path other, stricter families might have taken. "My father made me make an appointment with him to talk about this. I said, 'Dad, I want to talk to you about my choice of marriage,' and he said, 'I don't want to talk about it now. You have to make an appointment with me.' He was a doctor and he had an office. So, I made an appointment with him to sit down in his office — in that sterile environment — and talk to him about my future."

You had to make an appointment to talk about love! We are laughing.

"Love, I didn't mention," Shirlee corrects us quickly. "I just talked about what my plans were. I said, 'This is it,' and I was very definite. My mother didn't like it either; she cried a lot. My aunt said, 'After the war, when the men come back, there'll be plenty of men, you don't have to marry this guy.' I said no, I want to go. I had to emphasize the fact that I wanted to go, that for me this was the right plan."

Shirlee and Mohamed were married in June 1945 in a double ceremony along with another American woman and one of the Afghan friends from Shirlee's statistics class. "Well, it wasn't a wedding really. We'd gotten our licenses, had our tests. The four of us went to the city hall. My parents stood in the room at the back, and my aunt was there. They didn't come to our party, though. We had a little wedding party — two couples in this big apartment in Hyde Park. Our Turkish, Iranian friends — our international community, they all came. They were the ones who celebrated because they knew what it was all about."

Shirlee's parents were not alone in their ambivalent response to the marriage. Shirlee tells us how, shortly after the ceremony, her husband and his friend went to the Afghan consulate to inform the consul of their changed marital status. "So what happened? The guys were so excited about getting married that they took a train to Washington, which was very exciting in those days. And the consul said, 'OK, guys, your scholarships are over.'" Mohamed and his friend had forgotten that they had signed pledges agreeing not to marry Americans. They got nice presents from the consul — a linen tablecloth and a set of goblets — but they lost their scholarships.

Fortunately, however, Mohamed was able to complete his Ph.D. During his coursework, he'd met a woman, Flora Thurston, from Cornell University, who was in the department of rural education in the school of agriculture there. Within a few months, she was able to arrange a fellowship for him. The Tarakis moved in autumn, again aided by Dr. Thurston. "She was so wonderful to us, no prejudices. She had an active group of foreign students meeting in her apartment every week. She was like our family away from home."

While the couple's courtship seemed to have been marked by a freedom of thought and movement, their marriage, Shirlee discovered, would be something different. Shirlee was surprised and challenged by Mohamed's jealousy. "Until this point I was very comfortable with my husband. We hadn't any problems, any conflicts, but when we went to Cornell, I found all of a sudden that my husband was a jealous, possessive man. He couldn't stand my working. I had several jobs, and the one that was most irritating to him was my work with a Russian scientist, Alexis Romanov. I would tell my husband, 'I had a really bad day with Dr. Romanov,' and he would say, 'How are you getting so involved with this man? Is this gonna be some kind of emotional involvement here?' And I said, 'This is my job, we need the money,' because we only had a little bit of a stipend. But he didn't like that." Overcome by her husband's objections, Shirlee quit her job with Alexis Romanov and got a new job working at a statistics laboratory. Shirlee pauses for a moment then shakes her head, amazed anew at Mohamed's unreasonableness.

But Mohamed didn't like Shirlee's work in the statistics laboratory either. "So there I was sitting in a room that was an economist's office, sitting *here*" — Shirlee places one hand on the table, the other far away to emphasize the distance in the room — "and all the way over *there* was a guy. And Mohamed was even worried about my relations with *that* man! He'd say, 'Do you talk to him?' I'd say, 'Yes, I say hello.' Mohamed said, 'Don't say hello. Don't give him any ideas.' Oh boy. Then we'd argue about it. We'd have really heated arguments, and we might not speak to each other for a few days. I was getting in deeper and deeper. There I was, separated from my family. But I had a one-track mind as far as my future was concerned. Go to Afghanistan. I didn't always think it was going to get better. But my goal was to go."

Shirlee stops, her hands suddenly still, head tipped back as she thinks about this long-ago struggle. When she draws her chin down, she looks directly at us with a candor that seems the product of long retrospect. "At this point, if I had the feelings I have now about being a feminist, about being an independent woman, I would have broken off with him right there and then. I should have. I didn't."

These struggles, we learn, occurred while the couple still lived in the United States. Life would become even more difficult when they moved to Afghanistan in October 1947, though we get the impression that Shirlee did not immediately notice, caught up as she was in the adventure she had been so determined to have. If things were not always agreeable in Afghanistan, they were always vividly new, and Shirlee brightens again, as she tells us of her long journey and arrival in her new home. "We took a ship, then a plane, then a train to Karachi, Pakistan. Then finally we were met by his brothers in a small town, Muqur, in Afghanistan. They had brought me a *chadari*." Shirlee pauses, and when she speaks again, it is as though her voice has been subtly transformed — the Persian word unveiling accents and speech rhythms that weave in and out of our conversation, absorbed during her twenty-five years in Afghanistan. "In fact, I had thought I would have to wear the veil, and I was willing to accept that, actually. But my sisters-in-law told me, 'You don't have to wear this unless your husband wants you to, the foreign women aren't wearing them anymore.' I told my husband that I hoped he could get me out of wearing it, and he did."

Still, Shirlee was expected to adhere to other cultural rules about the conduct of women, and many freedoms were proscribed simply because of her gender. There were many places she could not go, for example, without a male escort — or at all. She could not drive a car. When walking the street or anywhere in public, she was to keep her eyes ahead, her face expressionless. She could not greet male friends or relatives on the street because such greetings would indicate wandering eyes. "When I would go out in Kabul unveiled, I would keep my eyes straight ahead. You don't look at people. You don't smile if you know them. Once I ran into one of my brothers-in-law, he was coming toward me. I didn't know what to do. I looked away.

"Here's what my husband said: If anybody saw me speaking to

a man in public, they would assume immediately that I was having an affair. You see? That's what a speaking relationship with another man meant in their culture."

Yet nothing Shirlee says gives us the impression that she suffered terribly from culture shock in these early days, despite the often dramatic cultural differences she was encountering. For one thing, the Taraki family eased her transition, welcoming Shirlee with a warmth that was immediate and genuine, making her feel quite at home. "That family was good to me. We lived with one of the brothers when we first arrived, for a couple of weeks. The fact that I was an American — there was a certain halo around me — even though they'd already fixed Mohamed up with the sister of his closest friend and that had to be undone. They didn't require us to have a second ceremony or anything; they didn't want to be bothered with that. Instead, they had a big party for us."

Life in Kabul was also never as primitive as Mohamed had led Shirlee to expect. "When Mohamed left, the family had been living in the village, and maybe they really did have a hole in the ceiling there." But soon after Mohamed's father died, Shirlee tells us, the family moved to Kabul, so they left the village. Many of his family members found jobs with the government, and, eventually, each brother bought a house for his family. In Kabul, Shirlee tells us, houses were "pretty primitive," but not like those her husband remembered.

By spring, Shirlee was pregnant. Women in the family who knew that the couple had been married for several years came and asked Shirlee why she hadn't had children earlier. "I said, 'Well, we wanted to start our family here.' Then they asked me, 'But how do you prevent it?'" Shirlee was surprised — the women were asking her about contraception. It was one of the moments that opened Shirlee's eyes to the problems of women in Afghanistan, but at that time she could not help the women. "My husband forbade me to talk about sex," she says.

In August 1948, Shirlee gave birth at home to a daughter, Lisa. Although women traditionally gave birth at home, this birth was attended by a Turkish woman doctor, a courtesy arranged by the minister of health, one of Shirlee's friends from the University of Chicago. Shirlee also prepared herself by reading a book from the Children's Bureau on how to prepare your home for delivery.

Were you nervous? we ask Shirlee.

"Sure! But I had my sister-in-law, she came and she helped me through my pains. My husband went to her house to be with his brother. She stayed through the whole delivery." Shirlee adds wryly, "Some visitors turned back when they heard it was only a girl." The Taraki's son, Yosuf, was born three years later.

Motherhood was a source of deep satisfaction for Shirlee. Pictures taken during this time in Shirlee's life portray a woman who appears happy and completely at home, her role as mother helping to weave her even more securely into the fabric of the Taraki family. We see sunny photographs of Shirlee and her friends with their own children; in one photograph, we see three-year-old Lisa smiling brightly, dressed in a traditional outfit, holding out her skirts. Shirlee tells us, "She even had her own little *chadari*, just for fun. Apparently the American relatives were quite shocked by this and thought she was required to wear the veil!"

At that point in her life Shirlee also had a part-time teaching job, and between this and caring for her own children, she kept busy and cheerful. "I had the best of both worlds," she says. We look at pictures of Shirlee with her children. In one, she sits with

Lisa and Yosuf, books in their laps, heads down and serious. They are learning English together, a circle of happy absorption.

It was clear from the beginning that the children would be raised Muslim, Shirlee tells us, since religion and education were inseparable in Afghanistan. "It's so simple for Afghan children to acquire Muslim identities, because the schools are all parochial. There's only one school, and the children are taught to be Muslims from the first grade. My kids learned the Koran so well that people thought I was teaching them. But they were getting it from school. They studied all the rituals. They were taught how to pray in school, they actually got on the ground and did prostrations and ablutions." Shirlee had no misgivings about her children growing up Muslim: "Oh, my kids were Afghan. I was very proud of my kids being raised Afghan, that they knew the culture."

What is not apparent in the sunny photographs of family outings, however, is how Shirlee's contentment in her family life was often overshadowed by Mohamed's continuing jealousy and possessiveness. Whatever distance Mohamed seemed to have from his culture while they lived in the United States — particularly from his culture's ideas about women — evaporated once the couple had settled in Afghanistan. Shirlee remembers feeling particularly indignant about her husband's behavior at international social events, which, because of Mohamed's government post, the couple often attended. Mohamed frequently spoke with women he met at such embassy parties, but he was furious when he saw Shirlee exchange even a word with another man. "Mostly the struggle was about foreign men — especially American men. Foreign men didn't know the rules, that this was the wife of an Afghan and you don't approach her, you don't speak when you're not spoken to. I looked like an American woman — which I was! But I had this problem; my Afghan husband was watching me from the corner. Maybe *he's* talking to a woman, but that's different."

Kabul's international community was large, and there were a number of American women married to men from Afghanistan who understood better than anyone the difficulties Shirlee faced. Like her, these women were often accustomed to significantly more freedom than they had in their marriages. What's more, many found a sexual double standard in place that was frustrating and demeaning. Shirlee tells us that several of the American women she knew discovered their husbands had lovers whom they made little effort to hide, such was their sense of entitlement. One man even took an Afghan wife, and his American wife attended the wedding. "I really feel that Afghan males who married Westerners felt deprived in a way," Shirlee speculates. "They hadn't experienced life with an Afghan woman!"

The women who, like Shirlee, had to live with all kinds of prohibitions in their social interactions were deeply angered and saddened. Most of them, furthermore, felt they had little choice but to stay with their husbands because they couldn't afford to be on their own, because they had children, or because marrying outside culture and religion had cost them their families of origin. Ironically, the struggles of these women occurred in the context of steady and significant advancements for Afghan women. After World War II, Afghanistan had turned to both the United States and the Soviet Union for development aid, receiving loans for an aid program from the former and military assistance, as well as help building roads, schools, and irrigation facilities from the latter. With this aid had come Westernizing influences that especially affected the women in cities like Kabul.

{ *Unveiled* }

Shirlee shows us pictures from this time. In dramatic contrast to earlier photographs where women appear in public only as anonymous shapes, thoroughly veiled and robed, we see women attending university, now recognizable as individual people, wearing what were the days' fashions — sunglasses, gloves, scarves. We are struck, imagining the difference this must have made to those women, feeling it ourselves as a kind of lightness, the warmth of sun on our faces. "After they lifted the veil," Shirlee tells us, "the university was desegregated and women were allowed to attend. So people could meet one another without elaborate arrangements from the families, and many new-style families resulted. These changes in the girls' schools were encouraged, and girls and teachers were applauded (literally) for their courage in coming out from behind the veils."

In fact, by 1959, when Eisenhower visited the country, the government, in an ironic twist, ordered all veiled women off the street for the day. Men were instructed that their wives could only view the motorcade if they were unveiled. The government, Shirlee tells us, didn't want any foreign photographers to capture a reality they were already ashamed of. "You see, they had advertised to the world that women didn't have to wear the veil anymore. So they didn't want it to look like women still did. Although," Shirlee notes dryly, "the woman herself could not make that decision without her husband's okay."

Shirlee vividly recalls the excitement of Eisenhower's visit. She was asked by her brother-in-law to escort her sister-in-law, Bibishirin, to the event. "This was still pretty early on, really. Eisenhower came at a crucial time, when a lot of women weren't ready to come out yet, maybe they didn't even have the wardrobe." Bibishirin wanted to see Eisenhower, however, and her husband was supportive of this desire, so Shirlee's brother-in-law brought Bibishirin to Shirlee's in a veil, and they headed out to see the motorcade together, unveiled. Seeing all those women's faces in public was a kind of shock for Shirlee. "It felt so strange to me. In fact, it took another six months for Bibishirin to get out from behind the veil after that. She had younger sisters, and they influenced her. Once I got over there and got used to seeing the *chadari*, I could never imagine seeing women like my sisters-in-law going around in public without a veil."

Despite what must have seemed like dramatic progress for Afghan women, it is not surprising that Shirlee frequently felt isolated, with all the prohibitions on speech, mobility, and social interaction. These were, after all, added to her separation from her home, her country of origin, her American friends and family. Her isolation from her family became especially intense because of a disagreement between her husband and her family members during a two-month visit home in 1956. "We only made this one trip together, and this was a very unfortunate one. Not only did Mohamed get appendicitis, but worse, a rift developed, precipitated — at least my husband claimed it was — by my brother-in-law." Mohamed felt that the American side of Shirlee's family got preferential treatment from her parents. "He felt discriminated against," says Shirlee. Though Shirlee wasn't at all sure that her husband's perceptions were accurate, she felt obliged to side with him in this dispute.

Not surprisingly, Mohamed's jealousy also surfaced on the trip. "He was watching me so carefully. Even contacts with cousins. He didn't want to see any affection at all. These were my *cousins*!" exclaims Shirlee. For Shirlee, of course, first cousins were "beyond the pale"; but, she explains, this is not so in Afghanistan, where first cousins are considered choice marriage partners. "So Mohamed had that feeling whenever we went to a family event. They had big dinners for us, and he was always watching. It was terrible. He left in a huff, and I was forced to go along with him."

After that, Shirlee did not communicate with her parents for about two years. "Finally, I sent a letter to my parents, telling them I felt very bad that things had gone like this, and I got a beautiful letter back, telling me that life was too short. I kept that letter. My father died only a few years later, so I was glad we had a kind of reconciliation."

Another source of isolation that Shirlee had not expected to feel with such poignancy was her separation from other Jewish people. Interestingly, it was Mohamed who first pointed her in the direction of the Afghan Jewish community, which eventually helped, in some ways, to ease her loneliness. Shirlee and Mohamed were walking in a park when they saw a group of picnickers under some trees. "My husband said to me, you know those people are Jewish. And I said, how can you tell, because they were quite a distance away. He said, I can see their children, they are wearing bangs. Afghan kids didn't wear bangs. So my husband said let's go over." Shirlee was surprised that Mohamed was willing to admit he had a Jewish wife and that he was interested in meeting this group of Jewish picnickers. "He said, 'This is my wife, and she's Jewish.' And they took me in their arms. They couldn't believe it. Here was this Afghan coming, confessing he had a Jewish wife. They called me *Beni Israel*. I had never heard that expression; it means 'child of Israel.'"

After that, the American community found out Shirlee was Jewish, but she doesn't feel that any of the Americans discriminated against her because of it. On the contrary, it helped her develop a wider range of connections because the Americans began directing newly arrived Jewish people to Shirlee. These connections were valuable but limited, however. Because of deeply entrenched anti-Semitic feelings in Afghanistan, Shirlee did not go to synagogue with them or form close attachments. Avowed Jewish women had to wear ugly veils "as a kind of punishment for being different," and they couldn't have servants because no Afghan was willing to work for them. "I had to keep our friendships pretty low-key," Shirlee tells us.

Despite the boundaries Shirlee had to construct, her relationships with other international women, with people of the Jewish faith, with Afghan sisters and family members formed the beginnings of an intercultural, interfaith community that would grow into a central passion later in Shirlee's life. In any case, it was these connections that sustained her through trying times to come. In 1965 Mohamed was forced to leave his prestigious job as the governor of the province of Kabul, a loss that radically altered the family's lifestyle. The Tarakis' misfortune occurred during what Shirlee recalls as a golden era for the country: "It was a really wonderful time; they had a new constitution, they had the first free — really free — elections, and a commoner was chosen by the king to be the prime minister. They had women elected to the parliament. The students could hold demonstrations."

In fact, Mohamed's professional demise was brought about by a tragedy that occurred during one of these student demonstrations. An army unit controlled by the king's son-in-law fired on the students to disperse them, inadvertently killing one. "It became a big scandal," Shirlee tells us, "partly because of the new freedom that allowed the papers to carry the story." The king decided to save face by blaming the scandal on Mohamed. The king called him the next day, blaming the incident on the police — who were Mohamed's responsibility — and asking Mohamed to resign.

"My husband said, 'Your Majesty, I can't do that. It was proven that my police did not shoot, it was the army. There were lots of witnesses.' The king said, 'Okay, so you refuse.' Mohamed went home with his car, this big black sedan we had. When he got home, there was a phone call from the palace. They told us there would be two drivers arriving tomorrow to take away our automobiles. That was the end of *that* job."

Mohamed was without work, so Shirlee was forced to find more lucrative employment herself. Eventually, she went to work with Columbia University Teacher's College as a language specialist and cultural liaison. Shirlee found this job positive and challenging but faced again the familiar problem of Mohamed's jealousy. "It was hell on earth for me. I had been working in the schools at a very minimal salary. But we lost a lot: Mohamed's big salary, a big entertainment allowance, and all sorts of perks. So I had to quit my job to get better employment." Mohamed was jealous of Shirlee's male colleagues, and because he was unemployed, Shirlee tells us, "he had nothing to do but worry about what I was doing in the office."

The Tarakis also faced the challenge of providing their children with the broader education they wanted for them, despite their reduced means. After Lisa graduated from twelfth grade in Afghanistan, the Tarakis decided to send her to college in the United States. Shirlee found her a scholarship through an organization called the American Friends of the Middle East. It was a wonderful scholarship with all expenses paid, including travel — to Mills College — a school for women. "We felt that would be best for her, since she'd had no contacts with men." Shirlee found a different scholarship for her son, Yosuf, to attend a private high school, Lake Forest Academy, near her family in Chicago. Yosuf would later attend Northwestern University, aided by scholarships that the university provided. "So we were kind of proud of our children," Shirlee finishes.

Lisa and Yosuf came back for a family vacation in Afghanistan in 1970. "That was our last time together." The Tarakis went on a northern tour of the country, traveling hundreds of miles in a Volkswagen bug to Mazar-e-Sharif. In these photographs, Lisa, a college student, looks like a young Shirlee, and Yosuf, a teenager still growing, has distinct characteristics from each parent. Shirlee wears sunglasses and a scarf, looks wiry and energetic, gestures at something, her hands caught in a blur of motion, while Mohamed leans back against the car, graying but still handsome, looking at the mountains, dramatic and crumpled in the distance.

In the fall of 1971, Mohamed was stricken with esophageal cancer, succumbing in a matter of months to the illness. Despite the challenges of being married to Mohamed, it was very difficult for Shirlee to lose her husband, and there was one more loss coming. As he was dying, Mohamed asked Shirlee to make two promises: that she would have no other men in her life and that she would leave Afghanistan. To comfort him, she made the first promise and to honor him, she made the second, even though it meant losing the country that had become home to her. Both requests were to the same end. It was a threat to Mohamed's honor and manhood for Shirlee to be with another, and even for her to be seen in the company of another man by those who had known him was too much for Mohamed to contemplate. To further assure his honor, Mohamed asked Shirlee to leave the country. "There's a word," Shirlee tells us, "*namoos*. A man's honor. I was my husband's *namoos* — even in death."

In a radical departure from custom, Lisa and Shirlee were permitted by Mohamed's brother to be present at the burial service. After the traditional forty-day period of mourning, Shirlee returned with her children to the United States.

This return was the beginning of a new life for Shirlee. She rediscovered her connection to her family of origin, though much had changed. Her own mother had become an artist after Shirlee's father died. "My mother was leading a great life," Shirlee tells us, "and when I came back to the states, I started up a different relationship with her. She was older — " Shirlee pauses to note with irony. "Well, my mother was younger than I am right now when I came back. She was living alone and wanted me to go with her, for us to do things together. She took me to temple and introduced me to all of her friends, convinced me to come to Evanston." Shirlee stops to show us a picture of her mother standing before an easel in a room full of objects, her posture expressing both a deep absorption and satisfaction. Later, Shirlee shows us the painting, too, its oil surface textured and complicated with tiny brushstrokes.

While her mother inspired her to find a new happiness, it was her daughter who introduced her to feminism. "She wrote me letters while she was still at Mills, 'I attended this or that demonstration.' Because it was the height of the women's movement — California! But I had a lot of catching up to do when I got to the United States," Shirlee says. She had become less assertive, she tells us, more subdued. "People at work were always saying 'we can hardly hear you.' I actually had speech therapy to help me speak." Soon after reading Betty Friedan's *The Feminine Mystique*,

Shirlee joined the women's movement. "I even sent copies of the book back to friends in Afghanistan."

Both of Shirlee's children have international identities. Lisa continued her education with graduate work at SUNY, obtaining her master's and her Ph.D. in sociology. There she met her future husband, who was also doing Ph.D. work. "He's from the Middle East. So she, following in her mother's footsteps, went to live in her husband's country." Shirlee smiles as she says this, perhaps enjoying the symmetry. Lisa teaches sociology in the West Bank, where she has a nine-year-old son.

Yosuf is married to a woman from Afghanistan, and the couple has a two-and-a-half-year-old son, Ilyas ("He's one-quarter American!"). Shirlee is an involved grandmother, spending most Saturdays with Ilyas. "This guy has several languages at two and a half," Shirlee tells us proudly. "He has Persian, very good Persian, using high-level words. He's also speaking English at a high level. Just yesterday he said 'hot' to me and I said, *kat*? (That means 'letter' in Persian). And he said, 'No, it's *hot*!'"

But perhaps the most urgent and compelling cause in Shirlee's life now is calling attention to the plight of women in Afghanistan and aiding women from that country. She assisted, for example, in relief efforts for refugees from the Soviet invasion of 1979, helping to settle refugees, sharing her apartment with new arrivals, teaching English and life skills.

After Soviet forces left Afghanistan in 1989, the fundamentalist resistance parties put back the veil in 1991. Since September 1996, the ruling fundamentalist Islamic sect, known as the Taliban, has systematically persecuted the women of Kabul. Shirlee tells us, "Thousands of widows (some of them my former students and colleagues) have had to resort to begging for food for their families, since they are no longer permitted to work outside the home. Women must be heavily veiled when they do go out, always with a male escort. Girls cannot attend school; the university is closed to women." The latest news is sadder still. According to Shirlee, the Taliban has banned "music, dance, storytelling, kite flying, and all other forms of entertainment."

Shirlee now holds presentations to aid one of the humanitarian organizations helping to ease the situation — PARSA, founded and run by an old Kabul friend of Shirlee's, Mary MacMakin. We attended one of Shirlee's fund-raising slide shows at Evanston's public library, "An American Woman in Afghanistan," and were impressed by the packed meeting room where the warmth and respect for Shirlee was palpable. With other women, she formed the Afghan Women's Task Force, which opposes the Taliban's strict religious fundamentalism.

After one such presentation, a young Polish woman came to visit Shirlee. "She asked me some questions about my presentation, but I sensed that she was there for another reason, so I just asked her, 'What do you really want to know?' It turned out she had fallen in love with a man from another country, and she wanted advice. I told her that she should first go to his country and see him with his family, then decide about marriage." She pauses for a moment, perhaps thinking, as we are, about that woman's choice, about her own choice and its life-changing consequences.

When we stand up to leave Shirlee's apartment, we feel disoriented, as though we have lost our temporal place. In the two short hours we have spent with Shirlee, her narrative has spanned five decades and two continents, weaving back and forth in time, dizzying us. As we leave, we shake hands with her, thank her.

It's a wonderful, amazing story we tell her, still trying to come back to 1998. Shirlee draws herself up slightly.

"Well, it's not a story, it's my life," she says with dignity.